Work, Organization, and Employment

Series editors

Tony Dundon, The University of Manchester, Manchester, UK
Adrian Wilkinson, Business School, Griffith University, Brisbane, QLD, Australia

The series publishes high-quality research in the related subject areas of work, employment relations, organizational studies and analysis, and human resource management. The series takes an overarching pluralist approach, debating and discussing topics via related theoretical lenses including political economy, ethics, and systems of governance.

A key focus of the series is how the imperatives for efficiency, quality and high performance can be configured so that equality, inclusion, good pay, dignity, well-being and social justice are also achieved in increasingly globalised work regimes.

The series investigates the connections between the world of work and the political economy and public policy that shape regulations, organizational and business environments, work experiences, and well-being within a new globalised model of consumerism.

More information about this series at http://www.springer.com/series/14359

Peter Holland · Julian Teicher
Jimmy Donaghey
Editors

Employee Voice at Work

Springer

Editors
Peter Holland
Department of Management and Marketing
Swinburne Business School, Swinburne University of Technology
Melbourne, VIC, Australia

Jimmy Donaghey
Warwick Business School
University of Warwick
Coventry, UK

Julian Teicher
School of Business and Law
Central Queensland University
Melbourne, VIC, Australia

ISSN 2520-8837 ISSN 2520-8845 (electronic)
Work, Organization, and Employment
ISBN 978-981-13-2819-0 ISBN 978-981-13-2820-6 (eBook)
https://doi.org/10.1007/978-981-13-2820-6

Library of Congress Control Number: 2018958342

This Springer imprint is published by the registered company Springer Nature Singapore Pte Ltd.
The registered company address is: 152 Beach Road, #21-01/04 Gateway East, Singapore 189721, Singapore

Contents

Editors and Contributors

About the Editors

Peter Holland is Professor of Human Resource Management and Director of the Executive MBA at Swinburne University of Technology, Melbourne, Australia. He has worked in the Australian finance sector and consulted to the private and public sector in a variety of areas related to human resource management and employee relations. His current research interests include employee voice, workplace electronic monitoring and surveillance, and talent management.

Julian Teicher is Professor Human Resources and Employment and Deputy Dean (Research) in the School of Business and Law at Central Queensland University, Melbourne, Australia. In the early part of his career, he worked as an industrial relations officer for two unions, one in the maritime and power industries and the other in nursing. His research is in two related fields: workplace (industrial) relations and public policy and management. He has published widely on a range of topics including: conflict management, employee participation, voice and industrial democracy, bargaining and dispute resolution, and training and skill formation.

Jimmy Donaghey is Professor of Employment Relations at the Industrial Relations Research Unit, Warwick Business School, University of Warwick, UK and Adjunct Professor at Monash University, Melbourne, Australia. His research interests focus on the internationalisation of employment relations and worker voice.

Contributors

Nikola Balnave Macquarie University, Sydney, Australia

Alison Barnes Macquarie University, Sydney, Australia

Chris Brewster Vaasa University, Vaasa, Finland; Henley Business School, University of Reading, Reading, UK; Radboud University, Nijmegen, The Netherlands

Alex Bryson University College London, London, England

John Burgess Melbourne, Australia

Julia Connell Newcastle, Australia

Brian Cooper Department of Management, Monash University, Clayton, Australia

Richard Croucher Middlesex University Business School, London, UK

Niall Cullinane Queen's University Management School, Queen's University, Belfast, UK

Tony Dobbins Birmingham Business School, University of Birmingham, Birmingham, UK

Jimmy Donaghey Warwick Business School, University of Warwick, Coventry, UK

Joe Dromey IPPR, Coventry, England

Tony Dundon Alliance Manchester, Business School, University of Manchester, Manchester, UK

Richard Freeman Harvard University & NBER, Boston, USA

Rafael Gomez University of Toronto, Toronto, Canada

Rob Hecker Tasmanian School of Business and Economics, University of Tasmania, Hobart, Australia

Eugene Hickland DCU Business School, Dublin City University, Dublin, Ireland

Peter Holland Department of Management and Marketing, Swinburne Business School, Swinburne University of Technology, Melbourne, VIC, Australia

Sarah Kaine Business School, University of Technology Sydney, Ultimo, Australia

Xiaoyan Liang Central Queensland University, Melbourne, Australia

Benjamin Manning Macquarie University, Sydney, Australia

Graeme Martin University of Dundee, Dundee, Scotland

Anthony McDonnell University College Cork, Cork, Ireland

Alan McWilliams Victoria University, Melbourne, Australia

Paula K. Mowbray Griffith Business School, Nathan, Australia

Emma Parry Cranfield, England

Thomas Prosser Cardiff University, Cardiff, Wales

Katherine Ravenswood Auckland University of Technology, Auckland, New Zealand

Julian Teicher Central Queensland University, Melbourne, Australia

Louise Thornthwaite Macquarie University, Sydney, Australia

Herman Tse Monash Business School, Caulfield East, Australia

Adrian Wilkinson Griffith Business School, Nathan, Australia

Paul Willman London School of Economics and Political Science, London, England

Introduction

Peter Holland, Julian Teicher and Jimmy Donaghey

Work is the dominant activity of most people's lives. Work acts as an enabler of economic activity for individuals and as the generator of wealth for corporations, nations and individuals and carries with it the important issues of redistribution and fairness. In addition to these economic functions, work also has important social functions in that it brings people together with very different personalities and moreover interests. At the heart of these economic and social interests is the ability of those at work to be able to articulate their position and also that these concerns are viewed vis-à-vis with those of others in the workplace. But as will be developed in this chapter and the remainder of the book, the content and context of voice in the workplace is changing. As such, the field of employee voice has gained prominence in the employment relations, human resource management and organisational behaviour literature in recent years. While these perspectives differ significantly in how they define voice, a common feature of all these literatures are the issues of why, how and when do workers influence what happens in their place of work. The purpose of this book is to add to the understanding of the changing nature of voice from an employment relations perspective.

The Employment Relations Approach to Voice

In the area of customer relationships, Hirschman (1970) introduced the idea of voice as an alternative to loyalty or exit. Voice was viewed as a mechanism through which those customers who did not wish to remain silent or seek alternative suppliers could lever their power as consumers. But while his work focussed on these consumption relations, in many ways, within the employment relationship, it is no surprise that the issue of voice comes more to the fore. As is long recognised, the employment relationship is more socially embedded than a simple, easily defined consumer relationship (Simon 1951) and thus voice or loyalty can be thought of as the defaults, with exit as being the last resort option.

A key feature of the employment relations approach to voice is that it is premised on the recognition that workers have interests independent to those of their employers. These interests may at times be common, may overlap or may be in conflict with those of their employers but as such, there needs to be a (voice) vehicle through which workers can advance their interests. From an employer perspective, it is also recognised that this is a valuable source of knowledge in an increasingly dynamic environment (Holland 2014). Taking this approach, the definition of voice adopted for the volume is that of Wilkinson and colleagues (2014:5) who define employee voice as,

> as the ways and means through which employees attempt to have a say and potentially influence organizational affairs relating to issues that affect their work and the interests of managers and owners.

For Budd (2004), voice, along with economy and equity, was one of the three key tensions which the employment relationship had to balance. This point was also emphasised by Marchington (2007), who described voice as the area of HRM where the tension between the various stakeholders of an organisation is most apparent. As such, the employment relations approach puts the concept of voice as a central tenet of its ongoing contractual nature.

The literature on employee voice in the area of employment relations, where this volume is situated, has developed out of a convergence between debates around representation, participation and involvement. One of the seminal arguments on voice was Freeman and Medoff (1984) who highlighted that while unions may exercise monopoly power in wage bargaining and extract economic rents, unions also provided economic efficiency through the provision of collective voice in the form of representation. But employee voice and the employment relationship are evolving and changing. Gone are the days when large numbers of workers on standardised contracts working for large-scale manufacturing companies were represented by trade unions. But this does not mean that interest in employee (or union) voice has decreased. In fact, the opposite is the case. The myriad actors and forms which have emerged have meant that voice has become established as one of the key areas of enquiry in the various approaches which use the employment relationship as its theoretical and employment focus. With the decline of union based forms of representation in many advanced economies, the voice literature has expanded to analyse those forms of representation based around non-union representation schemes (Dobbins and Dobbins 2014). These indirect forms of representative voice are not the only forms covered by the definitions of voice with what have often been labelled as 'involvement' and 'participation' also included (Dundon et al. 2004). These more direct forms of voice encompass systems such as teamwork, quality circles and the likes are generally more directly related to the work task than more representative systems.

The vibrancy of research into voice is due to a variety of interrelated factors. First, there is a body of literature that seeks to explore the links between employee voice, with increased commitment and competitive advantage, and this is particularly of interest to managers and many management academics (Batt et al. 2002;

Farndale et al. 2011). Second, the changing industrial landscape of the advanced market economies in recent decades, especially declining union membership and the associate need for voice has witnessed the emergence of managerially driven mechanism to fill the emerging voice vacuum (Terry 1999; Taras and Kaufman 2006; Donaghey et al. 2011; Dundon and Rollinson 2004). Third, and related to the preceding point, the rise of human resource management, with its focus on direct relationships between employees and employers, has led to a more strategic focus on managing the employment relationship (Boxall and Purcell 2016). However, this is not without its problems, because as management attempts to fill the voice vacuum, there is a legitimate concern that it seeks to 'crowd out' other more critical forms of voice, particularly those forms which challenge management control. Fourth, public policy actors have increasingly sought to regulate issues around the provision of worker voice. Two contrasting approaches can be seen. In the EU, for example, a series of pieces of legislation have been passed which set minimum levels of voice which workers are expected to be provided with in their workplace (Hall 2011; Gold 2011; Donaghey et al. 2013). In contrast, in the US for example, the rise of 'right to work' states has sought to champion the individual over the collective will with resultant benefits to employers. The infamous example of the Volkswagen plant in Chattanooga Tennessee where the German car maker was prevented from establishing a Works Council and recognising union was driven through an aggressive political campaign by those outside the employment relationship (Silva 2018). Therefore, it is important to look at what is happening in the contemporary workplace and how voice is being managed.

Change and Employee Voice

This book is firmly positioned to make a contribution to the employment relations literature on voice. This is not to say that the Organisational Behaviour (OB) based literature has not something valuable to say but that to keep a focus, our engagement is generally with the employment relations literature. Within our approach, a key focus is on the theme of voice and change. Three main cross-cutting, and often overlapping, aspects are present in this volume. First, the changing nature of the workplace and wider society, and how this affects voice; second, how voice systems have changed and transformed over time; and third, new ways to look at voice through an employment relations lens.

It is worth reflecting on these three themes at this juncture. First, without doubt, workplaces are changing. As is often highlighted, in the past 40 years, advanced economies have witnessed a shift from Fordist mass production to a more knowledge and services based post-Fordist economy (Rowthorn and Wells 1987; Coutts et al. 2007). Workplaces have seen greater diversity with emphasis on inclusion of women, people from multicultural backgrounds and disabilities. In addition, changing technologies and generational shifts in how such workers engage with each other and wider society make for changes in voice. It has been emphasised that this increased awareness of workplace diversity and interests shifts the nature of the representation which workers seek (Safford and Piore 2006). While in general, these may be viewed as positive developments, other employer-driven changes have also changed the workplace. For example, casual employment, zero-hours contracts, 'gig-economy' jobs and privatisation have all created underlying threats to job security in the workplace through the dislocation of work and employment. These changes carry with them potential changes to the nature of worker voice which need to be investigated (see for example, Dean and Greene 2017).

Second, as outlined above, a key driver behind the employment relations approach to voice has been the question of how workers are represented in an era of the decline of collective bargaining and union representation? much research has gone into understanding the emergence of these new systems and what types of changes take place within systems. How have voice systems within workplaces changed and how have changed workplaces witnessed changes in employee voice? Forces such as privatisation, deindustrialisation and outsourcing/offshoring all carry with them pressures towards change. But the extent of such change needs to be explored in greater depth. Whilst many books have identified and documented the evolution of voice in the workplace, we have always been aware that the dynamic and changing nature of voice has not quite been captured within the context of the changes we have seen in work and the workplace of the twenty-first century. For example, the rise of social media which effectively flattens the communication within the organisation and provides information instantly to a global audience is changing the way employees communicate and importantly is often outside the control of management. This can be juxtaposed with 'old style' union voice which is embracing such technologies through what is known as 'E-voice' (Balnave et al. 2014).

Third, as outlined above, the employment relations approach to voice exists alongside scholarship in fields such as organisational behaviour, human resource management and labour process theory. It is worth noting that the literature on voice has often 'borrowed' terms from other literatures: While many authors cite Hirschman (1970) as being the basis of employee voice, as we do above, it is worthwhile to point out that Hirschman's famous 'Exit, loyalty and voice' formulation was focussed on consumer/customer relations rather than employment relations. Thus, important lessons can be drawn from fields across the social sciences. In terms of voice, it has generally been thought of as being workers exercising their voice to their line managers or at least those with direct relationship to their employment who listen to their concerns. But the assumption of management wanting workers to have a voice or actually listening and taking it into account is not guaranteed. For example, a growing literature focuses on the extent to which management may wish to have silent workers (Donaghey et al. 2011) or management may exhibit 'dear ears' to the issues raised by workers (Harlos 2001). An emergent theme is that workers can have voice but their voice may be directed at those who they believe can influence the relationship but are not actually a participant in their employment relationship. This has particularly happened in the context of the Internet. With the Internet and associated social media, workers can now post public frustrations with their employer online with the desire of being heard or creating reputational damage. While ultimately these target the employer, they aim to do so through an indirect route of mobilising power such as consumer power rather than traditional methods of employment relations (Donaghey et al. 2014; Holland et al. 2016). This particularly is the case in supply chain relationships where NGOs and others seek to inflict reputational damage amongst consumers for breaches of labour rights (Reinecke and Donaghey 2015; Wright 2016).

Motivation for the Book

In recent years, a number of books have emerged which seek to provide an overview of research into worker voice (Wilkinson et al. 2014; Johnstone and Ackers 2015). The motivation for this book is slightly different. In particular, the book seeks to develop insights associated with the changing nature of voice from theoretical and practical perspectives through case study analysis of employee voice. In our title, we use 'voice at work' in the double meaning of workplace voice but also what this means in practical and empirical terms in the modern workplace.

Whilst this book focuses on advanced market economies, because of the breadth of the concept of employee voice, it lends itself to differing perspective on employment relations and human resources management. Often described as the Anglo-American and European perspectives, these approaches are underpinned by differing levels of participation and involvement in the workplace, which need to be understood as ways of enhancing or inhibiting voice. In this context, the increasing focus on silence and how it can be 'structured' into the workplace by management to negate effective voice is also considered an important aspect of voice patterns and practices in the workplace.

As noted, the scope of the book is intended not only to cover theoretical aspects of voice but also the practical aspects of employee voice. Irrespective of the nature of the channel, employee voice arrangements vary widely in terms of their design, employee coverage, the scope of issues covered and their depth or embeddedness and effectiveness in the workplace. To address these issues, the final section of the book focuses on the dynamic and changing nature of voice at the workplace through case studies to provide insight into the role and impact in the day-to-day interactions within and outside organisations. This we see as providing the reader with an insight into how voice actually works in practice and how the various actors interpret and work within the social structures voice creates.

The Structure of the Book

The book is divided into three parts. Part one starts with a bold approach by Mowbray, Wilkinson and Tse to unite the theoretical perspectives. As these authors note, such an approach will provide the HRM/ER and OB disciplines with new opportunities to advance the literature on employee voice with the potential of eliciting new findings. Noting the need to unite the field, the following chapters in this section highlight the structural differences that have emerged in what are seen as the Anglo-American and European models of voice.

Bryson, Freeman, Gomez and Wilman frame the Anglo-American model in the context of the decline of trade union density and traditional union voice, and the rise of direct voice which they argue has undermined collective voice. They highlight the emerging difference through a profile of the workforce, where 'new' workers are unlikely to join unions. This establishes their argument for a 'twin-track' model of employee voice. They however suggest that whilst many of the new workers or 'digital natives' are unlikely to join unions, the new e-platforms of the twenty-first century may provide a fertile environment to address workplace issues and problems. In contrast to this perspective, Brewster, Croucher and Prosser explore the European perspective on voice. Focusing on the European corporatist model of voice, the authors highlight the democratic approach which emphasises stakeholders rather than the shareholder, the proactive role of the state and the acceptances by management of the value of real consultation not just rhetoric. As such, voice is viewed as having a legitimate role in the workplace supported by legislation under the guise of legally supported collective voice or co-determination. However, these authors sound a word of caution to the long-term standing of established voice mechanisms, with the rise of right-wing governments across Europe, underpinned by neo-liberal ideology, which could see this model move closer to that of the Anglo-American model.

Part two explores what might be described as the new dimensions of voice. The first chapter by Holland, Cooper and Hecker looks at the increasing impact of social media as a new form of voice, building upon the points raised by Bryson et al. about these new platforms as a vehicle for workers who increasingly do not join unions. The research highlights the high and low road of these digital platforms for employers as something to fear and control or embrace as a real-time voice. The second strategy provides a framework to address issues as they emerge as a key HRM strategy to enhance involvement and participation. However, they note that such a strategy cannot operate in a vacuum, and key structural issues need to be in place such as mutual trust. Also picking up on the merging of old and new voice, Barnes, Balnave, Thornthwaite and Manning explore the impact of social media on union communication, member voice and democracy. They argue that these new digital platforms can enhance communications between the union and its members. This is a relatively new perspective on the use of digital platform by unions and the authors use a case study to explore this approach. They find that these platforms have the potential to engage members with the union, although this remains relatively limited.

Donaghey, Dundon, Cullinane, Dobbins and Hickland address the emerging structural aspect of how management silences workers. In line with the book focus of looking at voice issue in the workplace, they use three case studies to analyse the implementation of the EU's Information and Consultation Directive in the UK and Ireland. The case studies illustrate how management responded to avoid elements of the Directive to prevent worker voice and how management acted in silencing workers and they highlight the implications of this approach. The final chapter in this sections looks at the role voice can play in addressing one of the most significant issues in the workplace, that of bullying behaviour and culture. Holland explores the importance of voice in combination with ethical leadership to address these issues and develop a culture of transparency and good governance. The chapter is completed by a major case study into the how such an approach was used to address an endemic culture of bullying and silence in the health sector.

The final section of the book is devoted to case studies in voice across different sectors. The first chapter by McWilliams, Holland and Hecker focuses on the manufacturing sector and is unique in that the research was undertaken inside a car plant which was in the process of a staged closure. The chapter charts the development of voice through various stage of the 70 years of production, culminating in the key role of voice in ensuring that in the 3 year planned shut-down employees remained engaged and involved in the work and workplace issues. The service sector case study by Burgess and Connell addresses one of the most contentious of the contemporary workplaces of the twenty-first century—the call centre. Call centre work is highly monitored, scripted and subject to forms of close supervisor control with the work being monotonous and demanding with few opportunities for participation. The chapter draws upon studies of voice in call centres in Australia and the UK to examine forms of voice mechanisms used and the outcomes emerging in the ICT driven continuous service delivery context. In exploring the health sector, Kaine and Ravenswood look to one of the most deregulated and under resourced areas of the sector—aged care. Their study of voice is framed through the different regulatory environment of Australia and New Zealand. The chapter considers the different levels at which voice is exercised as a means to analyse different voice channels and their efficacy. The next chapter returns to the theme of voice in the digital era with Parry, Martin and Dromey, research exploring why some organisations have embraced this technology and how best to incorporate these new digital platforms. Looking at six organisations, they explore the role of power in controlling social media and how it impacts the levels of trust and encourages voice and collaboration. The final chapter by Teicher and Liang explores voice in a largely overlook but significant part of the workforce—Third Sector organisations, which deliver important services on a not-for-profit basis. The examination of voice within the context of a mixed employee and volunteer workforces identifies it as an important element in this workplace. Against this background, the case examined is a complex and long-running collective bargaining dispute in a rural fire service in Australia. A perceived lack of voice among volunteers underscored a legacy of poor management, which also impeded the resolution of the dispute.

References

Balnave, N., Barnes, A., MacMillan, C., & Thornthwaite, L. (2014). E-voice: How network and media technologies are shaping employee voice. In A. Wilkinson, J. Donaghey, T. Dundon & R. Freeman (Eds.), *Handbook of Research on Employee Voice: Edward Elgar* 439.

Batt, R., Colvin, A. J., & Keefe, J. (2002). Employee voice, human resource practices, and quit rates: Evidence from the telecommunications industry. *ILR Review*, *55*(4), 573–594.

Boxall, P., & Purcell, J. (2016). *Strategy and human resource management* (4th ed). Basingstoke, UK: Palgrave Macmillan.

Budd, J. W. (2004). *Employment with a human face: Balancing efficiency, equity, and voice*. Cornell University Press.

Coutts, K., Glyn, A., & Rowthorn, B. (2007). Structural change under new labour. *Cambridge Journal of Economics*, *31*(6), 845–861.

Dean, D., & Greene, A. M. (2017). How do we understand worker silence despite poor conditions–as the actress said to the woman bishop. *Human Relations*, *70*(10), 1237–1257.

Donaghey, J., Cullinane, N., Dundon, T., & Wilkinson, A. (2011). Reconceptualising employee silence: Problems and prognosis. *Work, Employment and Society*, *25*(1), 51–67.

Donaghey, J., Carley, M., Hall, M., & Purcell (2013). *National Practices of Information and Consultation in Europe*. Eurofound.

Donaghey, J., Cullinane, N., Dundon, T., & Dobbins, T. (2012). Non-union employee representation, union avoidance and the managerial agenda. *Economic and Industrial Democracy*, *33* (2), 163–183.

Dobbins, T., & Dundon, T. (2014). Non-union employee representation. In A. Wilkinson, J. Donaghey, T. Dundon, & R. Freeman (Eds.), *Handbook of research on employee voice: Elgar original reference* (p. 342).

Dundon, T., & Rollinson, D. (2004). *Employment relations in non-union firms*. Routledge.

Dundon, T., Wilkinson*, A., Marchington, M., & Ackers, P. (2004). The meanings and purpose of employee voice. *The International Journal of Human Resource Management*, *15*(6), 1149–1170.

Farndale, E., Van Ruiten, J., Kelliher, C., & Hope-Hailey, V. (2011). The influence of perceived employee voice on organizational commitment: An exchange perspective. *Human Resource Management*, *50*(1), 113–129.

Freeman, R. & Medoff, J. (1984). What do unions do? New York: Basic Books.

Gold, M. (2010). Employee participation in the EU: The long and winding road to legislation. *Economic and Industrial Democracy*, *31*(4_suppl), 9–23.

Hall, M. (2010). EU regulation and the UK employee consultation framework. *Economic and Industrial Democracy*, *31*(4_suppl), 55–69.

Hirschman, A. O. (1970). *Exit, voice, and loyalty: Responses to decline in firms, organizations, and states* (Vol. 25). Harvard University Press.

Holland, P. J. (2014). *Managing Voice an Employers Perspective*. In A. Wilkinson, T. Dundon, J. Donaghey, & R. Freeman (Eds.), *The Handbook of Research on Employee Voice* (2nd ed). UK: Edward Elgar (forthcoming).

Holland, P., Cooper, B. K., & Hecker, R. (2016). Use of social media at work: A new form of employee voice? *The International Journal of Human Resource Management*, *27*(21), 2621–2634.

Johnstone, S., & Ackers, P. (2015). *Finding a voice at work? New Perspectives on Employment Relations*. Oxford: Oxford University Press.

Harlos, K. P. (2001). When organizational voice systems fail: More on the deaf-ear syndrome and frustration effects. *The Journal of Applied Behavioral Science*, *37*(3), 324–342.

Marchington, M. (2007). Employee voice systems. In P. Boxall, J. Purcell, & P. Wright (Eds.), *The oxford handbook of human resource management* (pp. 231–250), Oxford: Oxford University Press.

Piore, M. J., & Safford, S. (2006). Changing regimes of workplace governance, shifting axes of social mobilization, and the challenge to industriall relations theory. *Industrial Relations: A Journal of Economy and Society*, *45*(3), 299–325.

Reinecke, J., & Donaghey, J. (2015). After Rana Plaza: Building coalitional power for labour rights between unions and (consumption-based) social movement organisations. *Organization*, *22*(5), 720–740.

Rowthorn, B., & Wells, J. R. (1987). *De-Industrialization foreign trade*. Cambridge: Cambridge University Press.

Silvia, S. J. (2018). The United Auto Workers' Attempts to Unionize Volkswagen Chattanooga. *ILR Review*, *71*(3), 600–624.

Simon, H. A. (1951). A formal theory of the employment relationship. *Econometrica: Journal of the Econometric Society*, 293–305.

Taras, D. G., & Kaufman, B. E. (2006). Non-union employee representation in North America: Diversity, controversy and uncertain future1. *Industrial Relations Journal*, *37*(5), 513–542.

Terry, M. (1999). Systems of collective employee representation in non-union firms in the UK. *Industrial Relations Journal*, *30*(1), 16–30.

Wilkinson, A., Dundon, T., Donaghey, J., & Freeman, R. (2014). Employee voice: Charting new terrain. In A. Wilkinson, J. Donaghey, T. Dundon, & R. Freeman (Eds.), *The handbook of research on employee voice: Participation and involvement in the workplace* (pp. 1–16).

Wilkinson, A., Donaghey, J., Dundon, T., & Freeman, R. B. (Eds.). (2014). *Handbook of research on employee voice: Elgar original reference*. Edward Elgar Publishing.

Wright, C. F. (2016). Leveraging reputational risk: Sustainable sourcing campaigns for improving labour standards in production networks. *Journal of Business Ethics*, *137*(1), 195–210.

Part I
Employee Voice: What's it all About?

Chapter 1
Evolution, Separation and Convergence of Employee Voice Concept

Paula K. Mowbray, Adrian Wilkinson and Herman Tse

Abstract This chapter discusses the early conceptualisation of employee voice within the human resource management, employment relations and organisational behaviour disciplines. The chapter identifies the significant turning points within the literature and the resultant divergent pathways that these disciplines took with regard to the conceptualisation and study of voice. The discussion then focuses on ways to better integrate the disparate voice literature. Following this, future directions are provided to guide new voice studies where an integrated concept of voice can be applied. Accordingly, it is proposed that future voice studies should consider both employer and employee interests and formal and informal voice.

Keywords Voice concept · Voice mechanisms · Voice behaviour
Informal and formal voice

1.1 Introduction

Over the past three decades, there has been burgeoning interest in the study of employee voice across a number of disciplines in management research (Greenberg and Edwards 2009; Johnstone and Ackers 2015; Kaufman 2014a; Morrison 2011, 2014; Wilkinson et al. 2014). This scholarly interest is aligned with changes over time in practice concerning how employee voice is operationalised within the organisations and the importance placed on it, which has been influenced by declining unionism around the world as well as a concern with better engaging with the workforce to help improve organisational performance. There have been many high-profile cases where the absence of voice is seen as having led to organisation crises, such as the Volkswagen emission scandal in Germany, the Bundaberg Hospital deaths

P. K. Mowbray · A. Wilkinson
Griffith Business School, Nathan, Australia

H. Tse (✉)
Monash Business School, Caulfield East, Australia
e-mail: herman.tse@monash.edu

P. Holland et al. (eds.), *Employee Voice at Work*, Work, Organization, and Employment, https://doi.org/10.1007/978-981-13-2820-6_1

in Australia, and in the US the Columbia space disaster, the collapse of Enron, and the British Petroleum oil-rig explosion (Morrison 2011; Wilkinson et al. 2015). Moreover, there is increasing evidence that employee voice has positive outcomes on organisational performance (Harley 2014) and employee well-being (Pohler and Luchak 2014). Thus, the research indicates that employee voice continues to be an important issue for both employers and employees (Burke and Cooper 2013; Klaas et al. 2012; Wilkinson et al. 2014).

Certainly, since Hirschman's (1970) seminal book on voice was published in relation to customers, and then the voice concept later applied to employees by Farrell (1983) and Freeman and Medoff (1984), we have developed a greater understanding of how employee voice mechanisms may be shaped by different factors inside or outside organisations (Kaufman 2015; Marchington 2015) and the behavioural antecedents to employees expressing voice (Morrison 2014). However, despite the early research on employee voice stemming from Hirschman's concept of voice, we have witnessed differences between the employment relations (ER), human resource management (HRM) and organisational behaviour (OB) disciplines with regard to how employee voice is conceptualised, and this has thwarted our understanding of employee voice. These differences extend beyond a focus on formal voice mechanisms within the HRM/ER voice field and informal voice behaviour with the OB voice field, and includes how scholars within these fields perceive the underlying motivation to voice (Mowbray et al. 2015). Consequently, employee voice has been studied in disciplinary siloes and there are significant gaps in particular in understanding how behavioural antecedents may apply to formal voice.

Studies within HRM/ER typically consider employee voice as a *formal mechanism* or system constructed by the organisation to provide employees with the *opportunity* to communicate with management and to have meaningful input into decisions (Lavelle et al. 2010; Pyman et al. 2006; Wilkinson and Fay 2011). Thus, there is recognition that employee voice may benefit both the employer and its employees, and that the issues raised may relate to both of these actors (Dundon et al. 2004; Dundon and Gollan 2007). However, the OB discipline primarily considers a managerial perspective of employee voice, i.e. that voice should benefit the organisation (Barry and Wilkinson 2016; Morrison 2011, 2014). Within this discipline, voice is typically considered a promotive and discretionary *behaviour* where employees communicate constructive ideas, suggestions, concerns and opinions with the intent to bring about improvement or change (Morrison 2011, 2014; Van Dyne and LePine 1998). The OB discipline also differs in its study of employee voice by primarily examining *informal* employee voice at the individual level of the employee or manager. Thus, aside from the separate body of work that examines remedial or justice voice (Klaas 1989; Klaas and DeNisi 1989; Klaas et al. 2012; Olson-Buchanan 1996; Olson-Buchanan and Boswell 2002, 2008), the OB discipline typically discounts voice raised through formal voice systems within their studies, regardless of whether those mechanisms are designed for voice related to the organisations' or employees' interests.

There have been a number of recent articles, book chapters and calls for special editions (Kaufman 2015; Knoll et al. 2016; Mowbray et al. 2015; Pohler and

Luchak 2014; Sumanth and Lebel 2016; Wilkinson and Barry 2016; Wilkinson et al. 2014), that have discussed the limitations and differences between the HRM/ER and OB voice concept and studies, and which have called for an integration of the voice concept in order for the disciplines to draw from each other's studies and to move the literature forward more cohesively. Therefore, it would appear that there is recent interest by employee voice scholars (although primarily HRM/ER scholars at this stage) to adopt a more common conceptualisation, which may indeed lead to a convergence of the disparate research on employee voice.

In order to move toward this integrated HRM/ER and OB concept of voice, it is important for us to understand the nature, characteristics and trajectory of employee voice research within these disciplines. In this chapter, we explore how the conceptualisation of employee voice has evolved within the HRM/ER and OB disciplines since Hirschman's seminal book on voice, demonstrating the early similarities and then the later divergent paths. Next, we look further at the recent interest in the convergence of the voice concept and recommendations to integrate the HRM/ER and OB voice literature. We end the chapter with a discussion on how voice scholars could use a more integrated HRM/ER and OB concept of voice to advance future voice studies and to help resolve practical organisational issues.

1.2 Significant Turning Points and Pathways Within the Employee Voice Literature

While the concept of employee voice and 'employees having a say' can be traced back more than two centuries (Kaufman 2014b, 2015), it is Hirschman's (1970) exit-voice-loyalty theory, that was originally related to customers, that has underpinned the HRM/ER and OB employee voice studies in the past three decades. According to Hirschman, dissatisfied customers could choose between either exit or voice, when there was 'an objectionable state of affairs'. Hirschman theorised that customers would be more likely to choose the voice option when they were more loyal to the firm. Hirschman (1970, p. 30) defines voice as:

> ....any attempt at all to change, rather than to escape from, an objectionable state of affairs, whether through individual or collective petition to the management directly in charge, through appeal to a higher authority with the intention of forcing a change in management, or through various types of actions or protests, including those that are meant to mobilize public opinion.

It wasn't until 1983 that Farrell applied Hirschman's (1970) voice theory to employees, and added an additional dimension, neglect, to the theory. Neglect refers to 'lax and disregardful behaviour' (Farrell 1983, p. 598) where employees choose to willingly underperform and which can be characterised by behaviours such as lateness, absenteeism and silent sabotage (Allen 2014). This was followed by Freeman and Medoff (1984), who applied the theory to employment relations and argued that voice mechanisms, such as grievance and arbitration systems, were accountable for lower quit rates in unionised work places and that trade unions were the key to a functioning voice system. Interest in employee voice then began to grow, and Spencer (1986) examined the relationship between employee retention and employee voice mechanisms, finding that formal voice mechanisms (even those without union representation) were positively related to employee retention. As illustrated in Fig. 1.1, much of the early research on voice predominantly focused on Hirschman's (1970) exit-voice theory applied to formal union voice mechanisms and grievances, with notable publications by scholars across the ER and OB disciplines including those by Lewin (1987), Rusbult et al. (1988), Withey and Cooper (1989), Klaas (1989), Klaas and DeNisi (1989). Moving into the 90s, this focus on grievances continued, with Lewin and Mitchell (1992), Olson-Buchanan (1996) and Boroff and Lewin (1997) making notable contributions.

However, as we can see from Fig. 1.1, there was also a different path that some voice scholars were taking. For some, such as McCabe and Lewin (1992), there was a subtle differentiation and shift, with a call to include participation within voice studies. In the UK and Continental Europe, voice was linked to a wider agenda and debates around industrial democracy (Brannen 1983; Heller et al. 1998; Poole 1983). Industrial Democracy is a more powerful concept than voice as it promises to alter the structure of authority by giving employees a right to share in decision—making with management. Also influential from this tradition was the work of Ramsay (1977). Ramsay stresses the historical character arising from 'cycles' of working class resistance, creating periodic crises of management legitimacy with participation designed to help management deal with this. However, once these moments have passed the interest in participation and voice fades (Ackers et al. 1992). In contrast, Marchington et al. (1993) argued that there were a wider range of management motives behind the development of participation and voice and management saw it as more than a safety valve.

As Mowbray et al. (2015) note in their integrative HRM/ER and OB literature review, this turning point where employee participation and involvement were now considered within voice studies, coincided with decreasing unionism and increasing individualised voice arrangements, along with the increasing significance of HRM and a unitarist and high-performance approach to the management of employees. Consequently, we see within later definitions that arise after 2000 that the HRM/ER voice scholars conceptualise voice as providing both direct and indirect means to have a say over employer and employee interests. Within the HRM/ER studies, voice is now typically categorised as follows:

Task-Based Participation, which includes redesigned work operations, teamwork and self-managed teams. Voice through this mechanism is prevalent in HPWS and is seen as an opportunity for employees to use their discretion at work rather than be closely supervised by managers (Applebaum et al. 2000). Voice is integral to task-based participation as it facilitates workers having a say in how work is organised and is an integral part of the job, providing workers with more control over their working lives (Marchington 2007).

Upward Problem-Solving differs to task-based participation, in that these voice mechanisms operate independently of the work process. This form of voice can

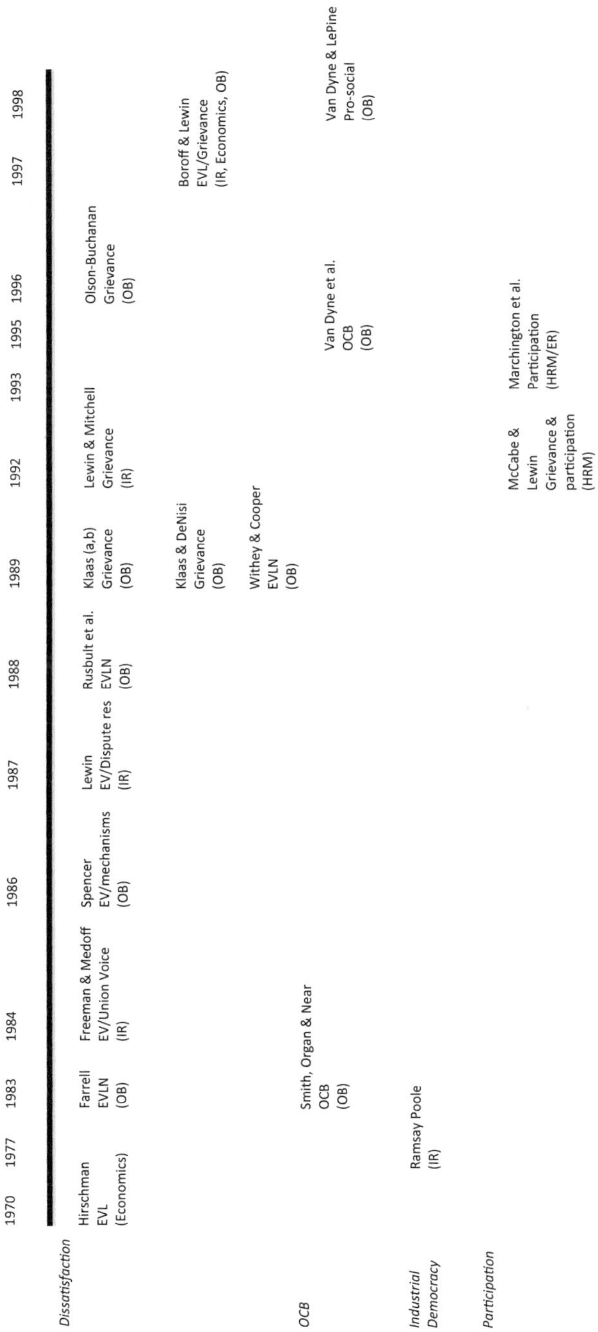

Fig. 1.1 Major turning points influencing current employee voice concepts

incorporate a range of mechanisms, designed to elicit employee knowledge and ideas, including offline teams, quality circles, suggestion schemes, attitude surveys and, problem-solving groups (Marchington 2007; Wilkinson et al. 2013).

The third category of employee voice is where workers *complain* to management about others' behaviour and performance at work, through **formal grievance procedures**. Marchington (2007) associates this form of voice as being the most closely related to Hirschman's Exit-Voice-Loyalty theory and notes that it provides employees an opportunity to articulate their concerns directly to management with the hope it will lead to changes in behaviour.

Downward communication is sometimes also identified as a form of direct involvement and voice. The primary purpose of this mechanism is to inform employees about work issues through either formalised written documents or face-to-face interactions between management and employees, cascading the information down the hierarchy. While technically not a form of employee voice itself, it can represent open communication and can be 'an important precursor to "fuller" employee involvement' (Wilkinson et al. 2013, p. 747) and enable two-way communication to take place.

Based on the definitions provided above, it can be seen that the HRM/ER discipline has conceptualised employee voice on the basis of plurality and mutuality, i.e. employee voice is conceived as providing formal mechanisms that enable employees to have a say over their own work life, while also providing mechanisms that encourage employees to contribute to the performance of the organisation, such as suggestion schemes. Thus, Boxall and Purcell (2015, p. 152) point to how voice can be critical to economic success particularly on those areas where staff have discretion in their jobs. More recent HRM/ER voice studies (Marchington and Suter 2013; Townsend et al. 2013) have also included informal voice as an additional channel for voice; thus, the concept of employee voice within this discipline has continued to expand.

From an HRM/ER perspective, the OB voice scholars took a unitarist approach to voice as it narrowed the voice construct from its original Hirschman beginnings. The organisational citizenship behaviour (OCB) literature had a significant influence over the OB voice concept and represents a significant turning point in the OB concept of voice. This shift in the concept of voice was influenced by the work of Smith et al. (1983), who identified the antecedents to OCB and included the statement 'makes innovative suggestions to improve the department' (p. 657) as a measure of altruism and later Van Dyne et al.'s (1995) identification of OCBs as extra-role behaviour. Using this as the basis for their research, Van Dyne and LePine (1998, p. 109) discussed the notion of helping and voice, defining voice as a 'promotive behavior that emphasizes expression of constructive challenge intended to improve rather than merely criticize… [it] is making innovative suggestions for change and recommending modifications to standard procedures even when others disagree'. This particular definition has shaped the construct and conceptualisation of employee voice within the OB discipline as evidenced by Morrison's (2014, p. 174) definition of employee voice as challenging, extra-role, informal, discretionary communication about work-related issues 'with the intent to bring about improvement or change'.

Perhaps the biggest legacy of the Van Dyne and LePine (1998) voice definition is that it shaped how OB scholars perceived employees' motive to exercise voice, which is that voice is driven by the pro-social need to bring about improvement or change for the organisation or other stakeholders, rather than as a result of dissatisfaction or the desire to complain or to obtain a positive outcome for the employee (Morrison 2014). This has meant that OB voice studies have largely focused on voice as a discretionary, promotive behaviour that will benefit the organisation, rather than a consideration of its role in providing employees with a voice concerning employee interests. In her reviews of the employee voice literature, Morrison (2011, 2014) argues that the HRM and IR literature streams do not define voice in a way that closely matches current conceptualisations (i.e. pro-social, improvement-oriented), and thus she excludes them from her review. However, in doing so, Morrison (2011) has excluded a body of literature that also considers dissatisfaction and grievances and the voice associated with remedying such situations. To some extent, the justice scholars (see, for example, Klaas 1989; Olson-Buchanan and Boswell 2008) have filled this gap by focussing on employee grievances concerned with alleged mistreatment or wrongdoing. However, given that the focus has been on pro-social voice within the OB discipline, the significant and important findings of OB scholars have been limited to a narrow construct of voice.

Human resource management/ER scholars, Barry and Wilkinson (2016), have critiqued this pro-social concept within OB and argue that this represents a purely unitarist perspective, which discounts the fact that formal voice mechanisms can provide the opportunity to create voice opportunities and thus alter the power imbalance between employer and employee in favour of the employee. These authors argue that this conceptualisation of voice is a managerial perspective, not dissimilar to the HRM strand, where managers decide whether or not employees have a voice and the mechanisms they can utilise. Therefore, even within the HRM discipline, despite its close association with ER, voice is often perceived as part of a management process to benefit the organisation and increase performance (Harley 2014). Where the HRM/ER and OB disciplines differ in this respect, is that because the HRM studies are more closely aligned with the pathway of ER, there is still the recognition that voice can hold multiple meanings and purposes. Consequently, within the combined HRM/ER discipline, there is the recognition that voice can empower individuals, while at the same time be defined by managers. Thus, there is also a pluralist sentiment to employee voice, whereby employees have the right 'to an effective voice in their own destiny, regardless of the consequences for management' (Donaghey et al. 2011, p. 55).

Looking back at the beginnings of employee voice studies, we can see that the pioneering voice authors have had a significant influence over how the HRM/ER and OB voice scholars have conceptualised voice and approached their studies, as illustrated in Table 1.1. However, a more management driven agenda, reflecting political and economic changes has led to employee voice being reoriented to become more about meeting the objectives of the employer. Consequently, this has driven voice researchers across both HRM/ER and OB to take more interest in the managerial view of voice. Next, given this similar managerial perspective, we look at how the

Table 1.1 Comparison of HRM/ER and OB conceptualisation of employee voice

Concept	Human resource management/employment relations	Organisational behaviour
Form	System	Behaviour
Motive	Dissatisfaction	Pro-social
	Pro-social	Justice
		Dissatisfaction
Expectation	In-role	Extra-role
	Extra-role	In-role
Beneficiary	Employee	Organisation
	Organisation	
Mechanism	Formal	Informal
Content and types	Task-based participation	Suggestions for change and improvement
	Upward problem-solving	Expression of concern about work issues harmful to organisation
	Grievance procedures	Communicating different points of view
Focus	Participation in decision-making	Improve organisational or unit functioning

Source Mowbray et al. (2015)

HRM/ER and OB concept of employee voice could be integrated in order to develop a more common conceptualisation of employee voice between the two disciplines.

1.3 Integrating the HRM/ER and OB Voice Literature

Because employee voice has typically been examined in disciplinary silos with different conceptualisations, there are limitations to our understanding of employee voice and how employee voice behaviour might be related to employee voice mechanisms and collective, formal voice. For example, in their examination of the embeddedness of employee participation and involvement within UK organisations, Cox et al. (2006) considered only the breadth and depth of formal direct and indirect voice mechanisms and overlooked the informal voice that may occur between employees and their managers/employer. Similarly, in their examination of employee voice behaviour by employees speaking up in groups, Morrison et al. (2011) used Van Dyne and LePine's (1998) typical measure of employee voice, which do not consider collective or formal voice. A number of voice scholars have argued that in order for the voice literature to move forward and to gain a better understanding of the antecedents, opportunities, and outcomes of voice, a broader concept of employee voice is needed that includes both systems and behaviour, and acknowledgement that voice may occur formally or informally to a variety of targets and through different channels (Kaufman 2015; Knoll et al. 2016; Mowbray et al. 2015; Pohler and Luchak 2014; Sumanth and Lebel 2016; Wilkinson and Barry 2016; Wilkinson et al. 2014).

While in recent times, OB voice scholars have generally maintained the notion of a pro-social motive to voice, and discounted voice that is raised via formal mechanisms, considered complaining, or used for self-determination purposes (McClean et al. 2013; Morrison 2011, 2014), there has been an expansion of the voice construct to include different types of voice. Morrison (2011) suggested three different types of voice revolving around the pro-social motive, namely *suggestion-focused* voice, which is voice associated with improvements to the work unit or organisation; *problem-focused* voice, which is voice concerned with issues that may be harmful to the organisation; and *opinion-focused* voice, whereby employees may express views regarding work-related issues that may differ to those held by others. Similar voice types have been proposed by Liang et al. (2012), who empirically demonstrated that the psychological antecedents of felt obligation and organisation-based self-esteem were related to *promotive* voice, which is voice associated with suggestions and ideas, and that psychological safety was related to *prohibitive* voice, a form of voice associated with concerns that may be harmful to the organisation. Other types of voice behaviour were identified by Burris (2012), who found that managers responded differently to employees who used *challenging* voice, which is voice that will challenge the status quo, compared to *supportive* voice, which is voice that supports existing practices and policies. A validated set of voice measures has also been developed by Maynes and Podsakoff (2014), which includes some similar voice types to those suggested by the previous authors, such as *supportive* and *constructive* voice. Maynes and Podsakoff also added two different voice types that may be considered more negative, including *defensive* voice, which is voice that opposes employer-driven changes to work policies and procedures, and *destructive* voice, which is where employees may harshly criticise work policies, practices and procedures. While all of these OB voice types are underpinned by a unitarist and managerial-driven perspective of employee voice, it would not be a great expanse of the literature to apply these voice types to a concept of voice that includes voice content concerning employee interests and voice raised using formal channels.

In their integrative review of pro-social, informal voice, whistleblowing and formal remedial/justice and grievance voice, Klaas et al. (2012) used an integrative perspective to examine the determinants of voice. While this review did not include contemporary HRM voice studies, there was the inclusion of some IR literature concerning dispute resolution and grievances. Klaas et al. discuss formal and informal voice across these various types of voice in some detail, noting that formal voice may be used to escalate issues and may be seen as provocative. These authors also highlight and discuss the differences between two different types of voice, i.e. pro-social voice and justice voice. Earlier in this chapter, we discussed how OB scholars have primarily studied pro-social improvement-oriented voice that will benefit the organisation, and that this concept of voice evolved from the OCB literature. There is a smaller body of literature on justice voice (see, for example, Harlos 2010; Klaas and Ward 2015; Olson-Buchanan and Boswell 2002, 2008), which is concerned with

	Voice Behaviour	Voice System
Promotive	Pro-Social Voice	High Involvement Work Systems Non-Union Employee Representation Worker Ownership/Directors
Remedial	Grievance Filing Whistle-blowing	Collective Bargaining/Unions Works Councils Alternative Dispute Resolution

Fig. 1.2 A typology of employee voice research. *Source* Pohler and Luchak (2014)

grievances and complaints, however, the two voice types are not studied together by OB voice scholars and it is pro-social voice which dominates the area. The separation of studies is due to the different motivations attached to the two types of voice, which primarily excludes dissatisfaction as a motivator of pro-social voice. However, Klaas and colleagues argue that an employee may be initially motivated by a justice orientation to file a grievance but at the same time may have a pro-social motive to modify supervisory behaviour that may negatively affect co-workers. Likewise, they argue that employees may have a self-promotional or political motivation to voice. These arguments provide a more expansive perspective of the motives for employee voice than those offered by pro-social voice scholars (Morrison 2011, 2014), however, the exclusion of HRM/ER literature has meant that the self-determination motivation that may underpin HRM/ER studies is ignored and formal voice mechanisms such as self-managing teams, consultative committees and quality circles, are not considered in relation to voice behaviour.

Recognising the need to integrate voice from a systems and behaviour perspective, Pohler and Luchak (2014) identified two dimensions by which employee voice could be examined and integrated from the HRM/ER and OB perspective: the underlying intention or purpose of voice (i.e. promotive or remedial) and the form of voice examined (i.e. human behaviour or system impact), as illustrated in Fig. 1.2. Pohler and Luchak's framework represents the first attempt within the literature to integrate the HRM/ER and OB conceptualisations of employee voice and to integrate pro-social and justice voice and is a useful advancement.

However, the Pohler and Luchak typology does not clearly delineate all of the factors that need to be considered for an integrated HRM/ER and OB conceptualisation of employee voice. According to Mowbray et al.'s (2015) integrative review, there are other factors that need to be considered, including a broader range of motives, voice types, content and mechanisms, and a consideration of both formal and informal voice, beneficiary, role breadth and targets. These authors have argued that, while there are some differences in the way employee voice has been conceptualised across the HRM/ER and OB disciplines, there are also similarities that would indicate that an integrated conceptualisation would not be too difficult to achieve. For example, they examined the OB literature pertaining to voice as an in-role or extra-role behaviour and found that several studies (Tangirala et al. 2013; Van Dyne et al. 2008) demonstrate that voice could also be considered an in-role behaviour (as it may be considered in HRM/ER studies), despite Morrison's (2011, 2014) contention that voice is conceptualised as extra-role within OB voice studies.

Similarly, Mowbray and colleagues found that, while there is a strong contention by many OB voice scholars that voice is motivated by a pro-social desire to improve the organisation rather than a motivation to voice due to dissatisfaction (Morrison 2011), the proactivity literature suggests that the dissatisfaction may be the primary motivation that fuels the pro-social behaviour, a concept supported by an empirical voice study by OB voice scholars Tangirala and Ramanujam (2008). Mowbray et al. also discuss the increasing prevalence of HRM/ER studies including informal voice within their empirical studies, showing that voice may occur within formal or informal voice channels, and often sequentially or in parallel (Marchington and Suter 2013). Consequently, Mowbray et al. provide evidence that a consideration of formal and informal voice channels and behaviour is needed when examining employee voice from a HRM/ER or OB perspective.

A further development of an integrative and more inclusive voice concept by Kaufman (2015) critiques Morrison's (2011) model, arguing that it omits key variables related to voice. Developing a more comprehensive model, depicted in Fig. 1.3, Kaufman argues for a wider conceptualisation of voice than provided by the OB discipline. Among other factors, Kaufman identifies that the Morrison (2011) model does not include a consideration of the goals, strategy and performance of the organisation and their managers, or the programmes, policies and strategies that companies create for HRM and employee involvement. Kaufman's model includes a consideration of both employee and employer decision-making, with regards to voice. This is an important differentiation to Morrison's models, which only consider the role of the employee in making voice decisions. As Kaufman (2015, p. 30) argues, 'surely, however, the breadth, depth and form of voice are also critically influenced by decisions of managers'. Kaufman identifies similar internal contextual factors as Morrison (2011, 2014), such as organisational culture and managerial quality, and employee psycho-social dispositions. With a greater focus on the employer, he also includes the external environment as well, i.e. economic, legal and social-cultural, along with organisational configuration and governance structure, strategy and ER climate. Kaufman contends that those external and internal contingencies and strategies then shape the employer and employees' desired level of voice and the type of voice structure to be used. Kaufman's integrated ER and OB model provides the foundation for understanding the determinants of employee voice and illustrates the need to consider both individual and institutional factors. However, this model does not demonstrate how these individual and institutional factors interact and thus, there is still the need to bridge the gulf between the HRM/ER and OB concept of voice.

Examining voice outcomes across the individual, group and organisational level, Bashshur and Oc (2015) integrated voice literature across a number of disciplines and

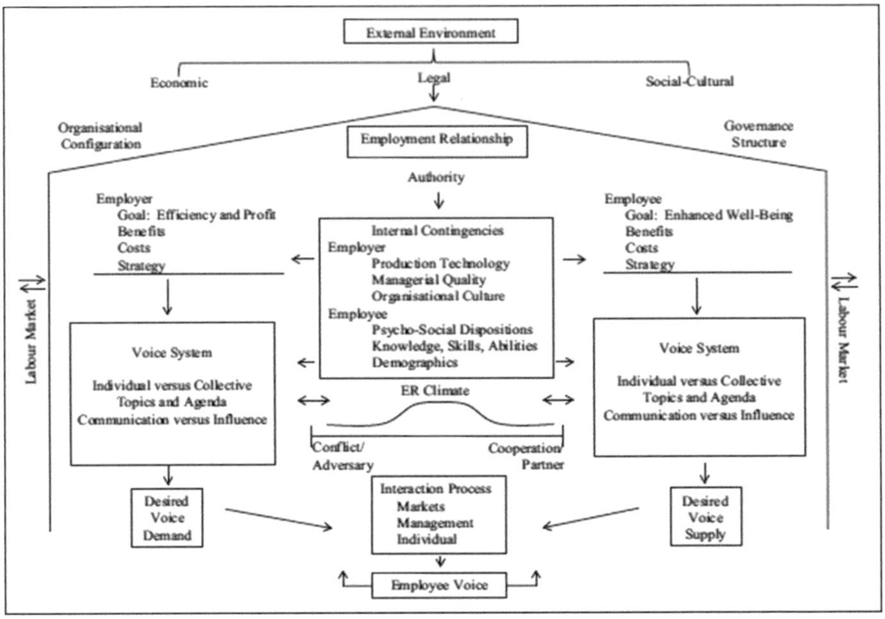

Fig. 1.3 Kaufman's (2015) employee voice framework. *Source* Kaufman (2015)

fields. Bashshur and Oc argue that because voice is conceptualised differently across the pro-social behaviour, organisational justice, HRM and IR fields, and because each field examines different dependant variables, there is a lack of integration across the literatures that makes it difficult to examine employee voice holistically. Accordingly, Bashshur and Oc suggest that instead of the OB discipline focussing on the distilling of the voice construct into 'smaller and distally related mini-constructs', there should be a 'return to definitions more closely rooted in Hirschman's (1970) original conceptualization of voice' (p. 1546).

With this sentiment to return to the root of Hirschman's concept of voice, while also considering the advances that have been made in the employee voice literature, we provide an integrated definition of employee voice that is based on the understanding that voice may be motivated by pro-social, justice, dissatisfaction or self-determination motives, that it may occur formally or informally, and that it may be discretionary or considered an in-role behaviour. This integrated HRM/ER and OB concept of employee voice is summarised is Table 1.2 and encapsulated in the following definition:

> Employee voice is speaking up with ideas, issues, concerns and opinions regarding employer or employee interests, through either formal or informal mechanisms or channels, and where doing so may be considered an in-role or extra-role behaviour.

Table 1.2 Integrated HRM/ER and OB conceptual framework of employee voice

Concept	Integrated HRM/ER and OB factors
Form	System
	Behaviour
Motive	Dissatisfaction
	Self-determination
	Pro-social
	Justice
Role Breadth	In-role
	Extra-role
Beneficiary	Employee
	Employer
Mechanism and channel	Formal
	Informal
Types	Task-based participation
	Upward problem-solving
	Grievance procedures
	Downward communication
	Suggestion-focused
	Problem-focused
	Opinion-focused
Behaviour	Supportive
	Constructive
	Defensive
	Destructive
	Complaining
Content	Contributions to decision-making
	Suggestions for change and improvement
	Concern about work issues harmful to organisation
	Opinions and different points of view
	Grievances
	Complaints
	Employees' individual interests such as personal development and conditions
Target	Executive and senior managers
	Middle and frontline managers
	Team leader
	Peers
	Union

Source Adapted from Mowbray et al. (2015)

1.4 Future Directions

An integrated conceptualisation of employee voice will provide the HRM/ER and OB disciplines with significant opportunities to advance the employee voice literature and to elicit new findings. The suggestion to converge these concepts of voice is not merely aspirational, but as discussed in this chapter, based on the recognition that greater integration is needed in order to develop a more holistic understanding of employee voice. It is recognised that the OB and HRM/ER voice scholars study employee voice differently, however, these differences should not be related to the concept of voice, just the *way* employee voice is studied.

One of the best ways to adopt a more holistic approach may be through cross-disciplinary collaboration on studies, which would enable scholars to utilise not only their own strengths but also to draw on the strengths of others. In doing so, it may be possible for the HRM/ER and OB scholars to contribute additional theoretical findings to the body of voice literature, both in isolation and collaboration. One area where there is the opportunity for the OB discipline to contribute to the voice literature is to incorporate formal voice mechanisms and channels within their studies related to pro-social voice to determine the relationship between formal employee voice systems and employee voice behaviour. This would provide the opportunity for OB voice studies to examine those relationships that have previously been determined between informal voice and behaviour, such as the leader member exchange (LMX) relationship (Botero and Van Dyne 2009; Burris et al. 2008; Van Dyne et al. 2008), and to examine these relationships in regard to formal voice.

One area of future research that could be undertaken is to examine the extent to which employees and employers consider that voice within formal voice mechanisms is a discretionary behaviour. Perceptions of role breadth and the extent to which voice is considered in-role or extra-role may differ significantly within formal voice mechanisms, such as staff meetings versus focussed improvement teams. Individual differences, such as duty orientation (Tangirala et al. 2013), may also contribute to perceptions of formal voice as discretionary. Generally, the HRM/ER scholars could benefit from the OB behavioural measures related to managing voice and employees voicing, such as leaderships types and personality and attitudinal characteristics, in order to better understand under what conditions employees are likely to voice using both formal and informal voice mechanisms and channels, across individual, team and organisational levels.

A significant future direction for the study of employee voice may be to consider a new definition and measurement of employee voice that is based on an integrated HRM/ER and OB concept of voice. However, we do need to be mindful as Barry et al. (2017) note that part of the difficulty of achieving integration is that in asking about the purpose of voicing leads us into normative terrain, where disciplinary perspectives will lock voice scholars into very different viewpoints.

There are a number of practical implications for organisations and their employees that can result from having a better understanding of how employee voice is operationalised. Organisations and their managers need to create an environment and avenues for voice where employees will feel confident and safe to engage in both improvement-oriented voice that will benefit the organisation and voice that is related to employee interests. Being committed and open to both types of voice may improve the LMX relationship between managers and employees, and employees may be more willing to voice on issues that will benefit the organisation and contribute to improved performance (Marchington 2007; Van Dyne et al. 2008). Providing informal opportunities for employees to voice, and perhaps doing so within formal mechanisms, may send the message to employees that they are able to speak up on more challenging or personal voice. Thus, having a theoretical understanding of how voice operates under multiple motivations and via various mechanisms and channels, is likely to assist employers to develop policies and practices that will not only benefit the organisation but will also contribute to employee well-being and the employee's need to express dissatisfaction and achieve self-determination alongside pro-social motivations.

References

Ackers, P., Marchington, M., Wilkinson, A., & Goodman, J. (1992). The use of cycles? Explaining employee involvement in the 1990s. *Industrial Relations Journal, 23*(4), 268–283.

Allen, M. (2014). Hirschman and voice. In A. Wilkinson, J. Donaghey, T. Dundon, & R. Freeman (Eds.), *The handbook of research on employee voice* (pp. 36–51). London: Edward Elgar Press.

Applebaum, E., Bailey, T., Berg, P., & Kalleberg, A. (2000). *Manufacturing advantage: Why high performance work systems pay off*. Ithaca, NY: ILR Press.

Barry, M., & Wilkinson, A. (2016). Pro-social or pro-management? A critique of the conception of employee voice as a pro-social behaviour within organizational behaviour. *British Journal of Industrial Relations, 54*(2), 261–284.

Barry, M., Wilkinson. A., & Dundon, T. (2017). Employee voice: Conceptualisations, meanings, limitations and possible integration. In: Wilkinson et al. (Eds.) *Routledge companion to employment relations*.

Bashshur, M. R., & Oc, B. (2015). When voice matters: A multilevel review of the impact of voice in organizations. *Journal of Management, 41*(5), 1530–1554.

Boroff, K. E., & Lewin, D. (1997). Loyalty, voice, and intent to exit a union firm: A conceptual and empirical analysis. *Industrial and Labor Relations Review, 51*(1), 50–63.

Botero, I. C., & Van Dyne, L. (2009). Employee voice behavior interactive effects of LMX and power distance in the United States and Colombia. *Management Communication Quarterly, 23*(1), 84–104.

Boxall, P. F., & Purcell, J. (2011). *Strategy and human resource management*. Basingstoke: Palgrave Macmillan.

Boxall, P. F., & Purcell, J. (2015). *Strategy and human resource management* (4th ed.). Basingstoke: Palgrave.

Brannen, P. (1983). *Authority and participation in industry*. London: Batsford.

Burke, R. J., & Cooper, C. L. (Eds.). (2013). *Voice and whistleblowing in organizations: Overcoming fear, fostering courage and unleashing candour*. Cheltenham, UK: Edward Elgar Publishing.

Burris, E. R. (2012). The risks and rewards of speaking up: Managerial responses to employee voice. *Academy of Management Journal, 55*(4), 851–875.

Burris, E. R., Detert, J. R., & Chiaburu, D. S. (2008). Quitting before leaving: The mediating effects of psychological attachment and detachment on voice. *Journal of Applied Psychology, 93*(4), 912–922.

Cox, A., Zagelmeyer, S., & Marchington, M. (2006). Embedding employee involvement and participation at work. *Human Resource Management Journal, 16*(3), 250–267.

Donaghey, J., Cullinane, N., Dundon, T., & Wilkinson, A. (2011). Reconceptualising employee silence problems and prognosis. *Work, Employment & Society, 25*(1), 51–67.

Dundon, T., & Gollan, P. J. (2007). Re-conceptualizing voice in the non-union workplace. *The International Journal of Human Resource Management, 18*(7), 1182–1198.

Dundon, T., Wilkinson, A., Marchington, M., & Ackers, P. (2004). The meanings and purpose of employee voice. *The International Journal of Human Resource Management, 15*(6), 1149–1170.

Farrell, D. (1983). Exit, voice, loyalty, and neglect as responses to job dissatisfaction: A multidimensional scaling study. *Academy of Management Journal, 26*(4), 596–607.

Freeman, R. B., & Medoff, J. L. (1984). *What do unions do?*. New York: Basic Books.

Greenberg, J., & Edwards, M. (Eds.). (2009). *Voice and silence in organizations*. Bingley: Emerald Group Publishing Ltd.

Harley, B. (2014). High performance work systems and employee voice. In: A. Wilkinson, J. Donaghey, T. Dundon, & R. Freeman (Eds.), *The handbook of research on employee voice* (pp. 82–96). London: Edward Elgar Press.

Harlos, K. (2010). If you build a remedial voice mechanism, will they come? Determinants of voicing interpersonal mistreatment at work. *Human Relations, 63*(3), 311–329.

Heller, F., Pusić, E., Strauss, G., & Wilpert, B. (1998). *Organizational participation*. Oxford, Myth and Reality: Oxford University Press.

Hirschman, A. O. (1970). *Exit, voice, and loyalty: Responses to decline in firms, organizations, and states*. Cambridge, MA: Harvard University Press.

Holland, P. (2014). Employers and voice. In A. Wilkinson, J. Donaghey, T. Dundon, & R. Freeman (Eds.), *The handbook of research on employee voice* (pp. 135–154). London: Edward Elgar Press.

Johnstone, S. P., & Ackers, P. (2015). *Finding a voice at work: New perspectives on employment relations*. Oxford: Oxford University Press.

Kaufman, B. E. (2007). The development of HRM in historical and international perspective. In: P. Boxall, J. Purcell & P. Wright (Eds.), *The Oxford handbook of human resource management* (pp. 19–47). New York: Oxford University Press.

Kaufman, B. E. (2014a). Explaining breadth and depth of employee voice across firms: A voice factor demand model. *Journal of Labor Research, 35*(3), 296–319.

Kaufman, B. E. (2014b). Employee voice before Hirschman: Its early history, conceptualization, and practice. In A. Wilkinson, J. Donaghey, T. Dundon, & R. Freeman (Eds.), *The handbook of research on employee voice* (pp. 17–35). London: Elgar Press.

Kaufman, B. E. (2015). Theorising determinants of employee voice: An integrative model across disciplines and levels of analysis. *Human Resource Management Journal, 25*(1), 19–40.

Klaas, B., & Ward, A. K. (2015). Formal, justice-oriented voice in the nonunion firm: Who speaks up and when? *Industrial Relations: A Journal of Economy and Society, 54*(2), 321–356.

Klaas, B. S. (1989). Determinants of grievance activity and the grievance system's impact on employee behavior: An integrative perspective. *Academy of Management Review, 14*(3), 445–458.

Klaas, B. S., & DeNisi, A. S. (1989). Managerial reactions to employee dissent: The impact of grievance activity on performance rating. *Academy of Management Journal, 32,* 705–717.

Klaas, B. S., Olson-Buchanan, J. B., & Ward, A. K. (2012). The determinants of alternative forms of workplace voice an integrative perspective. *Journal of Management, 38*(1), 314–345.

Knoll, M., Wegge, J., Unterrainer, C., et al. (2016). Is our knowledge on voice and silence in organizations growing? Building bridges and (re)discovering opportunities. *German Journal of Research in Human Resource Management, 30*(3–4), 161–194.

Lavelle, J., Gunnigle, P., & McDonnell, A. (2010). Patterning employee voice in multinational companies. *Human Relations, 63*(3), 395–418.

Lewin, D. (1987). Dispute resolution in the nonunion firm: A theoretical and empirical analysis. *Journal of Conflict Resolution, 31*(3), 465–502.

Lewin, D., & Mitchell, D. J. (1992). Systems of employee voice: Theoretical and empirical perspectives. *California Management Review, 34*(3), 95–111.

Liang, J., Farh, C. I., & Farh, J. L. (2012). Psychological antecedents of promotive and prohibitive voice: A two-wave examination. *Academy of Management Journal, 55*(1), 71–92.
Marchington, M. (2007). Employee voice systems. In P. Boxall, J. Purcell, & P. Wright (Eds.), *The Oxford handbook of human resource management* (pp. 231–250). Oxford: Oxford University Press.
Marchington, M. (2015). Analysing the forces shaping employee involvement and participation (EIP) at organisation level in liberal market economies (LMEs). *Human Resource Management Journal, 25*(1), 1–18.
Marchington, M., & Suter, J. (2013). Where informality really matters: Patterns of employee involvement and participation (EIP) in a non-union firm. *Industrial Relations: A Journal of Economy and Society, 52*(s1), 284–313.
Marchington, M., Wilkinson, A., Ackers, P., & Goodman, J. (1993). The influence of managerial relations on waves of employee involvement. *British Journal of Industrial Relations, 31*(4), 553–576.
Maynes, T. D., & Podsakoff, P. M. (2014). Speaking more broadly: An examination of the nature, antecedents, and consequences of an expanded set of employee voice behaviors. *Journal of Applied Psychology, 99*(1), 87–112.
McCabe, D. M., & Lewin, D. (1992). Employee voice: A human resource management perspective. *California Management Review, 34*(3), 112–123.
McClean, E. J., Burris, E. R., & Detert, J. R. (2013). When does voice lead to exit? It depends on leadership. *Academy of Management Journal, 56*(2), 525–548.
Morrison, E. W. (2011). Employee voice behavior: Integration and directions for future research. *The Academy of Management Annals, 5*(1), 373–412.
Morrison, E. W. (2014). Employee voice and silence. *The Annual Review of Organizational Psychology and Organizational Behavior, 1*(1), 173–197.
Morrison, E. W., Wheeler-Smith, S. L., & Kamdar, D. (2011). Speaking up in groups: A cross-level study of group voice climate and voice. *The Journal of Applied Psychology, 96*(1), 183–191.
Mowbray, P. K., Wilkinson, A., & Tse, H. H. M. (2015). An integrative review of employee voice: Identifying a common conceptualization and research agenda. *International Journal of Management Reviews, 17*(3), 382–400.
Olson-Buchanan, J. B. (1996). Voicing discontent: What happens to the grievance filer after the grievance? *Journal of Applied Psychology, 81*(1), 52–63.
Olson-Buchanan, J. B., & Boswell, W. R. (2002). The role of employee loyalty and formality in voicing discontent. *Journal of Applied Psychology, 87*(6), 1167–1174.
Olson-Buchanan, J. B., & Boswell, W. R. (2008). An integrative model of experiencing and responding to mistreatment at work. *Academy of Management Review, 33*(1), 76–96.
Pohler, D. M., & Luchak, A. A. (2014). The missing employee in employee voice research. In A. Wilkinson, J. Donaghey, T. Dundon, & R. Freeman (Eds.), *The handbook of research on employee voice* (pp. 188–207). London: Edward Elgar Press.
Poole, M. (1986). *Towards a new industrial democracy: Workers' participation in industry*. London: Routledge and Kegan Paul.
Pyman, A., Cooper, B., Teicher, J., & Holland, P. (2006). A comparison of the effectiveness of employee voice arrangements in Australia. *Industrial Relations Journal, 37*(5), 543–559.
Ramsay, H. (1977). Cycles of control: Worker participation in sociological and historical perspective. *Sociology, 11*(3), 481–506.
Rusbult, C. E., Farrell, D., Rogers, G., & Mainous, A. G. (1988). Impact of exchange variables on exit, voice, loyalty, and neglect: An integrative model of responses to declining job satisfaction. *Academy of Management Journal, 31*(3), 599–627.
Smith, C. A., Organ, D. W., & Near, J. P. (1983). Organizational citizenship behavior: Its nature and antecedents. *Journal of Applied Psychology, 68*(4), 653–663.
Spencer, D. G. (1986). Employee voice and employee retention. *Academy of Management Journal, 29*(3), 488–502.

Sumanth, J. J., & Lebel, R. D. (2016). Employee voice. In: *Oxford bibliographies in management*. New York: Oxford University Press. https://doi.org/10.1093/obo/9780199846740-0109.

Tangirala, S., Kamdar, D., Venkataramani, V., & Parke, M. R. (2013). Doing right versus getting ahead: The effects of duty and achievement orientations on employees' voice. *Journal of Applied Psychology, 98*(6), 1040–1050.

Tangirala, S., & Ramanujam, R. (2008). Exploring nonlinearity in employee voice: The effects of personal control and organizational identification. *Academy of Management Journal, 51*(6), 1189–1203.

Townsend, K., Wilkinson, A., & Burgess, J. (2013). Filling the gaps: Patterns of formal and informal participation. *Economic and Industrial Democracy, 34*(2), 337–354.

Van Dyne, L., Cummings, L. L., & Parks, J. M. (1995). Extra-role behaviors: In pursuit of construct and definitional clarity (a bridge over muddied waters). In L. L. Cummings & B. M. Staw (Eds.), *Research in organizational behavior, 17* (pp. 215–285). Greenwich: CT JAI press.

Van Dyne, L., Kamdar, D., & Joireman, J. (2008). In-role perceptions buffer the negative impact of low LMX on helping and enhance the positive impact of high LMX on voice. *Journal of Applied Psychology, 93*(6), 1195–1207.

Van Dyne, L., & LePine, J. A. (1998). Helping and voice extra-role behaviors: Evidence of construct and predictive validity. *Academy of Management Journal, 41*(1), 108–119.

Wilkinson, A., & Barry, M. (2016). Voices from across the divide: An industrial relations perspective on employee voice. *German Journal of Human Resource Management: Zeitschrift für Personalforschung, 30*(3–4), 338–344.

Wilkinson, A., Dundon, T., Donaghey, J., & Freeman, R. (2014). Employee voice: Charting new terrain. In A. Wilkinson, J. Donaghey, T. Dundon, & R. Freeman (Eds.), *The handbook of research on employee voice* (pp. 3–16). London: Edward Elgar Press.

Wilkinson, A., Dundon, T., & Marchington, M. (2013). Employee involvement and voice. In S. Bach & M. Edwards (Eds.), *Managing human resources (5th edn)* (pp. 744–761). Chichester: Wiley-Blackwell.

Wilkinson, A., & Fay, C. (2011). New times for employee voice? *Human Resource Management, 50*(1), 65–74.

Wilkinson, A., Townsend, K., Graham, T., & Muurlink, O. (2015). Fatal consequences: An analysis of the failed employee voice system at the Bundaberg Hospital. *Asia Pacific Journal of Human Resources, 53*(3), 265–280.

Withey, M. J., & Cooper, W. H. (1989). Predicting exit, voice, loyalty, and neglect. *Administrative Science Quarterly, 34*(4), 521–539.

Dr. Paula Mowbray is a Lecturer in the Department of Employment Relations and Human Resources at Griffith University. Her research interests are in the areas of employee involvement, participation and voice, organisational culture, high-performance work systems and employee engagement. Her work has recently been published in the International Journal of Management Reviews and International Journal of Human Resource Management.

Dr. Adrian Wilkinson is Professor and Director of the Centre for Work, Organisation and Wellbeing at Griffith University, Australia. He holds a visiting Professorships at Loughborough University and is an Academic Fellow at the Centre for International Human Resource Management at the Judge Institute, University of Cambridge. He has been shortlisted by HR magazine for the award of HR (Most Influential International Thinker). Adrian has authored/co-authored/edited 30 books and over 150 articles in academic journals. Recent books include HRM at Work: People Management and Development, 6th edition (CIPD, 2016); Case Studies in Global Management: Strategy, Innovation and People (TUP, 2012); Contemporary Human Resource Management (Pearson, 2016): The Oxford Handbook of Employment Relations (OUP, 2014) and the Handbook of Research on Employee Voice (Elgar 2014). Adrian served on the Australian Research Council

College of Experts from 2008–2010. He is a Fellow and Accredited Examiner of the Chartered Institute of Personnel and Development in the UK and a Fellow of the Australian Human Resource Institute. He is an Academician (Fellow) of the Academy of Social Sciences in the UK as well as a Fellow of the Academy of Social Sciences in Australia.

Dr. Herman Tse is an Associate Professor and the ECR network Director at Monash Business School. His research interest includes interpersonal relationships, emotions in teams, multilevel issues in organisations and leadership effectiveness. He has published a number of articles in leading journals such as Journal of Applied Psychology, the Journal of Organisational Behaviour, the Leadership Quarterly and the Human Resource Management. He has also served on the editorial board of the Journal of Organisational Behaviour, the Management Organisation Review and the Journal of Business Research.

Chapter 2
The Twin Track Model of Employee Voice: An Anglo-American Perspective on Union Decline and The Rise of Alternative Forms of Voice

Alex Bryson, Richard Freeman, Rafael Gomez and Paul Willman

Abstract This chapter will review the major studies undertaken in the twenty-first century to assess the changing nature of employee voice in the Anglo-American context. These studies are predominantly based on employee perceptions but also include employer surveys and multilevel analysis.

Keywords Workplace voice · Unions · Employment relations

2.1 Introduction

The effect of trade unions on firms and workers has been a core concern of labour and industrial relations (IR) scholarship ever since IR emerged as a distinct field of study (Webb and Webb 1897; Dunlop 1944). One of IR scholarship's earliest recommendations was for workers to have some mechanism for collective representation at the workplace (Feldman 1928) and independent trade unions were seen as the closest embodiment of this goal (Commons 1935). Although IR scholars no longer use terms like 'industrial man' or the 'labour problem' (Dunlop 1958) to frame the debate over unions and worker representation, current concerns about employees lacking voice are remarkably similar to those of nearly a century ago. In particular, the fostering of industrial democracy (the original term for employee voice and representation used

A. Bryson (✉)
University College London, London, England
e-mail: a.bryson@ucl.ac.uk

R. Gomez
University of Toronto, Toronto, Canada

P. Willman
London School of Economics and Political Science, London, England

R. Freeman
Harvard University & NBER, Boston, USA
e-mail: freeman@nber.org

P. Holland et al. (eds.), *Employee Voice at Work*, Work, Organization, and Employment, https://doi.org/10.1007/978-981-13-2820-6_2

by scholars like the Webb's (1897) and Commons (1935)) was actively debated well into the 1970s (Derber 1967, 1970) and is now, after a long period of dormancy, making a return (e.g. the 2016 British government green paper on Corporate Governance Reform with its call for worker representation on public company directorships). The main problem facing scholarship in the area of employee voice today is that the main vehicle for providing a voice to workers (i.e. the trade union) has witnessed a near universal decline (see Fig. 2.1). This raises the question of just how important voice and representation is in the context of post-Fordist economies (Thompson and Newsome 2004).

We begin this chapter by presenting a simple framework for understanding union decline that follows some of our own work in this area (Freeman 1998; Freeman and Rogers 1999; Bryson and Gomez 2005; Willman et al. 2006, 2017). We model the decline in unionization in Britain, Canada and the US—three countries that form the bulk of our research—as a shift by workers and firms from representative (collective) to direct (individual) voice. We discuss the channels that link a rise in 'direct (individual) voice' with a commensurate fall in 'representative (collective) voice' to specific subgroups of firms and workers, focusing on two alternative hypotheses: (1) the loss of unionized jobs and a decline in union density in established firms and among older workers versus (2) new workers and new firms adopting alternative forms of non-union voice or no voice at all. We show that it is the latter channel, the rise of so-called 'never-membership' and rise of alternative voice systems in newly established firms, which has contributed to the majority of union density decline.

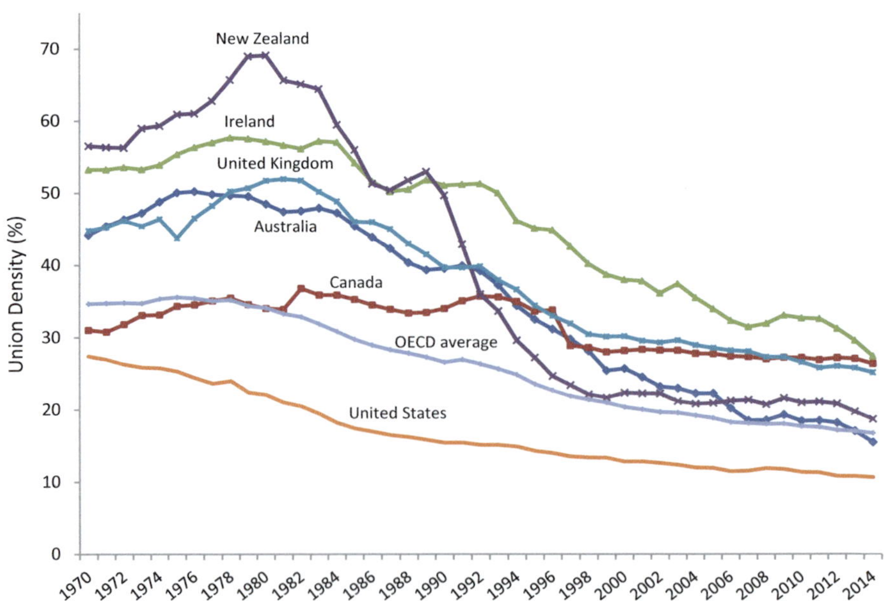

Fig. 2.1 Union density in six English speaking countries, 1970–2014. *Source* OECD, accessed on *OECD.stat* June 7 2017

This is especially so in Britain where we have the longest time series on workplace voice, but is also apparent in the US (Booth et al. 2010) where never-membership rates have been increasing amongst new labour market entrants (e.g. in the mid-1980s 58.1% of 23 year olds had never been unionized, but by the mid-2000s, that figure had risen to 70.6%, even after adjusting for demographic and structural changes).

We end with a discussion of how the decentralized form of industrial relations that prevails in the Anglo-American world—specifically, the Wagner Act model with its emphasis on organizing individual workers and workplaces—not only accounts for rising never-membership but has also fostered a 'twin track' model of employee voice. Twin track refers to the split that exists between workers with relatively high rates of union representation (e.g. those employed in sectors with high barriers to entry, stable product markets and/or service delivery monopolies) and with workers in smaller private sector firms, where the majority have no union representation. These latter workers are often voice free, but in some cases have access to employer-provided voice and increasingly, it seems, access to self-organized online worker forums and social-justice campaigns led by non-governmental organizations (NGOs). The difficulty in this area is that it is very hard to move beyond anecdotal cases given that these new employee advocacy groups have not appeared in a systematic way on many nationally representative surveys. The challenge then becomes to locate these new forms in the data we do possess and in the context of the theories and models discussed in this chapter.

2.2 Decentralized Bargaining and the Rise of Twin Track Unionism

The early 1980s was the high-water mark for union representation across most of the Anglo-American world (see Fig. 2.1). In 1980, for example, 51% of workers were represented by trade unions in Britain but by 2014 that number had fallen to 25%. In the United States, representation was always on the low end of the cross-national scale, but this overall decline masked an even sharper fall in private sector unionism. Whereas, union density rose in the public sector during the 1960s and 1970s in the private sector it has been falling since the mid-1960s (Fig. 2.2). The same pattern of high public sector density and declining private sector membership prevails in Britain and Canada.

The three panels for the US, Canada and Britain look very much like unionism has been on a 'twin track' for sometime. Several questions arise.

- First, why is the decline in collective representation concentrated amongst private sector workers?
- Second, does this decline call into question the relevance of trade unionism or the need for any other form of employee voice?
- Lastly, given the shifting nature of work and employment under what has come to be known variously as the 'gig economy' or 'new world of work', what forms

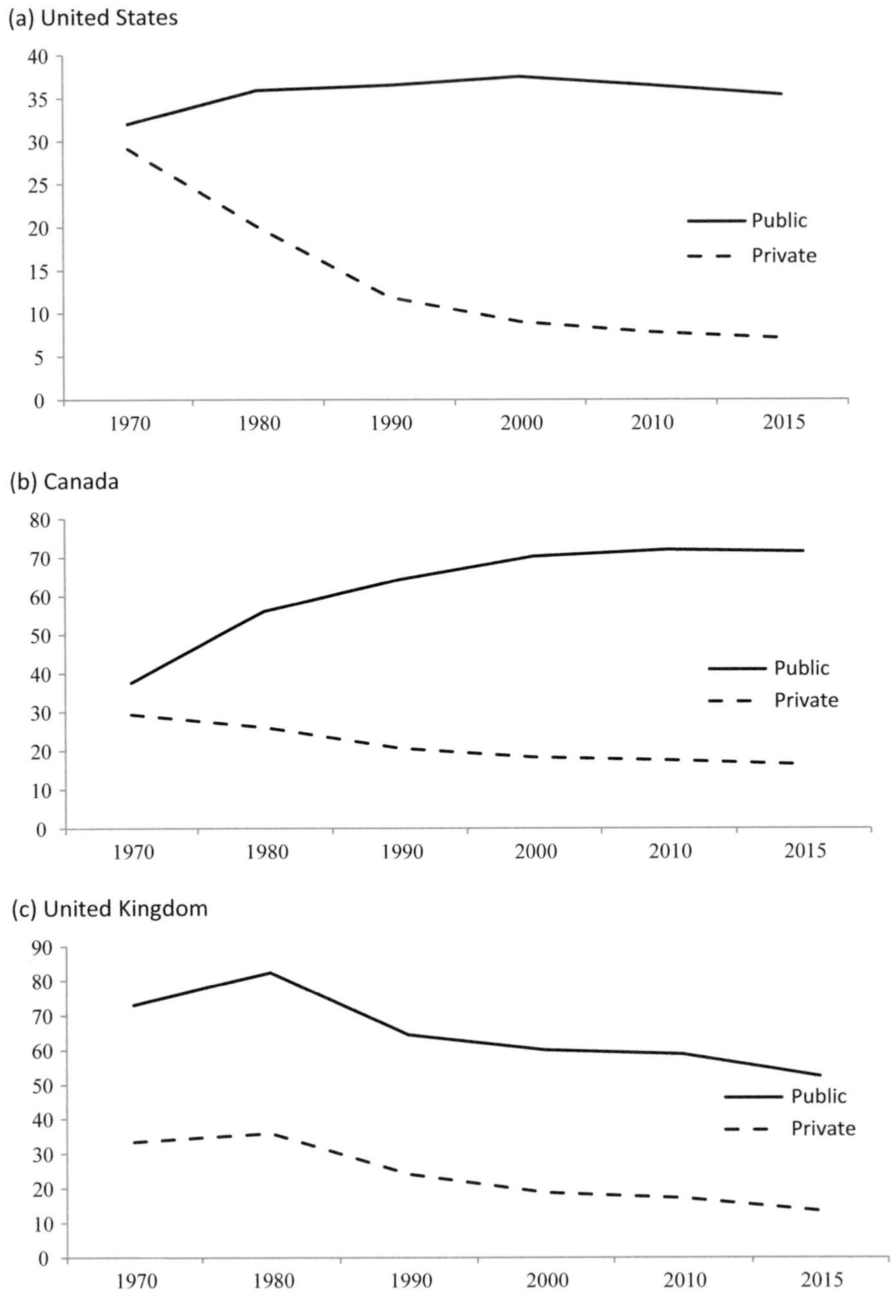

Fig. 2.2 Union density (%) in public versus private sector, 1970–2015. *Source* Bureau of Labor Statistics (BLS); Statistics Canada (StatsCanada); and Office of National Statistics (ONS)

(if any) of collective representation and voice might be possible in the Anglo-American world?

To answer these questions, we first examine the Anglo-American model by which employees secure union representation and voice. Though each country differs, this model contains a set of features common to all systems in which certified bargaining agents acquire exclusive representation rights and the employer has no statutory obligation to deal with sectoral bargaining agents or minority unions. Though different mechanisms exist for securing trade union representation (e.g. some jurisdictions invoke easier certification processes while others prevent agency provisions), the Anglo-American model in its essential form displays seven characteristics (Weiler 1989):

a. ***'Seven' Key Features of Representation Systems in the Anglo-American World***

(i) A non-union/no-voice default setting for employees such that whether working in a bank branch or retail outlet there is no system of worker representation in nascent organizations. As a result, private sector employees mostly work in non-union workplaces and have no access to formal representation systems.

(ii) If an employee has access to collective representation within the workplace, it is because the majority of workers were first organized to undertake the process of joining an independent union, securing certification from a labour board and then signing a first collective agreement with the employer. For the typical worker, possessing no experience with unions or certification procedures, this process can appear lengthy and complicated. In cases where employers are opposed to unionization, the process tilts against workers gaining certification (Doorey 2013). In particular, the use of mandatory vote certification procedures (as opposed to card-based certification, which exists across some Canadian jurisdictions) has had a negative effect on certification success rates and on union density (Johnson 2002, 2004). Slinn and Hurd (2011) show that in Canada certification delays often arise from unfair labour practices (ULP) applications and hearings related to employer conduct during organizing while in the US a similar pattern prevails (Ferguson 2008). Moreover, there is evidence that employer ULPs are more effective at defeating unionization under mandatory elections than undercard check certification (Riddell 2001).

Though British employees face similar hurdles in organizing their employer, getting to the first contract is not an issue in the same way because, although in law a collective agreement can be directly binding, usually collectively agreed upon terms are *implied* terms in individuals' contracts of employment.

(iii) Non-union employers can be averse to unionization drives and deploy a variety of tactics to head off incipient unionism (Riddell 2001; Slinn 2008; Doorey 2013). Though these tactics have been associated more closely with US industrial relations (Logan 2006), managers in other countries report at least equally negative attitudes towards unions than their American counterparts (Beaumont 1986; Beaumont and Harris 1994; Campolieti et al. 2007, 2013; Lipset and Meltz 1997; Saporta and Lincoln 1995; Taras 2002). Many non-union employers also engage in sustained efforts to persuade and supplant independent trade unions while others will coerce and suppress incipient unionism (Thomason and Pozzebon 1998). Furthermore, although there is evidence that major companies headquartered outside of the US have a lower likelihood of opposing unions (Thompson 1995), union acceptance amongst employers in Canada and elsewhere, as Rose and Chaison (1996, p. 92) presciently observe, 'is most likely the result of a low probability of escaping unions rather than a [less inherent antagonism]'. There is also a British employer response to unions, which can best be termed 'apathy'; a recognition that organizing a workplace is difficult and that expending valuable resources in opposing a union is unnecessary and possibly counterproductive (Amossé et al. 2016).

(iv) As a result of these difficulties in establishing collective representation, unionization can be conceived of as 'experience-good', meaning any good or service whose quality cannot be truly discerned before purchase (Nelson 1970). For workers (and employers), unionization is an experience good in that most union benefits (procedural justice, job security and the provision of family-friendly policies) are hard to observe before joining a union or working in an organized workplace. By definition, experience goods have properties making them hard to 'market' to potential adopters who have never-sampled membership. Consequently, groups like young workers or immigrants are likely to bypass union organizing unless already employed in a unionized workplace and otherwise compelled to join (Gomez and Gunderson 2004). In essence, the indeterminate nature of benefits associated with unionization can generate hesitation/scepticism on the part of non-union workers. This is why some unions in the UK and Australia (e.g. the Independent Education Union (IEU)) have experimented with a 'try-before-you-buy' approach offering 'free' membership for students and newly hired teachers (Costa and Hearn 1997).

(v) Most unionised workers are members of large (more than 100,000 members) unions. This is natural given that large national (or international) unions have ample resources to overcome the fixed costs associated with new certification drives and have experience organizing under the WAM, enabling them to lower the marginal costs associated with representing new workers. Large national/international unions are less successful, however, at unionizing new firms and small-to-medium-sized enterprises in the private sector; instead deploying scarce organizing funds to certify public sector organizations or large well-established firms with large bargaining units (Willman 2001). Rightly or wrongly, many non-union employees therefore perceive larger unions as having a distinctly impersonal and bureaucratic flavour (Weiler 1989).

(vi) Partly as a result of the above characteristics, there has been a steady decline in unionization in the private sector and a growth in 'frustrated demand' for employee representation (Freeman and Rogers 1999). This is generally greater for younger workers. Bryson et al. (2005, p. 165) found youth (<25 years) representation gaps of 36% in Britain, (i.e. 50% wanted union representation but only 16% had access), 44% in Canada and 42% in the US. The corresponding adult (25–64 years) representation gaps were 11%, 12% and 37%, respectively, in Britain, Canada and the US, respectively.

(vii) This large representation 'gap' has been filled, in part, by a growing array of statutory provisions (e.g. minimum notice periods), regulatory mechanisms (e.g. minimum wage laws), employer initiatives (e.g. joint consultative committees) and bottom-up social movements/'alt-labor' groups (Economist 2013; Hackman 2014; Eidelson 2013). Unfortunately, universal regulatory standards are subject to the problem of 'unfulfilled legal promise' (Weil 2007). Unless there is an indigenous base of union representation or workplace oversight, the vigilance required to make the universal employment standards programme a reality is often lacking and compliance is attenuated (Barbash 1989; Meltz 1989). Similar problems bedevil employer-led initiatives and social organizing models, i.e. without independence or statutory enforcement, alternative worker participation schemes tend to fail over time.

Given the problems associated with decentralized majority-based collective bargaining outlined above, the rest of the chapter identifies an analytical framework to understand union decline in Anglo-American economies.

2.3 A Framework for Understanding Union Decline and The Rise of Non-union Voice

We argue that the fall in private sector unionism and the high and relatively stable rates in the public sector can be accounted for by a model where union growth (or decline) is part of a 'bottom-up' process (Freeman 1998) embedded in a wider set of competing and complementary voice channels—all of which exist in a *solution market* for employee voice. Each voice channel—union, non-union or some hybrid form—has a bundle of attributes, requires a set-up 'cost' and has to be experienced in order to discern true quality and the full scope of benefits.

The idea of a *solution market* is captured by the 'experience-good model of employee voice' (Bryson and Gomez 2003, 2005; Gomez and Gunderson 2004; Budd 2010) which borrows some basic elements of consumer theory to predict the way in which voice provision differs amongst groups and how voice provision has shifted over time. In terms of union voice, the 'experience good' in question has three essential attributes: (1) a right to have a say over the conditions of work and pay, (2) some measure of bargaining power such that a greater share of profits flowing to workers than would otherwise be the case (wage premium) and (3) some job security provided via internal grievance procedures and just cause termination provisions insurance. All three elements reveal themselves to workers only after they have secured representation; that is, they are hard-to-observe attributes that are unknown prior to 'purchase'.

We highlight both supporting and conflicting evidence for this model. Bryson and Freeman (2013) find a correlation between increasing problems at work and the desire for 'union-like' solutions, suggesting that there is clear evidence of a union representation gap. However, as with any desire, there are costs that workers have to overcome in order to be unionized, and relative to benefits, union costs may be too high. Troy (2000) and other authors have used this fact to advance the claim that collective representation has simply been overtaken by self-representation and individualized contracting as the preferred (lower cost) employee modes of employment. We disagree with this reading and instead rely on the 'incumbency effect' (Diamond and Freeman 2001), which states that any established employee voice system (provided it meets a minimum standard of acceptability) will typically prevail over a proposed alternative, even if that alternative is preferred and better in some objective way. The reality of switching costs for workers (and firms) is one of the key elements in experience-good theory that ties the incumbency and experience-good models together with the incumbency effect being captured by the added 'cost' and/or 'risk' of switching out of one employee voice system to another of uncertain quality (Willman et al. 2014). Switching costs can keep employees locked-into sub-optimal employment relationships just as they can keep consumers locked-into sub-optimal mobile service contracts or bad banking relationships.

Our conclusion is that the experience-good hypothesis is an accurate depiction of why unionism has slowly ebbed as the default form of voice in Anglo-American economies. It falls short, however, as a full explanation for the decline of unions and the evolution of alternate forms of voice from the early 2000s to the present. A theory compatible with experience-good unionism and the rise of alternate voice forms is one which sees the emergence (or decline) of unions as part of a 'bottom-up process' in which individual actors make decisions, adopt new strategies and/or engage in behaviours that (cumulatively) generate sharp changes in trends or likewise contribute to long periods of union stagnation or decline. This is the so-called 'spurt-theory' of union growth and decline (Freeman 1998).

Though it seems like union decline has been the dominant theme for some time, this is not to say that traditional unions have become irrelevant, or that recent changes to their organizing strategies have had *no* effect on certain groups of previously unorganized workers (e.g., organizing public sector workers in the 1960s and 1970s or extending their reach through Justice for Janitors campaigns in the 1990s in the US). There were clearly innovations in union organizing over the past 30 years and these changes had *some effect* on new groups of workers (Erickson et al. 2002). Rather, while existing models of unionization can account for the presence of a pretty stable group of unionized workers and firms, industrial relations theory has not been particularly helpful in understanding the shifts in the structure of new forms of voice and the birth of 'do-it-yourself' organizing that has occurred in Anglo-American labour markets over the last decade.

We believe it is time to re-evaluate the rise of individualized and increasingly digitally infused forms of worker voice that have emerged in the first quarter of the twenty-first century. We begin, however, with a look at 'never membership'.

2.3.1 The Rise of the 'Never-Member'

We wish to focus on a finding first observed in Britain in order to point out that the proximate cause of union decline is largely a result of Wagner-style representation systems. Bryson and Gomez (2005) tracked the rise in the percentage of employees in Britain who were never members since the mid-1980s (see Fig. 2.3). The data for show that never-membership increased markedly between 1986 and 2006 while ex-membership remained roughly constant. By the early 2000s, never joining a union had grown steadily for the average 30-year-old worker, outstripping changes in other major life-course events such as marriage and university attendance. Bryson and Gomez (2005) went on to show that it was this reduced likelihood of ever becoming a member and not the loss of existing members which accounted for the decline in overall union membership in Britain since the 1980s.

In the US, though we do not have a comparable never-membership figure, we know from Booth et al. (2010, p. 42) analysis of successive waves of US Bureau

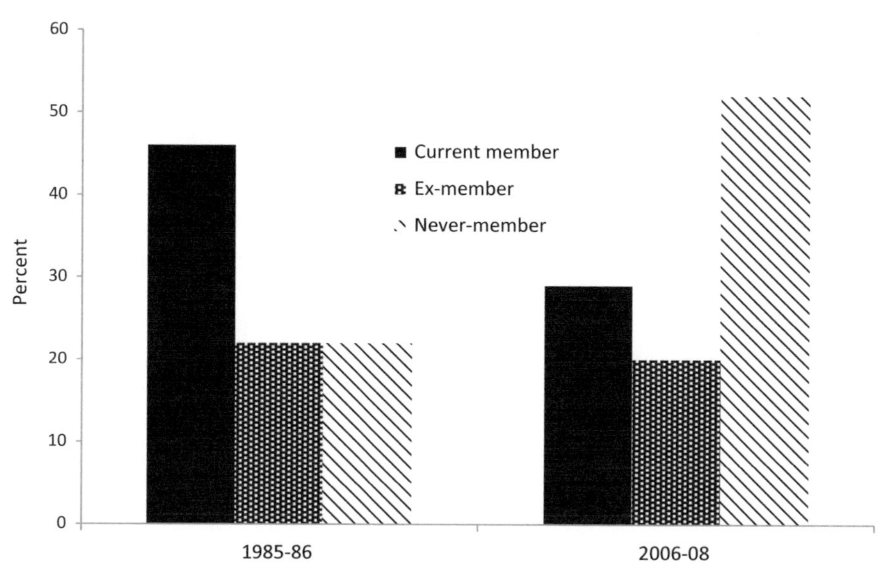

Fig. 2.3 Current, ex and never union membership rates in Britain, 1986–2008. *Source* Adapted from Bryson and Forth (2010)

of Labor Statistics NLSY data that it 'does indeed appear that never-unionization rates in the United States are increasing as new cohorts enter the labour market, even after adjusting for demographic and structural changes.' This view is consistent with what has occurred in Canada, where since 1997 the unionized workforce has grown in absolute terms (Baker 2012) but union density declined across Canada. The reason is that the growth of the non-unionized workforce, which grew by about 2.5 million over the same period, outstripped union membership expansion. In other words, never-membership is rising in Canada as it has in Britain and in the United States (Booth et al. 2010).

The rise in never-membership, however, is still only the 'proximate' cause of union decline in Anglo-American economies. To understand the deeper processes at work, we need a more 'general theory' of union growth (and decline).

2.3.2 The 'Spurt Theory' of Union Growth

As noted by Freeman (1998), two types of models can generate changes in union growth. The first, and probably most often used in IR scholarship, are models in which massive shocks or environmental changes generate commensurately large responses in otherwise stable union membership. The second are models in which the *process of growth* creates nonlinearities that produce 'phase transitions' when certain conditions are met, generating models of tipping-point, contagion, and self-organized complexity.

A more recent 'catchall' term refers to these latter models as 'agent-based' (Dawid and Neugart 2011) because of their stress on the cumulative effect of individual actions taken by agents, and in this case, individual workers, unions and firms. The focus of agent-based modelling is on how organization occurs and the behaviour of many individual actors acting in response to one another. The first set of models stress the exogenous shock, usually generated by political forces which is perhaps why legal scholars and labour historians gravitate to these explanations and generally interpret the growth or decline of union is as resulting from one (or more) of these 'one-off' legislative changes. Hence, it is argued that unions declined in the United States because of President Reagan's firing of PATCO strikers, in Britain because of Prime Minister Thatcher's crushing of the coal miners, in Canada they grew because of the passage of Order in Council PC 1003 and so on. Without denying the importance of particular laws or external events as catalysts for the growth process, Freeman (1998) lays out a model in which sudden positive changes in union density ('spurts') do not depend upon 'external environmental changes' but rather arise endogenously from individual actions and the process of union organization.

There is an affinity between Freeman's spurt model and a related theory of industrial mobilization proposed by Kelly (1998), which generates a similar tendency for explosions in industrial militancy and union growth. These shift changes coincide with critical turning points in 'long wave' political-economic developments. In particular, Kelly's model emphasizes the importance of workers acquiring a collective awareness of injustice emanating from the social relationship between capital and labour where employers and employees pursue different and/or opposing sets of interests. The question is how can this collective awareness emerge or be 'mobilized'? Mobilization, according to Kelly, depends on the accessibility of effective worker organizations and the availability of labour leaders willing and able to lead workers' struggles. The opportunity to take collective action, however, can be curtailed by employers via 'sticks' (threats such as firings and plant closures) or 'carrots' (inducements like profit sharing or internal grievance procedures). The state can also enter the labour–capital relationship typically (though not always) on the side of employers with legislation and actions that thwart worker organizing efforts.

What's interesting is that Freeman's (1998) model identifies the same forces of 'union mobilization' (organizing) and 'employer threats' (opposition) identified in Kelly's theory of discontinuous union growth and decline, but formalizes them into union 'organizing' and employer 'opposition' behavioural functions. The key to Freeman's model, however, is that employer opposition is linear in that anti-union efforts decline as union density rises, while union organizing is non-linear; that is, it is weakest at both the lowest and highest union density levels. Because at low-density levels unions lack resources to mobilize, whereas at high levels there is little incentive for unions to organize as the small number of non-union workers have little incentive to join given positive union spillover effects. The union organizing function therefore rises and falls in an inverted-U fashion with increasing union density.

There are two stable equilibria in the Freeman model, a zero union density equilibrium (though Freeman acknowledges that in practice there would naturally be some unionism at the theoretical 'zero' mark due to the difficulty in removing unions where they are present) and a high (though not 100%) union density equilibrium. A low (non-zero) union density level generates instability in a positive or negative direction for unionization. Moves in a negative direction are initiated by employers given their opposition to union's increases as density declines (no employer wants to be the single employer encumbered by a collective agreement or having to pay a union premium). Due to the difficulties in organizing at the best of times, moves in a positive direction from a low union starting point generally coincide with a confluence of external factors, but more importantly with union innovations in organizing that appear to shift the organizing function upward. The strategic-choice approach developed by Kochan et al. (1984) to explain how differences in labour-management outcomes can emerge under similar external environments is therefore compatible with the spurt theory of union growth. Innovations can emerge locally from actors facing otherwise similar external constraints but it is only when they spread in quick succession to others that innovations in worker organizing become transformative.

The empirical evidence highlighted by Freeman (1998) shows that all union density spurts were generated by unions (new and old) adding members. However, a much larger proportion of the growth in the 1930s and 1940s (the largest era of union growth in the US) occurred through 'new' CIO industrial unions emerging and organizing *new* workers in *new* ways, which explains the uniquely large growth experienced in that period relative to previous spurts. Similarly, the spurt in public sector unionism that occurred in North America and in the UK in the 1960s and 1970s was characterized by rapid expansion of unionism into new areas with new or changed organization forms such as the switch of employee associations like the National Education Association (NEA) into certified unions and growth of existing unions under the help of legal changes (Freeman and Ichniowski 1988). It is interesting to note that the levels of unionization achieved in the public sector across most of the Anglo-American world (see Fig. 2.2) have been high and stable for sometime. It might be that they have reached (for a given level of employer opposition in each national context) the high-level equilibrium anticipated in Freeman's model. In Britain, US and Canada, the public sector unionization rate is roughly five times the rate present in the private sector and the gap has persisted for over 40 years in the case of the US and Canada and even longer in the case of Britain.

2.3.3 Spurt Theory and the Rise of Right-to-Work Laws

Given that bottom-up processes rather than external shocks are implicated in Freeman's (1998) theory of long-run changes to union growth, one would expect that employer (and or state) opposition to unions is triggered when organized labour is already weak and in decline rather than when unions are strong and on the ascent. Such a tendency emerges when we look at the US in more detail, especially since the 1960s. It was a decade or more after this membership peak that individual states began enacting right-to-work (RTW) laws, which limited trade unions ability to collect dues from workers and apparently hampered unions' ability to organize. The passing of the Taft-Hartley Act in 1947 led to an immediate adoption of RTW laws by historically low-density Southern states, but then a 30-year period of stasis emerged during which not a single State enacted an RTW law until 1976 whereupon states began enacting RTW laws and by 2017, more states had RTW laws than did not.

We compiled data (see Table 2.1) on when states (since the post-1960s union peak) enacted RTW laws and compared union density at the time of the law passing. Invariably, a RTW law was passed only when union density was *below* (and well below in most cases) historical highs. Rather, laws 'restricting' union organizing emerged when density was at or near the state's historical low.

What can we infer from the RTW experience? From Fig. 2.4, we see that the first four states that enacted RTW laws were Louisiana [1976], Idaho [1985], Texas [1993] and Oklahoma [2001]; they were the four lowest density states and were below the US average at the time they enacted RTW laws. In fact, in all cases but one—Michigan—US states enact a RTW law only *after* state union density falls *below* the US average. This supports Freeman's model of bottom-up processes rather than external shocks through legal changes as leading the decline of unions. Recall as well that the union opposition function in Freeman's model predicts just such behaviour in that union opposition is inversely related to union density. Laws and legal changes are more like trailing indicators of organizational or movement strength/weakness rather than generators of them.

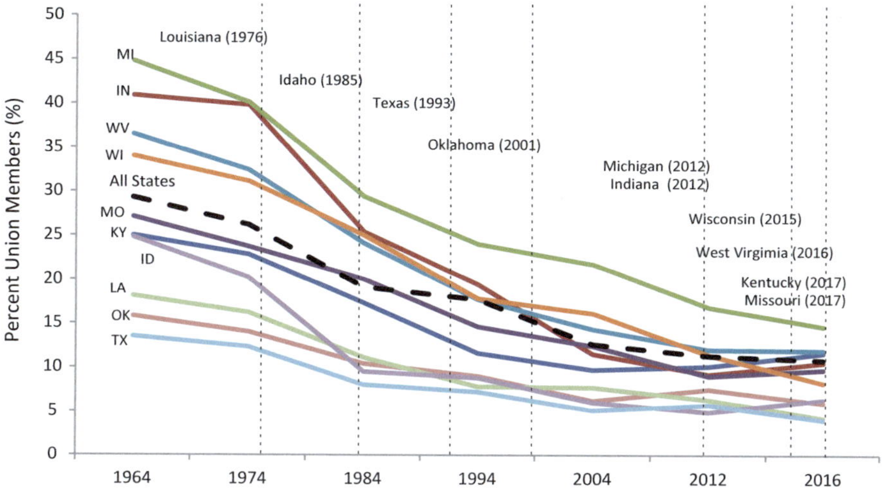

Fig. 2.4 Union density and timing of U.S. state-level right-to-work laws, 1964–2017. *Source* Barry T. Hirsch, David A. Macpherson, and Wayne G. Vroman, 'Estimates of Union Density by State,' *Monthly Labor Review*, Vol. 124, No. 7, July 2001, pp. 51–55. Accompanying data for 2001–2016 online at www.unionstats.com. *Notes* Figures represent the percentage of each state's non-agricultural wage and salary employees who are union members. The vertical lines indicate the year when the state 'right-to-work law' was passed outlawing union shop (which allows for hiring non-union employees, provided that the employees then join the union and pay dues within a certain period) and agency shop (in which employees must pay the equivalent of the cost of union representation, but need not formally join the union) provisions in their jurisdictions

2.3.4 The Experience-Good Model of Unionization and Implications for Employee Voice

The rise in never-membership, decline in overall density and the spurt model of union growth documented above have several important implications for the future of traditional collective representation.

First, when unions are present in an establishment they extend the benefits of union representation to a wider set of workers than just the ones they represent. Whether it is through the 'threat effect' (i.e. the inclination of non-union employers to match or even supersede certain contractually bargained outcomes in an effort to forestall union interest) or by lobbying government for improved legislated outcomes, a strong union movement also affects labour conditions outside of the organized sector.

Second, unions are successful in organizing workplaces when workers possess considerable knowledge of what unions can do through mobilization (Kelly 1998) or when there is strong demand for collective representation amongst workers (enough to overcome the significant hurdles associated with majoritarian representation). As a result, any decline in the number of workers who have ever sampled unionism makes the task of organizing individual workplaces harder.

Table 2.1 Union density and timing of state right-to-work (RTW) laws, 1964–2017

State	Right-to-work law		Union density	
	Year passed	Union density	High (year)	Low (year)
Louisiana	1976	17.3	18.1 (1964)	4.2 (2016)
Idaho	1985	12.2	25.0 (1968)	4.7 (2013)
Texas	1993	7.6	13.8 (1970)	4.0 (2016)
Oklahoma	2001	8.5	16.8 (1970)	5.4 (2016)
Michigan	2012	16.8	44.8 (1964)	14.6 (2016)
Indiana	2012	9.2	40.9 (1964)	9.2 (2012)
Wisconsin	2015	8.4	34.0 (1964)	8.2 (2016)
West Virginia	2016	11.9	36.5 (1964)	10.6 (2014)
Kentucky	2017	11.2	25.4 (1970)	8.7 (2008)
Missouri	2017	9.7	27.1 (1964)	8.4 (2014)
Overall average	2004	11.3	28.2 (1966)	7.8 (2014)

Source Hirsch et al. (2001) Estimates of Union Density by State. Monthly Labor Review, 124(7):51–55, July. Accompanying data for 2001–2016 online at www.unionstats.com

Third, to the extent that unionism is an experience-good, worker and sector composition matters. If the bulk of workers who have never-sampled union membership are concentrated in new sectors of the economy and amongst new workers, it is hard to see how the majority-based workplace model—designed as it was to organize workers with some knowledge of how unionism functions and how certification is achieved—can ever recover in a private sector dominated increasingly by new (often hostile or apathetic) employers and new (often uninformed) workers.

In short, gradual union decline is more likely when the default representation system is one in which workers have to continually organize individual workplaces, however, small or newly established, with a majority vote. As Bryson and Gomez (2003, p. 73) assert, "a 'key feature of unionization' in decentralized majority-based union representation systems is that 'increasing the flow of members into unions is far more difficult than maintaining the existing stock'" (Bryson and Gomez 2003). This statement assumes that the trade union movement is incapable on its own to educate and attract workers in small firms and new industries, but this is not a given and a new strategy by unions may emerge to target these workplaces and workers. Indeed, the last section of our chapter is devoted to just such possibilities.

In order to fully account for the declines in unionization witnessed in the private sector and the wide disparity of trade union representation observed between the public and private sectors, two caveats in the experience-good/never-membership story bear mentioning. The first issue revolves around the role of employer opposition (e.g. requiring employees to attend anti-union speeches by the employer, meetings between supervisors and small groups of bargaining unit employees, the distribution of anti-union literature, and threats against union supporters). There is evidence that public sector employers do not resort to the same degree of employer opposition as private employers do (Freeman and Kleiner 1990). The second issue has to do with establishment size. As seen in Fig. 2.5, for the largest establishments in Canada (500+ employees), the incidence of unionization is well over 50%. In contrast, the level of union representation for the smallest employers (those employing fewer than 20 employees) is 14%, or roughly one in 7 workers, a figure almost in line with the overall union density rate observed in the US. Small employers also contain the largest concentration of private sector employment (close to 30%) as compared to just over 17% in the public sector (see Statistics Canada, Table 282-0075). The average establishment size in the public sector is, therefore, larger than it is in the private sector, i.e. more public sector workers are employed in large establishments than is the case in the private sector (26 vs. 12%, respectively). There is necessarily then a confounding relationship, suggesting that part of the reason the public sector is more heavily unionized has to do with a 'need for voice' (arising both on the employee and employer side) that emerges in any large establishment. These data are even more striking in their consistency across jurisdictions sharing decentralized workplace model of representation (with Britain and the US sharing similar gradients in union density as firm size increases).

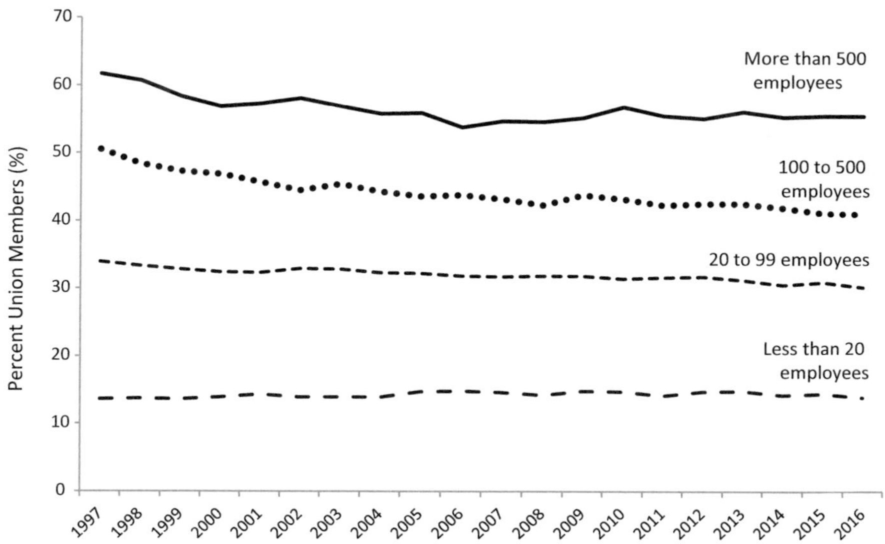

Fig. 2.5 Union density by size of establishment in Canada, 1997–2016. *Source* Statistics Canada. Table 282-0224—Labour Force Survey estimates (LFS), employees by union status, and establishment size, Canada, annual (persons unless otherwise noted). *Notes* Union density is calculated by members of a union and/or covered by a collective agreement as a proportion of all employees. Beginning January 1997, the number of employees at the location of employment (for example, building or compound) is collected from employees. Responses are recorded according to the following size groups: less than 20, 20–99, 100–500, more than 500. The concept of location of employment approximates the concept of establishment used by many Statistics Canada business surveys

One implication of the data in Fig. 2.5 is that as newer (and presumably) smaller private sector workplaces form; it becomes difficult and inefficient for large national unions to organize these workers. This could, therefore, provide a justification for a number of remedies such as allowing more informal voice mechanisms to emerge gradually, a 'broader' bargaining model and/or expanded powers for labour relations boards to revamp and resize bargaining units. This is essentially the argument first advanced by Willman (2001)—himself a former union organizer—and made in the context of why British unions were in decline amongst small private sector establishments. A more detailed elaboration of this idea—formalized as an extension of the Baumol 'cost-disease' argument—is put forth by Willman et al. (2017) and discussed next.

e. *The Union 'Cost Disease' Argument*

Union organization processes are not costless. In order to develop representation structures around an existing membership, unions must solve two collective action problems. The first is to encourage employees to join unions under circumstances where the benefits of such collective action may be available to free riders (Olson 1965; Olson and Zeckhauser 1966). The solution to this problem is twofold: (1) selective incentives via the introduction of private goods dependent on membership to supplement the public benefits of collective action and (2) special conditions to coerce or form constraints to encourage membership. Where these are possible, free riding is curtailed since membership may be consistently preferable to non-membership.

However, this sets up the second collective action problem: provision of such mechanisms has costs, and these costs must remain lower than the benefits of union membership to avoid the free-riding problem. A central organizational problem for unions is how to control such costs, and a central dilemma is how to balance the costs of servicing existing membership with those of recruiting a larger one (Willman 2004).

This is exacerbated because union organizations suffer from what Baumol and colleagues have termed the 'cost disease' (see Baumol and Bowen 1966; Baumol 2012; Flanagan 2012). This affects several sectors of the economy that deliver personal services—the main examples are health care, education and the performing arts—in which costs tend to rise consistently faster than productivity and inflation, because the labour input of service delivery is difficult to replace with capital and technology.

Baumol characterizes these as 'stagnant sector services' because of low productivity growth in contrast with 'progressive' sectors in which technology leads to rapid increases in productivity, reduction in real unit costs and thus the prices of goods. The problem is rather *relative* productivity growth. Salaries in the 'stagnant' sector tend to rise at broadly the same rate as those in 'progressive' ones, but since the percentage of total costs represented by labour costs is falling rapidly in the latter, but maintained in the former, only the former suffers from the 'cost' disease. Cost-disease organizations tend to experience cost and price rises, such that their services require an ever higher proportion of disposable income.

The evidence from Britain, using one of the longest-running and most extensively analysed datasets shows that unions taken together display consistent long-term real expenditure increases (Webb and Webb 1907; Roberts 1956; Latta 1972; Willman et al. 1993, 2017). However, they also suffer from pressures not to increase prices (membership subscriptions or dues) in real terms; these pressures are primarily from competition between unions and never-membership. The result is a consistent pressure on union financial reserves such that, in Britain, the trade union movement in the aggregate is asset-poor and reserves are at historical lows. This affects the ability of unions to seek membership expansion over servicing of existing members.

Put simply, what the cost-disease argument reveals is that the 'business model' of British and other Anglo-American unions is extremely fragile, pointing to the need to develop other revenue streams and organizational models that avoid (or suffer less from) cost disease in order to sustain collective voice.

f. *Make-or-Buy Dynamics in Explaining Employer Voice Choices*

Finally, what role does the employer play in this discussion? We know from the analysis of 'spurts' in union growth that their behaviour can be a contributing factor in union decline or ascendency. The question is whether they, in fact, thwart unionization by negative (anti-union) or positive (employer-provided non-union voice) means or by some combination. Before we can answer this question, we need to look a little closer at the nature of voice and its provision by either unions or employers.

Defining voice as any formal mechanism for communication between management and workers, we can distinguish *voice regimes* from *voice types*. A voice regime refers to whether a union or the firm provides the voice mechanism for workers and a voice type refers to whether the voice is direct or representative in nature. Non-union voice can be representative (such as statutory works councils or a joint consultative committee) or direct (such as employer-led team briefings or problem-solving groups) whereas union voice is always representative in nature. Voice regimes and types mix at the workplace level such as when an existing managerial practice that provides voice to workers mixes with a collective agreement. There is also the possibility of *no voice* employers in which unions are absent and there is no formal mechanism for engagement with employees.

If we assume that firms play a key role in the provision of workplace voice, then we need to know why some workplaces provide 'no voice', opt to create their own joint consultative committees ('make'), allow unions to form and provide voice ('buy'), or allow for both employer-provided systems to coexist with union voice ('dual').

Answering this question relies on transaction cost economics and institutional theory. In essence, we are dealing with bounded rational choices by employers who subsequently face high switching costs once a voice regime/type is chosen. A short primer on the transaction costs approach is followed by an application to workplace voice.

Transaction cost economics suggests that in exchanges characterized by asset specificity, high frequency of interaction and uncertainty, choices about transaction governance structures are required. In particular, the choice whether to make or buy, or, more accurately, own or contract. All else equal, the more idiosyncratic the investments, the greater the frequency of interaction (and duration of exchange) and the greater the uncertainty facing the buyer, internalizing the function rather than buying from the market will be preferred (Williamson 1975, 1987, 2013). The vertical integration decision by the firm is the paradigmatic example.

This choice of governance mechanism is made by parties operating under bounded rationality, faced with the possibility of seller opportunism and operating on a risk-neutral basis. The unit of analysis is the transaction and variance in governance modes are generated by differences in, and the interaction among, three-actor variables: (i) boundedness of rationality, (ii) trust between parties (i.e. expectation of opportunism) and (iii) risk preference. Where one allows for variance in risk preferences, as in Chiles and McMackin (1996), one in effect shifts the unit of analysis from ecological to cognitive, focusing directly on managerial decision-making and operating with a subjective conception of costs, i.e. as experienced by managerial decision makers. Focusing on conditions at the moment of regime choice allows consideration of different patterns among the three actor variables, but at the expense of predictive power. However, it also allows consideration of cohort effects and switching costs.

We can read this over into the analysis of employer voice regimes in the following way. With no idiosyncrasy, single interactions (the temporary employee paid by the piece) and no uncertainty, the employer will not need any voice and will therefore likely be a 'no voice' workplace; the classic example might be the longshore hiring hall while a contemporary one would be Uber and its platform economy which can recruit drivers on a daily basis and monitor their quality through customer feedback. However, the employer not operating under these narrow conditions and wanting voice faces a governance choice problem when seeking to 'obtain' a voice-producing workforce. Such an employer faces three options. The first is 'making', which would involve the provision of non-union voice through internal employer-made structures (direct or representative). 'Buying' voice is the second option and would, in extremis, involve the subcontracting out to a union of all aspects of voice provision. 'Dual' involves a mixture of union and non-union voice, is a third possibility and might be differentiated in terms of variance in the nature of the transaction (asset specificity, frequency and uncertainty) or of the purchasing party (boundedness of rationality, expectation of opportunism and risk preference).

Our central concern in this section is with explaining differences in voice regimes and types across employers and we argue this difference can be partly explained in terms of employer decision-making under uncertainty. Such an approach can explain a central feature of the evolution of voice regimes in Britain and elsewhere in Anglo-American economies, specifically the move towards non-union voice as part or all of workplace voice regimes.

Competition in product markets appears to encourage the shift towards non-union voice. Traditionally, this would be interpreted as a rent issue; in competitive product markets rent sharing possibilities disappear and the benefits of unionization for employees diminish. But for employers, the disappearance of a union wage premium should have made union voice more attractive suggesting that an explanation relying on risk management is at least worth considering; that is, employers facing high product market risk seek to control labour supply risk through internal voice-making decisions. This move was likely to have been accelerated by the 'hollowing out' of union density itself, raising questions about unions' ability to aggregate worker preference and increasing the risk of 'buying' over 'making' voice in the period under analysis.

One conjecture is that there have been declining costs (and risks) in employer-provided voice in Anglo-American economies over time, from the paradigmatic choice of union voice in the 1960s (buying) to the non-union dominated world of the 1990s (making). This decline in cost of 'making' voice, perhaps through the increasing availability of Human Resource (HR) professionals and the spread of HR benchmarking, has had the effect of lowering the make/buy threshold for firms across all risk appetites. Supporting evidence for this conjecture comes from a meta-analysis of union effect studies which concludes that the 'decline in the union effect on productivity in manufacturing, from … positive … in Brown and Medoff (1978) to … negligible … in later studies, could reflect the spread of "good labor practices" over time as non-union firms copied attributes of union workplaces … [such as] seniority systems, job posting, … systems for filling vacancies rather than relying on supervisors to promote workers, establishing formal wage scales, grievance systems and mechanisms for employee voice and so on' (Doucouliagos et al. 2017, p. 155).

Indeed, many studies have documented the spread of high-commitment workplace practices in the 1980s and 1990s, pioneered by unionized firms but adopted in non-union settings. To the extent that these practices provided a productivity edge to union firms, their spread to the non-union sector eroded the union advantage over time (Foulkes 1981; Lewin 1990; Colvin 2012). Another factor in explaining the shift away from 'buy' to 'make' and from 'representative' to 'direct' voice is the deregulation of economies and the opening up to global trade that increased product market risk, thus compounding the move away from representative union voice towards employer-provided direct channels. It is clear that in the private sector at least, the default option in the choice of voice regime has shifted from union to non-union, from make to buy, from representative to direct, according to changes in the values of risk and cost variables (assuming of course that returns were equal). The presence of switching costs in our model, however, makes regime choice 'sticky' rendering radical switching (from union to non-union and vice versa) rare. This, as we shall see, is consistent with the evidence presented in Sect. 2.4.

2.4 Filling the Void: Changes in Employee Voice in the Early Twenty-First Century

a. ***The Shift from Union to Non-union and from Representative to Direct Voice***
Relying on the best available dataset for charting voice over time, the Workplace Employment Relations Survey (WERS), we display the evolution of workplace voice regimes in Britain for the private sector since the 1980s. The US and Canada have

had their versions of WERS over the years but nothing close to the consistency of measures found in the British survey.

Table 2.2 Panel A, shows that the proportion of workplaces with no voice has been roughly constant over nearly three decades (e.g. 24% in 1984, 22% in 2004 and back to 24% in 2011). The first three rows of Table 2.2 demonstrate the growing share of non-union voice over the period 1984–2011. The most common form of voice at the start of period was dual voice (at 30%) but by the end of the period, dual voice had fallen to 14% and non-union voice constituted 58% of all private sector workplace voice regimes in Britain. This stands in sharp contrast to the steep decline in union-only voice (18–3% between 1984 and 2011).

Panel B of Table 2.2 shows the parallel shift from representative forms of voice (whether union or non-union) to direct forms since 1984. Direct forms of voice which include regular meetings with employees, to team briefings and problem-solving groups now occupy the majority of voice provision at 43% in 2011, as compared to just 9% with representative voice alone.

While the *scale* of the decline in private sector union voice and representative voice has been well documented, the *scope* of the decline is often overlooked. In Table 2.3, we see that, whereas almost 60% of private sector workplaces had at least some union members at the start of the period, union presence dropped dramatically to 28% in 2011. On-site union representation declined continuously, falling from 38% in 1980 to 13% in 2011, suggesting a loss of unions' ability to represent workers effectively even where unions continue to be recognized by the employer (Willman and Bryson

Table 2.2 Prevalence of voice in British private sector workplaces, 1984–2011

	1984 (%)	2004 (%)	2011 (%)	Percentage point change
Panel A: voice regimes				
Union voice only	18	5	3	−15
Dual voice[a]	30	17	14	−16
Non-union voice only	25	55	58	+33
No voice	24	22	24	No change
Panel B: voice types				
Representative voice only	23	11	9	−14
Representative + direct voice	35	26	24	−11
Direct voice only	17	40	43	+26
No voice	24	22	24	No change

Source Authors calculations. WERS survey various waves
Notes This voice typology is constructed using the voice items which are present in the data throughout the period 1984–2011 for private sector workplaces with more than 25 employees. All values are column percentages. Columns may not add up to total voice percentages due to rounding and missing information on some workplace.
[a]Dual voice refers to presence of union and non-union voice systems in the same workplace

Table 2.3 Prevalence of voice types in British private sector workplaces, 1984–2011

	1984 (%)	2004 (%)	2011 (%)	Percentage point change
Panel A: non-union voice				
Representative voice Join consultative committee (JCC)	26	20	21	−5
JCC that meets regularly	24	15	16	−8
Non-union employee representative	10[a]	16	15	+5
Direct voice Regular meetings with employees	34	37	37	+3
Team briefings	31	48	51	+20
Problem-solving groups[a]	30	28	25	−5
Panel B: union voice				
Any union members	60	35	28	−32
Any recognized union	50	22	17	−33
Any on-site lay union representative	38	14	13	−25

Source Authors calculations. WERS survey various waves
Notes This voice typology is constructed using the voice items which are present in the data throughout the period 1984–2011 for private sector workplaces with more than 25 employees. All values are column percentages. Columns may not add up to total voice percentages due to rounding and missing information on some workplace
[a]This question was only asked starting in 1990

2009). Finally, we see a fall in union recognition across British workplaces from 50 to 17% between 1984 and 2011.

The type of voice has also changed. From Table 2.3, we see that the decline in representative voice was more general, extending to non-union (employer-sponsored) forms. For instance, the percentage of workplaces with a functioning joint consultative committee (JCC) meeting at least once a quarter fell from 26% in 1984 to 16% by 2011. Though there was a small increase in non-union employee representatives at the workplace, the decline in JCC's suggests that both forms of representative voice suffered a substantial decline in the private sector from 1984 to 2011. By contrast, direct voice types have been constant or increasing in coverage since 1984. The incidence of team briefings, for example, has risen from (31 to 51%) over the 27-year period. Regular meetings between employees and senior management became more prevalent over the period 1984–1990 and have remained common (37%) ever since. Overall, the decline in representative voice has been gradual in the private sector whereas the incidence of direct voice rose dramatically between the 1980s and mid-2000s and has remained high ever since.

b. ***Notable Developments in Workplace Voice Since the 1980s***

What can we conclude from the British data? Three developments stand out.

First, voice coverage was as extensive in 2011 as in 1984 and on balance, non-union forms have filled the void left by declines in unionization, with the number of workplaces offering no voice to workers stable.

Second, whereas employers chose voice regimes up to the 1960s in circumstances where union-based voice regimes were common exemplars and where there were normative and mimetic pressures to avoid non-union-only regimes, the costs of opposing unions were also higher. The risk-averse option was therefore dual voice. Over time, the compositional shift from manufacturing to services and inward investments by companies with higher levels of asset specificity offered examples of non-union voice to many employers. By the 1990s, cohort effects dominated, with almost all new entrants choosing non-union voice. Where union voice persists, it is highly likely to be found as part of a dual channel voice regime and very rarely on its own.

Finally, in North America, a divergence has emerged. In Canada, private sector companies are free to establish non-union labour relations approaches, which facilitate (and mimic) formalized union mechanisms for employee voice outside of a union-only structure. This is not a system that is legally available to US employers and employees because of the peculiarities of section 8 (a)(2) of the National Labor Relations Act (NLRA), which prevents most non-union forms of workplace voice that are not certified unions (Taras 2006). Typically, such non-union forms of employee voice take place via employer-sponsored groups and committees that may deal with issues that are of particular interest to employers such quality, cost issues, or issues related to improving organizational outcomes (Taras 2006). These approaches also allow for voice on working conditions and offer a platform for employee management on workplace productivity and innovation related issues.

c. ***Some Possible Futures for Employee Voice***

Millennials are the first generation to be fully immersed in digital technologies (Harris 2017). Accordingly, e-platforms become a standard, 'second-nature' technology that they are willing to access at any time for nearly any type of need. The obvious question is whether new generations will utilize this new technology to tackle workplace problems. Initial signs suggest the answer is 'yes'. Various 'alt-labor' groups (Economist 2013; Hackman 2014; Eidelson 2013) now pursue the once 'far-out notion' of workers sharing information openly about organizing campaigns and gaining collective power to improve their economic situation through modern communication technology (Bryson et al. 2010; Freeman and Rogers 2002). If firms like Uber and AirBnB can upend traditional business practices and grow suddenly through Internet-based networked platforms (Parker et al. 2017), it seems reasonable that groups of workers can use similar technologies to upend traditional union practices, resurrect collective action, and improve worker well-being.

The group that has obtained the most attention in this regard is OUR Walmart, which originally adopted a Facebook-based strategy for campaigning within Walmart and has now developed an App technology with support from IBM Watson as a virtual expert and advisor. The App can be modified by other workers depending on their labour practices and policies and thus can be viewed as an experiment with potential extensions to other firms. OUR Walmart has a miniscule staff (4 people) and comparably small budget and by necessity operates by providing platform tools for workers to self-organize. When the App was unveiled in 2016, Walmart advised workers not to download it—a sure sign that the firm viewed it as a potential danger to its mode of operating. OUR Walmart believes that its activities over the past 2 years spurred the February 2016 increase in minimum pay at Walmart, which induced its main competitors to increase their pay commensurately. Even if OUR Walmart was only a partial factor, it is a remarkable achievement as Walmart is the largest employer in the US, with 1.5 million 'associates', whose labour practices influence those of other retail firms throughout the country. It is also adamantly opposed to traditional unions.

OUR Walmart and some of these 'alt-labor' groups receive traditional union support—such as Workers Action Centres (WACs) in Ontario and Worker Centers (WCs) in the US that have led the 'Fight for 15' campaigns across many North American cities—but most are on their own, with few resources. They resemble the start-ups of the dot.com period; all it takes is for at least one of them to succeed and traditional unions will likely imitate their strategies or amalgamate/merge and transform the way they operate.

The union explosion that occurred during the Great Depression was initiated by groups using the 'new' CIO industrial union model of the time, which was then copied by the more 'conservative' AFL craft unions. We have clearly been here before, but just as history never repeats itself in exactly the same way, there is room for yet another employee representation 'track' to emerge which can channel the views and interests of workers for the century ahead.

2.5 Conclusion

This chapter reviewed the evidence on union decline in the Anglo-American world, focusing on the connection with the provision of employee voice, with a particular emphasis on the rise of alternative forms of workplace voice and representation. Our conclusion is that trade union representation and employee voice have been on a 'twin track' for sometime in Canada, Britain, and the United States, the focal countries of our work. The most obvious case is the difference in unionization found in all major Anglo-American economies between the private and public sectors, with the latter seemingly able to achieve a high and stable union density coverage rate while the first has been in decline for over for 30 years and approaching historically low levels. In addition, there is other evidence of 'twin-track' unionism such as the division found between large well-established employers (where representative union voice still prevails) and smaller newer organizations that seem to have eschewed unions and representative forms of voice completely.

We found that an agent-based model of unionism—the 'spurt' model of union growth—is consistent with these trends. This model with its emphasis on bottom-up processes of organizing and union and employer responses to union density level changes is also consistent with other approaches such as mobilization theory (Kelly 1998), strategic-choice theory (Kochan et al. 1984), the experience-good model of unionism (Gomez and Gunderson 2004) and the make-or-buy dynamics of transaction cost theory applied to employer-provided voice choices (Willman et al. 2014).

We also consider some possible futures for employee voice, having concluded that the decline in traditional workplace-based collective bargaining does not portend the 'end' of representative employee voice as some have suggested (Troy 2000). The periods of representative voice explosions (up-to-now all union-based) have coincided with innovations in institutional forms and new grassroots organizing, something we contend is still possible given the evidence over the past century in Anglo-American economies. We know that theoretically labour innovations can reduce the union cost-disease problem by 'farming out' union organizing and services to committed volunteers—the so-called 'off balance sheet' work of unions. But perhaps more importantly, there appears to be a fluidity in organizational form that these new on-line union tools take which means they do not conform to standard models of trade union representation that pivot around collective bargaining rights at a specific workplace. In militaristic terms, the analogy we have in mind is conventional ground forces (old unions) versus guerilla forces (new unions). Given that these new 'guerilla' forms of worker representation are emerging from young union activists who sense an opportunity to help non-union workers with particular issues, it is perhaps an opportune time for labour relations scholars to begin tracking the prevalence of these new organizing models, analysing their outcomes and identifying correlates of their success or failure.

References

Amossé, Th., Bryson, A., Forth, J., & Petit, H. (Eds.). (2016). *Comparative workplace employment relations: An analysis of practice in Britain and France*. London: Palgrave MacMillan.

Baker, D. (2012). Canada proves the decline of unions is not inevitable. http://www.aljazeera.com/indepth/opinion/2012/09/201291103825936625.html.

Barbash, J. (1989). Equity as function: Its rise and attrition. In J. Barbash & K. Barbash (Eds.), *Theories and concepts in industrial relations* (pp. 114–122). Columbia: University of South Carolina Press.

Baumol, W. J., & Bowen, W. G. (1966). *Performing arts, the economic dilemma: A study of problems common to theater, opera, music, and dance*. New York: Twentieth Century Fund.

Baumol, W. J. (2012). *The cost disease: Why computers get cheaper and health care doesn't*. New Haven: Yale University Press.

Beaumont, P. B. (1986). Management opposition to union organisation: Researching the indicators. *Employee Relations, 8*(5), 31–38.

Beaumont, P. B., & Harris, R. I. D. (1994). Opposition to unions in the non-union sector in Britain. *International Journal of Human Resource Management, 5*(2), 457–471.

Booth, J. E., Budd, J. W., & Munday, K. M. (2010). Never say never? Uncovering the never-unionized in the United States. *British Journal of Industrial Relations, 48*(1), 26–52.

Brown, C., & Medoff, J. (1978). Trade unions in the production process. *Journal of Political Economy, 86*(3), 355–378.

Bryson, A., Forth, J. (2010). Trade union membership and influence 1999–2009. CEP Discussion Paper No 1003, Centre for Economic Performance, LSE, London.

Bryson, A., & Freeman, R. B. (2013). Employee perceptions of working conditions and the desire for worker representation in Britain and the US. *Journal of Labor Research, 34*(1), 1–29.

Bryson, A., & Gomez, R. (2003). Buying into union membership. In H. Gospel & S. Wood (Eds.), *Representing workers: Trade union recognition and membership in Britain* (pp. 72–91). London: Routledge.

Bryson, A., & Gomez, R. (2005). Why have workers stopped joining unions? The rise in never-membership in Britain. *British Journal of Industrial Relations, 43*(1), 67–92.

Bryson, A., Gomez, R., & Willman, P. (2010). Online social networking and trade union membership: What the Facebook phenomenon truly means for labor organizers. *Labor History, 51*(1), 41–53.

Bryson, A., Gomez, R., Gunderson, M., & Melt, N. (2005). Youth-adult differences in the demand for unionization: Are American, British, and Canadian workers all that different? *Journal of Labor Research, 26*(1), 155–167.

Budd, J. W. (2010). When do US workers first experience unionization? Implications for revitalizing the labor movement. *Industrial Relations: A Journal of Economy and Society, 49*(2), 209–225.

Campolieti, M., Gomez, R., & Gunderson, M. (2013). Managerial hostility and attitudes towards unions: A Canada-US comparison. *Journal of Labor Research, 34*(1), 99–119

Campolieti, M., Riddell, C., & Slinn, S. (2007). Labor law reform and the role of delay in union organizing: Empirical evidence from Canada. *Industrial and Labor Relations Review, 61*(1), 32–48.

Chiles, T. H., & McMackin, J. F. (1996). Integrating variable risk preferences, trust, and transaction cost economics. *Academy of management review, 21*(1), 73–99.

Colvin, A. J. (2012). American workplace dispute resolution in the individual rights era. *The International Journal of Human Resource Management, 23*(3), 459–475.

Commons, J. R. (1935). Communism and collective democracy. *American Economic Review, 25*(2), 212–223.

Costa, M., & Hearn, M. (Eds.). (1997). *Reforming Australia's unions: Insights from Southland magazine*. Sydney: Federation Press.

Dawid, H., & Neugart, M. (2011). Agent-based models for economic policy design. *Eastern Economic Journal, 37*(1), 44–50.

Derber, M. (1967). *Research on labor problems in the United States*. New York: Random House.

Derber, M. (1970). *The American idea of industrial democracy, 1865–1965*. Urbana: University of Illinois Press.

Diamond, W. J., & Freeman, R. B. (2001). Liking the workplace you have: The incumbency effect in preferences toward unions. CEP Working Paper 115, Centre for Economic Performance, LSE, London.

Doorey, D. J. (2013). Graduated freedom of association: Worker voice beyond the Wagner model. *Queen's Law Journal, 38*(2), 511–521.

Doucouliagos, H., Freeman, R. B., Laroche, P. (2017). The economics of trade unions: A study of a research field and its findings. Routledge, Taylor & Francis Group, London.

Dunlop, J. T. (1944). Wage determination under trade unions. Macmillan & Co, New York.

Dunlop, J. T. (1958). Industrial relations systems. Holt & Co, New York.

The Economist. (2013). New labour, Alt-labour. http://www.economist.com/news/unitedstates/21586287-believe-it-or-not-union-movement-starting-embrace-innovation-new-labour.

Eidelson, J. (2013). Alt-Labor. The American prospect (2013, January 29) (pp. 15–18). http://prospect.org/article/alt-labor.

Erickson, C. L., Fisk, C. L., Milkman, R., Mitchell, D. J., & Wong, K. (2002). Justice for janitors in Los Angeles: Lessons from three rounds of negotiations. *British Journal of Industrial Relations, 40*(3), 543–567.

Feldman, H. (1928). *Survey of research in the field of industrial relations*. New York: Social Science Research Council.

Ferguson, J.-P. (2008). The eyes of the needles: A sequential model of union organizing drives, 1999–2004. *Industrial and Labor Relations Review, 62*(1), 3–21.
Flanagan, R. J. (2012). *The perilous life of symphony orchestras*. New Haven: Yale University Press.
Forth, J., Bryson, A., & George, A. (2017). Explaining cross-national variation in workplace employee representation. *European Journal of Industrial Relations, 23*(4), 415–433.
Foulkes, F. (1981). How top nonunion companies manage employees. *Harvard Business Review*, September Issue.
Freeman, R. B., & Ichniowski, C. (1988). *When public sector workers unionize*. Chicago: University of Chicago Press.
Freeman, R. B., & Kleiner, M. M. (1990). Employer behavior in the face of union organizing drives. *Industrial and Labor Relations Review, 43*(4), 351–365.
Freeman, R. B., & Rogers, J. (1999). *What workers want*. Ithaca, NY: ILR Press.
Freeman, R., & Rogers, J. (2002). Open source unionism: Beyond exclusive collective bargaining. *Working USA: The Journal of Labor and Society, 7*(2), 3–4.
Freeman, R. B. (1998). Spurts in union growth: Defining moments and social processes. In M. D. Bordo, C. Goldin, & E. N. White (Eds.), *The defining moment: The great depression and the American economy in the twentieth century* (pp. 265–295). Chicago: The University of Chicago Press.
Gomez, R., Gunderson, M. (2004). The experience good model of trade union membership. In Wunnava, P. V. (Ed.), The changing role of unions: new forms of representation (pp. 92–112). M.E. Sharpe, Armonk, NY.
Hackman, R. (2014). Alt-labor: A new union movement or the same old song? The Guardian (2014, May 1). https://www.theguardian.com/money/2014/may/01/low-wage-new-unionwalmart-fast-food.
Harris, M. (2017). *Kids these days: Human capital and the making of millennials*. New York: Little, Brown and Company.
Hirsch, B., Macpherson, D., & Vroman, W. (2001). Estimates of union density by state. *Monthly Labor Review, 124*(7), 51–55.
Johnson, S. (2002). Card check or mandatory representation vote? How the type of union recognition procedure affects union certification success? *The Economic Journal, 112*(2), 344–361.
Johnson, S. (2004). The impact of mandatory votes on the Canada–US union density gap: A note. *Industrial Relations, 43*(2), 356–363.
Kelly, J. (1998). *Rethinking industrial relations: Mobilisation, collectivism and long waves*. London: Routledge.
Kochan, T. A., McKersie, R. B., & Cappelli, P. (1984). Strategic choice and industrial relations theory. *Industrial Relations: A Journal of Economy and Society, 23*(1), 16–39.
Latta, G. (1972). Trade union finances. *British Journal of Industrial Relations, 10*(2), 392–411.
Lewin, D. (1990). Grievance procedures in nonunion workplaces: An empirical analysis of usage, dynamics, and outcomes. *Chicago-Kent Law Review, 66*, 823.
Lipset, S. M., & Meltz, N. (1997). Canadian and American attitudes towards work and institutions. *Perspectives on Work 1*(3), pp.14–20.
Logan, J. (2006). The union avoidance industry in the United States. *British Journal of Industrial Relations, 44*(4), 651–675.
Meltz, N. M. (1989). Industrial relations: balancing efficiency and equity. In J. Barbash & K. Barbash (Eds.), *Theories and concepts in comparative industrial relations* (pp. 109–113). Columbia: University of South Carolina Press.
Nelson, P. (1970). Information and consumer behavior. *Journal of Political Economy, 78*(2), 311–329.
Olson, M. (1965). *The logic of collective action; public goods and the theory of groups*. Cambridge: Harvard University Press.
Olson, M., & Zeckhauser, R. (1966). An economic theory of alliances. *The Review of Economics and Statistics, 48*(3), 266–279.

Parker, G. G., Van Alstyne, M. W., & Choudary, S. P. (2017). *Platform revolution: How networked markets are transforming the economy—and how to make them work for you*. New York: W.W. Norton.

Riddell, C. (2001). Union suppression and certification success. *Canadian Journal of Economics/Revue canadienne d'économique, 34*(2), 396–410.

Roberts, B. C. (1956). *Trade union government and administration*. London: Bell and Sons.

Rose, J. B., & Chaison, G. N. (1996). Linking union density and union effectiveness: The North American experience. *Industrial Relations: A Journal of Economy and Society, 35*(1), 78–105.

Saporta, I., & Lincoln, B. (1995). Managers and workers' attitudes toward unions in the US and Canada. *Relations Industrielles/Industrial Relations, 50*(3), pp. 550–566.

Slinn, S. (2008). No right (to organize) without a remedy: Evidence and consequences of the failure to provide compensatory remedies for unfair labour practices in British Columbia. *McGill Law Journal, 53*(4), 687–736.

Slinn, S., & Hurd, R. W. (2011). First contract arbitration and the employee free choice act: Multi-Jurisdictional evidence from Canada. *Advances in Industrial and Labor Relations, 18*(1), 41–86.

Taras, D. G. (2002). Alternative forms of employee representation and labour policy. *Canadian Public Policy, 28*(2), 105–116.

Taras, D. G. (2006). Non-union representation and employer intent: How Canadian courts and labour boards determine the legal status of non-union plans. *Socio-Economic Review, 4*(2), 321–336.

Thomason, T., & Pozzebon, S. (1998). Managerial opposition to union certification in Quebec and Ontario. *Relations Industrielles/Industrial Relations, 53*(4), 750–771.

Thompson, P., & Newsome, K. (2004). Labor process theory, work, and the employment relation. In B. Kaufman (Ed.), *Theoretical perspectives on work and the employment relation* (pp. 133–162). Champaign: Industrial Relations Research Association.

Troy, L. (2000). Beyond unions and collective bargaining. *Working USA, 3*(5), 102–134.

Webb, S., & Webb, B. (1897). *Industrial democracy*. London: Longman Green.

Webb, S., & Webb, B. (1907). I. Longman Green, London.

Weil, D. (2007). Crafting a progressive workplace regulatory policy: Why enforcement matters? *Comparative Labour Law & Policy Journal, 28*(2), 125–154.

Weiler, P. C. (1989). *Governing the workplace*. Cambridge: Harvard University Press.

Williamson, O. E. (1975). *Markets and hierarchies: Analysis and antitrust implications: A study in the economics of internal organization*. New York: The Free Press.

Williamson, O. E. (1987). *The economic institutions of capitalism: Firms, markets, relational contracting*. New York: The Free Press.

Williamson, O. E. (2013). *The transaction cost economics project: The theory and practice of the governance of contractual relations*. Cheltenham: Edward Elgar Press.

Willman, P. (2001). The viability of trade union organization: A bargaining unit analysis. *British Journal of Industrial Relations, 39*(1), 97–117.

Willman, P. (2004). Structuring unions: The administrative rationality of collective action. In Kelly, J., Willman, P. (Eds.), Union organisation and activity (pp. 73–85). Routledge, London.

Willman, P., & Bryson, A. (2009). Accounting for collective action: Resource acquisition and mobilization in British unions. In Advances in industrial and labor relations (pp. 23–50). Emerald Group Publishing Limited.

Willman, P., Morris, T., & Aston, B. (1993). *Union business; trade union organisation and financial reform in the Thatcher years*. Cambridge: Cambridge University Press.

Willman, P., Bryson, A., & Gomez. R. (2006). The sound of silence: Which employers choose no employee voice and why? *Socioeconomic Review, 4*(2), 283–299.

Willman, P., Bryson, A., Gomez, R., & Kretschmer, T. (2014). Employee voice and the transaction cost economics project. In A. Wilkinson, J. Donaghey, T. Dundon, & T. Freeman (Eds.), *Handbook of research on employee voice* (pp. 52–65). Cheltenham: Edward Elgar.

Willman, P., Bryson, A., & Forth, J. (2017). *UK unions, collective action and the cost disease*. LSE, London: Department of Management.

Dr. Alex Bryson is Professor of Quantitative Social Science at University College London's Department of Social Science. He is a research fellow at IZA, NIESR and Rutgers. His research interests span labour economics, industrial relations and programme evaluation https://iris.ucl.ac.uk/iris/browse/profile?upi=ABRYS65.

Richard B. Freeman holds the Herbert Ascherman Chair in Economics at Harvard University. He is Faculty co-Director of the Labor and Worklife Program at the Harvard Law School, and a Senior Research Fellow at the LSE's Centre for Economic Performance. He directs the NBER's Science Engineering Workforce Projects, and is Co-Director of the Harvard Center for Green Buildings and Cities. His research interests include the job market for scientists and engineers; the transformation of scientific ideas into innovations, Chinese and Korean labor markets; the effects of AI and robots on the job market; and forms of labor market representation and employee ownership.

Dr. Rafael Gomez is Professor of Employment Relations and Director of the Centre for Industrial Relations and Human Relations at the University of Toronto. He has co-authored and co-edited 4 books and over 70 articles and chapters in prestigious academic publications, and won research grants from the Social Sciences and Humanities Research Council to study worker preferences at the workplace.

Dr. Paul Willman is Emeritus Professor of Management at London School of Economics and Political Science. His main research areas are in Labour relations and the analysis of organizational risk.

Chapter 3
Employee Voice and Participation: The European Perspective

Chris Brewster, Richard Croucher and Thomas Prosser

Abstract The development of works councils has been a singularly European development but it has not taken the same trajectory in each country. In some such as Denmark, it has been as an outgrowth of the national culture, whereas in others, works councils were brought into being by legislation. In the German case for example, initially, it was as a political counterweight. An associated development has been the appointment of worker directors. To some extent, these national-level initiatives have been overtaken by the enactment of European Directives which mandate forms of employee voice. While these forms of voice are well entrenched, it remains that they are under challenge from the emergence of new forms of employment and from the changing attitudes and expectation of workers in Europe.

Keywords Europe · Works councils · Worker directors · European Directives Challenge · Change

3.1 Introduction: Voice and Participation in Europe

Arguably, Europe is at the centre of some of the most fascinating developments in employee voice and participation. Definitions of 'Europe' vary: the term can refer

---

C. Brewster (✉)
Vaasa University, Vaasa, Finland
e-mail: c.j.brewster@henley.ac.uk

C. Brewster
Henley Business School, University of Reading, Reading, UK

C. Brewster
Radboud University, Nijmegen, The Netherlands

R. Croucher
Middlesex University Business School, London, UK

T. Prosser
Cardiff University, Cardiff, Wales

P. Holland et al. (eds.), *Employee Voice at Work*, Work, Organization, and Employment, https://doi.org/10.1007/978-981-13-2820-6_3

to the 28 states of the European Union (EU), the 32 countries of the European Free Trade Area, which includes, in addition to the EU states, Iceland, Lichtenstein, Norway and Switzerland and the 47 countries in the Council of Europe or the wider geographical definition of 'the Atlantic to the Urals'. Here, we refer to the European Free Trade countries and the countries immediately to the East of them. We, therefore, include the ex-communist countries now bordering Russia, because we recognise the relevance of their model of corporatist employee voice for countries to their West (Upchurch et al. 2015; Croucher 2016). Although we will note developments in all of these states, our focus will be on the European Union countries and the specific experiments in employee voice and participation there largely because these are the countries best covered by researchers. We do not discuss Russia, which has increasingly distanced itself from Europe and the USA. It has recently sought to build alliances with other post-Soviet countries through the Eurasian Economic Union which it sees as a potential counterweight to the EU with an alternative social model.

Europe is significant not just in its own right as a major world trading bloc but as an exemplar for other countries. The colonial legacy of countries like the UK, France, the Netherlands, Spain and Portugal continues to have an impact on HRM, including ER, practices in other countries (Wood et al. 2016) and experiments on this continent are carefully watched elsewhere. While Germany's colonial presence was less important than that of the other countries listed, its long traditions of economic involvement in Central and Eastern Europe, historic relationship with Turkey and its status as an economic 'high road' powerhouse means its model carries great weight internationally. South Korea's works councils, for example were initially modelled on their German equivalents (Croucher and Miles 2009).

3.1.1 What Is Distinctive?

The significance and appropriate forms of employee voice and participation have long been debated at the European level. From the launch of European integration in the 1950s, it was understood that deepening European economic integration necessitated Europe-wide structures for employee voice and participation. Though initial efforts to develop such structures were rather tentative, the launch of the European single market project in the mid-1980s led to more sustained attempts. Such efforts reflected the 'special', *sui generis* nature of European integration. Unlike regional integration arrangements in other parts of the world, the European project was predicated upon a deepening of integration between member states which, in the sphere of social policy, implied the development of common social policy institutions (Falkner 1998).

Europe, therefore, provides a specific context for examining voice and participation. Several factors make its approach to voice and partnership distinctive (Brewster et al. 2018). These factors originate in European history and the fundamental idea that democratic rights exist in the workplace as well as in society. The result is a number of differentiating elements at the European level: its 'stakeholder' rather than shareholder model; the role of the state; the notion of 'rights' to and in a job; and an acceptance by managers of the value of consultation. There are also very considerable differences not only between European countries but also within the different country groupings that have been proposed and are discussed further below. Even in the 'Nordic' countries, where many features of the European model find their strongest expression, very considerable differences exist between nations (Gooderham et al. 2014). Yet despite this diversity, a discernible model exists and although none of its components are unique, the combination makes Europe different. We comment briefly on each component in turn in order to set the scene for the rest of the chapter.

The idea of democratic rights at work and in society. The essential origins of Europe's distinctive set of practices lie in a long history of creating democratic institutions and applying them to industry and society. Europe had a centuries-long history of industrial activity and wage labour even before the development of capitalism, giving rise even then to a dense body of trading and employee institutions. The more immediate origins of the distinctive elements we identified above lie in the development of strong workers' movements during industrialisation in the nineteenth century. These built and exchanged well-articulated ideologies of industrial democracy, workers' control of industry and social reform. In all Continental European countries, trade unionism developed from workers' movements from below which were steered and shaped either by social democratic parties or by more radical activists. British history showed the reverse tendency: the Labour Party was formed by trade unions and stamped by their more pragmatic ideologies. All of these parties, both the British and Continental European versions, sought to reform society in more egalitarian and inclusive directions. They encouraged, brokered and participated in national and then, international social settlements between capital and labour throughout the twentieth century and down to the present. They were integrated into European countries' polities, became parties of government and then provided strong and even essential legal support for trade unionism and worker voice more widely (Western 2000). Their reforms were generally accepted by other political parties as they were seen as providing social and industrial stability, and during the Cold War as building a bulwark against Communism. The social settlement was underpinned by the prosperity and full employment of the post-war boom years: the *Trente Glorieuses*. This unique 'social contract' weakened as the memory of war receded and was called into question by a resurgence of conservative politics and neo-liberal economics after the 1970s oil price shock. The sheer strength of the challenge meant that social democratic parties began to abandon much of their pro-worker agenda even before the collapse of Communism removed the failed alternative model from the political landscape. The post-1945 settlement was then largely dismantled during the last quarter of the twentieth century, a process accelerated by the aftermath of the 2008 Global Financial Crisis. Nevertheless, as we suggested above, that settlement reflected longer-term continuities and many Europeans had absorbed and continued to hold its values. Large employers had come to see utility in parts of the social contract and incorporated elements into their everyday management practice. These continuities underlie the seismic changes in European labour markets and social attitudes that threaten it. They are reflected in other, more contingent, elements of the 'European model' as we show below in more detail.

Stakeholders. Many constitutions and legal systems in Europe, and certainly all those within the EU, give significant rights in businesses to a range of stakeholders (Beer et al. 2015) other than just the owners of the business. The firm is seen as a part of society as well as a private entity belonging to its owners. Groups are seen to have a legitimate 'stake' in organisations, therefore, include employees, trade unions, customers, local and national governments and indeed society at large. All have a collective interest in the organisation, with regard to, for example decisions about employment, the environment and business's role in society. In some countries, certain groups have a legal basis for influencing organisational decisions. For example, in the Germanic countries, co-determination through works councils and trade unions is comparatively strong and legally regulated. The stakeholder concept has also been crucial to the EUs approach to social policy, as we detail below.

Role of the state. It has been argued that state regulation and the more limited autonomy of employers distinguish HRM, particularly employment relations, in Europe from those in the USA (Pieper 1990: 82) and this remains an accurate assessment. Of course, the comparison could equally well be made with many other countries and regions besides the United States of America. In Europe, the state intervenes directly in the economy. National, regional and local governments either own or part-own larger parts of the economy and, overall, the state is, therefore, a more substantial employer (employing up to half the working population in Norway, for example). The state also provides more services that are common elsewhere: to employees to help them develop their skills, find work and understand their rights; to employers to help them meet legal requirements; and to employers and trade unions to resolve their differences. It does so directly, through conciliation services, for example to regulate industrial disputes. It also does so indirectly through support to employers via state-aided vocational training and labour market programmes, including retraining and job transition support, job creation schemes and efforts to help younger people and the long-term unemployed access the labour market across the EU. Employment practices, including for example, wages, working hours and holidays, are at least in part regulated by the state—as is, as we shall show, employee communication. These interventions are frequently on a very large scale, like the financial subventions made by the German state in supporting the extent and quality of vocational education and training (Croucher and Brookes 2009).

Taken together, the stakeholder approach and the role of government ensure a more comprehensive approach to education, social welfare and health, for example that is found in many other regions in the world. These 'background' factors influence voice and participation in Europe fundamentally. They mean that, in general, people are educated enough to have valuable opinions and confident enough not be frightened of speaking up.

Rights to and in a job. In Europe, the state generally accepts and guarantees individual's rights to and in their jobs. Pieper (1990), making this point, included the greater regulation of recruitment and dismissal, the formalisation of educational certification and the quasi-legal characteristics of the industrial relations framework in comparison to the USA. We could also include, or specify, legislative requirements on pay, on hours of work, on forms of employment contract, rights to trade union representation, requirements to establish and operate consultation or co-determination arrangements—and a plethora of other legal requirements. We might also include the more common legislation on equality or health and safety, which impact the employment relationship on both sides of the Atlantic. In addition, the state has historically provided better-developed welfare provision in European countries than elsewhere, underpinning a greater sense of employee income security. Although these arrangements are becoming less generous in international comparative terms, they remain distinctive, especially when compared to those in, for instance, most of Asia.

There have been significant and even dramatic changes to these arrangements in many European countries since the Global Financial Crisis. The most obvious example is that of Greece, although there have been considerable changes to labour markets in many other countries, particularly in the Mediterranean. In the extreme case of Greece, the impact of the crisis and the associated legislative and workplace changes has been severe. Considerable changes to the law have facilitated the imposition of part-time contracts of employment, the decentralisation of bargaining from industry level together with pay decreases (Eurwork 2013). Further, alongside reductions in numbers employed, an increase in work pressures and growing negative effects on health, many of these changes appear to become 'institutionalised' so that improvements in the economic situation will not reverse them. Nevertheless, strong elements of stability remain in much of the rest of Europe. The European model may be subject to erosion, but it remains an important background to employee voice and its exercise at work, a subject we turn to next. We begin with trade unionism, as Europe historically has globally been its main redoubt.

3.2 Forms of Voice

Voice generally, as readers of the book will be well aware, takes many forms, however, we examine four that show distinctive factors.

Legally supported collective voice (1) Trade unions. It is often claimed that collective representation has become increasingly irrelevant to current workplace realities given employee individualisation and the active promotion of neo-liberal models, particularly since the Global Financial Crisis that began in 2008. Yet, this argument has recently been convincingly challenged as inadequately reflecting their continued importance to worker voice in Europe and more widely (Meardi 2014). Collective bargaining results are extended well beyond those directly concerned, through the industry-wide bargains common in many European countries; France provides the most extreme example as nine out of ten workers are covered by them even though nine out of ten are not union members. Perhaps even more importantly, collective forms of voice provide workers raising concerns with a degree of protection from hostile management reacting to them as individuals. Trade unions are one of the two main forms of collective employee representation in Europe, along with 'co-determination' or the system of ensuring that all employees voices are heard both at workplace through works councils and in some countries at the strategic company Supervisory Board level. Here, we deal with trade unions.

Europe has more people in free trade unions than other regions of the world. This is a highly unionised continent. Union memberships range from almost everyone in some of the Nordic countries to almost no one in France and some of the ex-communist countries. Thus, there is great diversity in levels of union membership in different countries but there is no direct correlation between the levels of membership and employee representative influence. To make one comparison: although German unions are widely and indeed correctly thought of as powerful, their overall density level among economically active employees (at 17.7%: 2013) is rather lower than in Britain (25.4%: 2013) where they are often thought of as relatively weak (EIRO 2015). A key determinant of union influence is the level of support for trade unionism provided in national legal frameworks and this is much stronger in France, Belgium, the Netherlands, Germany and the Nordic countries than in Britain (Charlwood 2006). Even in France, the fragmented unions have a significant influence on employment issues, wages and working conditions. The central reason for French union influence is the Republican tradition, which has long encouraged constant negotiation between the state and society, now including 'social partners', that crosses political parties. Britain has neither strong legal foundations for trade unions nor entrenched state traditions supporting them.

'Trade union', even in Europe, is a single term that covers many different forms of organisation with varying implications for employee voice. Although many commentators operate with a West European default model of trade unionism, i.e. of a body seeking to develop self-activity and voice among workers themselves in order to bargain collectively, this is quite different from the model assumed by many workers in Eastern Europe where a more instrumental attitude and welfare-based attitude exists. We examine first the West European situation. Where works councils and other forms of employee representation are often used by managers in different countries in pragmatic ways, to supplement less formal communication channels on certain issues where they need to strengthen employee 'buy-in' to their initiatives; this practice has been shown to remain common in Europe's larger companies (Brewster et al. 2007a, b). The opportunistic use of collective representation by managers demonstrates that there is a degree of utility to them in that a single representation channel is useful to employers, challenging the supposedly 'universal best practice' individual voice models suggested by some commentators (Brewster et al. 2007a, b). Further, it seems that higher levels of trade unionism are associated with a more strategic approach to HRM by employers (Vernon and Brewster 2012).

There has been considerable deterioration in the density and quality of workplace representation in many Western countries since the 1970s, particularly since the Global Financial Crisis. Britain is an extreme case in this respect with workplace representation through shop stewards declining markedly in its incidence and quality across the period (Arrowsmith and Pulignano 2013). The 'big picture' is that trade unions across Europe have been in a period of decline over the last thirty years that has been uneven across nations but is nevertheless visible in most EU countries.

The unevenness is very evident: in a few cases, such as in Malta, membership has increased (EIRO 2016). But in others, the Nordic countries continue to exhibit well-established voice and co-determination mechanisms. However, in the UK, France and Germany, there has been a steady decline, while in Southern Europe, it has been a steep decline, especially since the financial crisis (EIRO 2016). This trend cannot simply be equated to a decline in collective voice; indeed, it has stimulated other forms of collective voice such as employee networks. An example has been the Siemens employee network, an important example of one of a number of grass roots employee self-organised bodies which have emerged in response to major management re-structuring actions in the twenty-first century. The Siemens network grew in the company to deal with management's far-reaching plans aimed at reducing the number of jobs and radically altering knowledge workers' working lives. The body emerged not in opposition to but rather in symbiosis with the trade union and works council, assisting the latter in dealing with workers' issues and responses. The Siemens employee network organised large-scale demonstrations and took legal action in support of large numbers of individual employees against the company with some success since almost all of the cases were won (for a detailed account and assessment see Croucher et al. 2007).

In those countries which entered the European Union as post-communist 'accession countries' between 2007 and 2013, and also in the countries bordering them—-Belarus, Ukraine and Moldova—very different systems existed immediately after 1989. In all of them, the communist legacy and arguably longer-term social factors continue to play a role in workers' mentalities. Trade unionism was and to some extent still is considered as a way of administering welfare to workers; it is considered less a means for informing, mobilising and supporting workers in seeking to exercise voice than as operating on behalf of management. Majority 'official' (government approved) unions therefore still live with this legacy of not offering workers voice but rather providing them with benefits. Unions deal with this legacy in different ways: many have made serious efforts to move away from the communist model of unions and to take on more of a bargaining role. A small group of 'independent' unions exists in some countries, but these remained an embattled minority restricted to a few industries; they have offered more participation to members and always had a more democratic ethos but also limited membership. Through their national-level federations, the mainstream official unions have long been involved in tripartite arrangements which Ost (2000) characterised as 'illusory corporatism' which integrated the unions into government without offering real democratic opportunities. Meardi (2007) largely confirmed this verdict just before the Global Financial Crisis, pointing to a weakening in countries where trade unionism had previously been more effective. Negotiation at all levels is often simply formal and tokenistic.

However, in these 'accession countries', links have long existed with western unions through training programmes and therefore, although still stamped by their history, they have gradually reformed, taking on more democratic procedures and much of the bargaining role of their western counterparts (Croucher and Rizov 2012). Contrary to many western perceptions, studies show that Central and Eastern European unions in the ex-communist countries there are capable of exercising some influence in companies, particularly in large public sector organisations and when the business cycle is in a downturn (Croucher and Rizov 2012). Nevertheless, workers remain comparatively weak in the employment relationship in relation to their western counterparts and unhappiness with local employers has increasingly taken the exit, i.e. migration, routes. This has, in turn, strengthened the hand of those who remain by creating labour shortages (Meardi 2007). Nevertheless, the examples of collective action by workers, although limited, were increasing prior to the onset of the financial crisis (Meardi 2007).

A contrast exists between these countries and those to their immediate East since the possibilities there both for exit and collective employee voice are less. Workers in the former Soviet Union states (FSUs) certainly have few voice options. Even before Ukraine was devastated and its trade unions divided by war, employers simply used many workplace-based unions as 'rubber stamps' for approving 'collective agreements' as required by law (Croucher 2010). In Belarus, workers continue to express anger at their unions having become ineffective vehicles for expressing their views on issues of great importance to them (Danilovich et al. 2015). In Moldova, those unions previously showing some independence of government and an increasing capacity to involve workers and build their confidence to exercise voice at work have suffered from government hostility and have been marginalised while communist-style welfare unions have been encouraged (Morrison and Croucher 2010). Thus, voice expectations between workers in Eastern and Western Europe remain very different, increasing the difficulty of building common European approaches.

Legally supported collective voice (2) Co-determination. The most distinctive of the European contributions to voice is probably the existence of works councils. Works councils originated in Germany immediately after the revolutionary upsurge at the end of the First World War, were abolished by the Nazis and reconstituted again after 1945 as a significant aspect of democracy. They, therefore, have deep historical roots. Works councils carry out more day-to-day representation of employee interests and 'oil the wheels' of manager–worker interaction. They have rights to 'co-determine' certain important issues with management, and must be consulted or informed on a further range of matters (Croucher and Singe 2004). Their legal rights are also the basis for works councillors to conduct informal bargaining with managers. German works councils, or *Betriebsräte*, in common with the *comités d'entreprises* system in all larger French businesses, potentially provide a means for ensuring that employee voice is heard. The German approach has been the basis for providing employee voice in numerous other countries.

There are few detailed studies showing the system in action as a form of worker voice, but it is clear from these studies that there is very wide variation between workplaces in terms of how well the works council system operates. In his first classic study, Kotthoff (1981) identified six types of works council, three of which he regarded as effective in achieving worker voice and participation. A further study (1994) focused on links with wider democracy in Germany, but also revealed wide variation in works councillors' actual relations with managers. Ten years later, Croucher and Singe (2004) examined the system's detailed workings in two finance companies and found a sharp contrast between works council effectiveness in the two firms which was largely linked to the effectiveness of links with trade unions in the two workplaces. As a form of 'voice', the system is relatively effective compared to employer-driven consultative committees or individual voice, as works councillors have strong legal protection and workers in large companies are well aware of their value (Croucher and Singe 2004).

Despite declining collective bargaining coverage, trade unions in many European countries, including France and Germany, continue to bargain over pay and conditions at industry level, thereby externalising conflict on these issues beyond the workplace and permitting the development of a cooperative atmosphere at workplace level through co-determination. Unions also provide training and informational support to works councils which can improve their effectiveness (Croucher and Singe 2004). Despite concerns that work councils might act as substitutes for trade unions, it is clear that trade unions and works councils supplement each other (Brewster et al. 2007a, b). Strong unions are extremely positive for the main form of collective employee voice which complements trade unionism: works councils.

The co-determination system, once an unquestioned fact of industrial life in many European countries, has increasingly been debated, particularly in its board-level dimension. This is a widespread practice in European countries both inside and outside the EU and indeed is required in firms registered as 'European' companies recognised under the EUs 2001 European Company Statute. It is a system of worker representation on boards, often applying to larger companies and in some countries extending to smaller firms. It does not exist in the UK, although that country's Trades Union Congress currently advocates its extension to companies there. In some countries, co-determination permits some inputs into company strategy, in others such as the Francophone and Nordic countries, worker representatives have a more restricted role both de jure and in practice and have less input into strategy (Waddington and Conchon 2015).

Some aspects of these arrangements have been challenged by employers. The German employers' association, the BDA, has been critical of its alleged hampering of German employers' capacity to compete internationally. As a result, earlier demands that the system of equal numbers of worker and other directors operated in mining and heavy industry be extended more widely have receded. Recent comprehensive survey research across 16 European countries and a sample of European companies conducted for the European Trade Union Institute shows that on occasions, these directors can achieve a significant role in board debates, ensuring that employee views are more salient than they might otherwise be, although in others this is less apparent (Waddington and Conchon 2015). These researchers find that a key consideration in the effectiveness of these worker board members is how well linked they are to other systems of worker representation.

Beneath the large company level, in smaller companies and in many workplaces in the German *Mittelstand*, or smaller and medium-sized enterprises, a sizeable 'co-determination free zone' has developed and in this large group of organisations employees have no formal collective voice mechanisms with any degree of independence from the employer. They, therefore, have only weaker forms of voice to fall back on: employer-driven forms and the possibility of exercising voice in an individualised and in that sense unprotected way. We deal with the former immediately below and then turn to individual voice in the following section.

Employer-driven collective voice. From the mid-1990s onwards, these forms of employee voice, typically known by names such as 'company councils' or 'non-union joint consultative committees' (although less widespread than those that are legally supported) became more common, especially in the UK and parts of Eastern Europe. There has been little research on them and very little on their effectiveness. Case study research provides some potential explanation for why such initiatives have been limited in the UK. Upchurch and his colleagues document a 'paradox of intention': that employers seek to gain from employee involvement while structural limits, inter alia a wish to avoid unionisation, restrict what can be achieved (Upchurch et al. 2006). Second, other work shows that these forms of representation can have some utility for employees, including those in unionised situations but also that rather than displacing a need for union representation it has a complementary effect (Gollan 2006), thus showing in this detailed case study a similar effect to that found by Brewster et al. (2007a, b) across Europe. This research was carried out at Eurotunnel (UK), which instituted non-union representation prior to acquiring union representation later and studied its workings across a 5-year period. The Company Council had an informational and consultative role, and also managed a social welfare budget. Initially, the council also had a collective bargaining role, although this function later passed to the trade union. These particular circumstances allowed the Company Council to establish itself prior to unionisation. Although support for the Company Council among employees, as reflected in surveys, declined over the 5-year period, and the union increased its membership, overall employees felt that the two bodies were complementary.

In some Eastern European countries outside of the EU, such as Ukraine, some employers have also pursued a strategy of seeking to build non-union forms of voice as an alternative to existing workplace unions, which continue to have a certain legal role. They have created (in local parlance) 'yellow unions', using them as channels for welfare distribution and approval of legally required 'collective agreements' (Croucher 2010).

Individual voice. The use of individual voice, in various forms, is almost ubiquitous across Europe (Brewster et al. 2014). However, we are unaware of any comprehensive survey allowing us to estimate its effectiveness with any pretensions to accuracy. The 'direct' expression of employee voice, unmediated by representatives, is a preference of US-style HRM. It is encouraged by the international neo-liberal consensus and has increasingly appeared preferable to many European managers. Managers' calculation has increasingly been that the costs of collective voice outweigh the benefits, although this is more the case in some countries and industries than in others (Willman et al. 2006). These costs—and especially the high start-up costs associated with collective employee voice—may well deter employers in small and medium-sized enterprises, such as those common in Mediterranean countries but also famously important in Germany, from instituting these measures. Managers also suggest that there is a lack of interest from employees in the more formalised, collective and 'indirect' forms of voice. This may be the case among some types of employee in strong labour market positions and without strong occupational traditions of representation (Willman et al. 2006). However, many employee surveys continue to show a demand for some or improved representation beyond what they currently experience. We, therefore, follow Willman et al. (2006) in preferring an explanation of the increasing emphasis on such forms as a result of management choice, while recognising that worker attitudes play some role (Charlwood 2006).

Contrary to theories postulating convergence of practice in European firms towards a US-style model of individual voice, research provides little or no support for the 'convergence' argument, at least in larger firms. And the paternalistic individualism in smaller, particularly family managed, firms that is widespread across Europe is very different from the US-style HRM stereotype. Research examining firm-level practice in Britain, Germany and Sweden before the financial crisis demonstrated that managers continued to make substantial use of collective voice mechanisms of all kinds. There was only very limited evidence of directional convergence towards individual voice in any of the major industrial countries examined (Brewster et al. 2007a, b).

In some companies with relatively flat hierarchies, such as in many small companies in the digital economy, individual voice may be more frequent and effective than in more hierarchical or lower trust environments. This is particularly likely to be the case where workers have specific skills that are in high demand. However, the pervasive increasing weakness of employees in the employment relationship across all European industries has become increasingly evident and hints that employees are likely to feel less confident about raising concerns than they were previously. The experience of many 'whistleblowers' appears to bear this out. 'Whistleblowing' refers to individuals raising issues about unethical, unfair or illegal corporate or organisational practices, and is one, albeit very specific, form of individual voice (see Chap. 10 in this book). It is one that seems clearly in the public interest and therefore desirable in principle. The issues raised may include matters of interest to employees, but also encompass subjects such as fraud and corruption. The adequate protection of whistleblowers is, therefore, a matter of good corporate governance (Lewis and Vandekerckhove 2011). Legally backed 'whistleblowing' procedures exist in 29 countries around the world and are not exclusive to Europe, although many European countries have them (Lewis and Vandekerckhove 2011). Yet experts on whistleblowing from Norway, where employment protection is strong even in European terms, suggest that some whistleblowers, and even people contemplating it or associated in some way with the whistleblower, experience retaliation and bullying. The experts, therefore, recommend stronger legislation to deal with the issue (Bjørkelo and Mathiesen 2011).

3.3 The EU, Legislation and Social Dialogue: History, Development and Controversy

As we outlined in the introduction, a distinctive aspect of Europe as a regional bloc has long been the idea that such a bloc required transnational institutions for worker voice. A key European innovation was the development of European works councils (EWCs). There had long been recognition of the need for firm-level organs that would inform and consult workforces on a European scale. Some companies had indeed adopted such institutions voluntarily, and there was increasing demand for European regulation. The result was the 1994 EWC Directive. This directive stipulated that EWCs were to be established in undertakings with 'at least 1,000 employees within the Member States and at least 150 employees in each of at least 2 Member States', and set out voluntary and prescribed modes of compliance with the directive. Providing they covered the entire European workforce, 'article 13' EWCs established prior to 22 September 1996 need not comply with the directive's terms. Those EWCs set up after this date, known as 'article 6' EWCs, were obliged to follow a model set out by the directive.

The proliferation of EWCs has inspired a large literature. Though some accounts focused on the weakness of such institutions in comparison to national works councils (Streeck 1997), and the lack of interest shown by companies based in the UK, others were more sanguine and emphasised the innovativeness of EWCs and their capacity to develop (Ramsay 1997). German unions insisted that EWCs did not represent co-determination vehicles, but were simply consultative bodies. The directive itself was also subject to revision precisely because some were critical of its limitations. The following years of trade union lobbying for fortification of its terms, a 2009 revision more clearly demarcated divisions of labour between EWCs and national works councils, better defined the rights of EWCs to information and consultation and gave more influence to trade unions. A European Company Statute (ECS) is also now available, giving such companies certain legal and fiscal rights but requiring further consultation. Following adoption by the EUs Employment and Social Policy Council in 2001, the ECS required employee involvement through board-level participation and 'representative bod[ies]'. Though such rights were not revolutionary, they were nonetheless an important supplement to existing forms of employee representation (Gold and Schwimbersky 2008).

European regulation also strengthened information and consultation rights at member state level. The following concern is that existing arrangements in certain countries were insufficient, the 2002 Information and Consultation Directive stipulated that institutions for the information and consultation of employees be established in 'undertakings employing at least 50 employees in any 1 Member State, or establishments employing at least 20 employees in any 1 Member State'. Nine sequential stages for the information and consultation of employees, from the transmission of data to discussion 'with a view to reaching an agreement on decisions', were set out. The directive was criticised, as sceptics pointed to its weak terms and the preexistence of stronger institutions in several member states (Koukiadaki 2010;

Hall and Purcell 2011). Nevertheless, it at least established works councils in countries without such institutions, arguably a major permissive contribution to social dialogue at national level.

Social dialogue has also become established at European level in recent decades. As part of the first Delors Commission's attempts to combat social dumping, summits between representatives of European labour and business were organised from 1985. The results of the so-called *Val Duchesse* dialogue, a name inspired by the Brussels château in which meetings were held, were nonetheless non-legally binding and tended to concern topics at the margin of the employment relationship. European-level social dialogue was strengthened in the early 1990s. The Social Protocol, annexed to the Maastricht Treaty in 1992 as a result of the UK Conservative Government's opposition, set out procedures for the conclusion of legally binding and non-legally binding European collective agreements. In the years following the Social Protocol three agreements, on Parental leave (1995), Part-time work (1997) and Fixed-term work (1999), were implemented via legally binding Council Directives. Many were optimistic about these developments. A series of authorities underlined the dialogue's procedural and substantive achievements and potential to develop, and the onset of Euro-corporatism was even heralded (Falkner 1998; Welz 2008).

Others were sceptical. These authorities pointed to the exclusion of crucial competences such as pay from the dialogue's scope, the organisational weakness of the European social partners and the dialogue's dependence on the European Commission. Developments after 2000 appeared to vindicate the sceptics. In response to the EUs impending enlargement and the increasing popularity of non-legally binding 'soft' European governance methods such as the Open Method of Coordination (OMC), the dialogue assumed a 'softer' form. It became known as the 'new phase' (Prosser 2006). Agreements concluded during the 'new phase' were implemented via the non-legally binding implementation route outlined in the Social Protocol. The Telework Agreement (2002), Work-related Stress Agreement (2004), Harassment and Violence at Work Agreement (2007) and Inclusive Labour Markets Agreement (2010) were all implemented via the 'procedures and practices specific to management and labour in the member states', and therefore depended on national social partners for implementation. Potential problems with this implementation route were soon foreseen (Keller 2003). Social dialogue structures in several member states were uncoordinated and/or fragmented, and studies of implementation outcomes typically arrived at pessimistic conclusions (Larsen and Andersen 2007; Prosser 2011).

Attempts at European sectoral-level social dialogue suffered from similar problems. Though the 1998 launch of European sectoral social dialogue committees (SSDCs) inspired the creation of a number of such institutions, the output of SSDCs was rather disappointing (Prosser and Perin 2015). Agreements subsequently implemented by Council Directive were concluded in certain sectors in which there were integrated markets and Europeanised sectoral policies (Leisink 2002), but in most sectors, these outcomes were absent. Many SSDCs contented themselves with the production of non-legally binding texts aimed at the European public authorities, and it was argued that they functioned primarily as lobbying forums (De Boer et al. 2005).

A variety of policies and institutions that guarantee the European-level participation of employees thus exist. Though they have been the subject of criticism, such forums for the transnational consultation of employees are unique and can point to numerous achievements. These institutions will therefore continue to function, although will evolve to meet the challenges and the power relationships of the twenty-first century.

A particular challenge will be the decision of the UK to leave the EU. Though it has been suggested that the exit of the traditionally neo-liberal UK might allow remaining member states to strengthen legislation guaranteeing European-level employee participation, it is difficult to see such a scenario materialising in the short-term. Not only is the attention of the EU fixed on the resolution of a series of existential challenges, but considerable opposition to the fortification of such regulation exists in other quarters. Implications for employee participation in the post-Brexit UK are also intriguing. Even if certain figures in the governing Conservative party favour the repeal of European regulation in this area, the apparent desire of the May Government to guarantee employee protection, not to mention logistical challenges associated with the abolition of such legislation, make this eventuality improbable.

Comparative capitalisms and voice. Attempts have been made to apply wider analyses of corporate governance systems within different varieties of capitalism to explain the variations in employee voice across Europe. The comparative capitalisms literature (Jackson and Deeg 2008) draws distinctions between the ways that capitalism works in different contexts. Typical categories include the Anglo-Saxon liberal market economies (LMEs) and the coordinated market economies of Rhineland Europe (Hall and Soskice 2001). It is argued that the former are characterised by competition, a requirement enshrined in law, a lesser role for government and hence lower taxation and limited state provision of welfare benefits and health. The latter are characterised by greater coordination between firms, more involvement of government with firms and better welfare provision. These differences go through into the relationships between employers and employees with higher degrees of interdependence and delegation (Whitley 1999) in CMEs. Higher interdependence means that people stay longer with the same firm, therefore training and development make more sense to both parties and voice becomes more important. Higher delegation means that people are trusted more, and have greater participation in their work and their firm. We have seen some of these factors at work in our discussions of Germany and the Netherlands versus the UK and Ireland.

There are multi-category versions of the comparative capitalisms theories. Thus, Amable (2003) identified within Europe social democratic capitalism, in the Nordic countries, Mediterranean capitalism and the emerging economies of Central and Eastern Europe. Again, we have seen how these contextual factors influence employee voice: the Nordic countries have much higher levels of trade union membership, including trade union membership for many managers, excellent social security, government support for, for example retraining and there is an expectation (little legislation is required) that people will be consulted about their work and their voice will be heard in the organisation they work in. The Mediterranean countries, characterised by a split between high levels of small, often family run, businesses and a more rule-bound public and large firms sector, have low levels of trade union membership, poor social security and paternalistic human resource management. Independent employee voice is limited. We have discussed the vast range of practices developing in the, often institutionally weak, former communist states and former Soviet Union states.

Test of internal relationships and voice (Brewster et al. 2014, 2015) seem to show support for these different categories and help to explain why they exist. The comparative capitalisms literature has, like much of the institutional and regulation literature been criticised because although it provides a much better understanding of how firms (and unions, etc.) are embedded in their context, it struggles to cope with change—if everything is embedded in a series of complementarities and path-dependent, then how do things change? The literature is attempting to respond to this critique. Thus, Amable and Palombarini (2009) emphasised the importance of power and politics in the development of systems and Streeck (2010), following the same ideas, has argued that pressures from the LMEs are causing the CMEs to move towards them, weakening the institutional complementarities. Nuanced accounts by Thelen (2009, 2014) attempt to unpick the detail of changes within specified countries, and foreign private equity does seem to have an impact on changing individual organisations towards patterns which include less voice (Guery et al. 2017). However, although there is inevitably change, the evidence (Mayrhofer et al. 2011) seems to be that human resource management practices, including employee voice, still remain distinct in each variety of capitalism.

3.4 Summary and Conclusions

There is no area of employee voice in which Europe is unique, except obviously its history and the influence of the European Union. In all other areas, even the use of works councils and the strength of the legislation requiring employers to allow and respond to employee voice, there are other examples around the world—most of them, of course, heavily influenced by the example of Europe. But the combination of still strong trade unions, legislative support, a belief in stakeholders' rights, powerful institutional demands and continent-wide, multi-country legislation is unique. And, it creates a unique environment for employee voice. The general right-wing shift amongst European governments and the increasing acceptance of the neo-liberal logic place this legacy at risk. It will be worth paying close attention to developments in voice in Europe over the next few years.

References

Amable, B. (2003). *The diversity of modern capitalism*. Oxford: Oxford University Press.

Amable, B., & Palombarini, S. (2009). A neorealist approach to institutional change and the diversity of capitalism. *Socio-Economic Review, 7*(1), 123–143.

Arrowsmith, J., & Pulignano, V. (2013). *The transformation of employment relations in Europe*. London: Routledge.

Beer, M., Boselie, P., & Brewster, C. (2015). Back to the future: Implications for the field of HRM of the multi-stakeholder perspective proposed 30 years ago. *Human Resource Management, 54*(3), 427–438.

Bjørkelo, B., & Mathiesen, B. S. (2011). Preventing and dealing with retaliation against whistle-blowers. In W. Vandekerckhove & D. Lewis (Eds.), *Whistleblowing and democratic values* (pp. 127–149). London: International Whistleblowing Research Network.

Brewster, C., Brookes, M., Croucher, R., & Wood, G. T. (2007a). Collective and individual voice: convergence in Europe? *International Journal of Human Resource Management, 18*(7), 1246–1262.

Brewster, C., Wood, G. T., Croucher, C., & Brookes, M. (2007b). Are works councils and joint consultative committees a threat to trade unions? *A comparative analysis, Economic and Industrial Democracy, 28*(1), 53–81.

Brewster, C., Brookes, M., Johnson, P., & Wood, G. T. (2014). Direct involvement, partnership and setting: A study in bounded diversity. *International Journal of Human Resource Management, 25*(6), 795–809.

Brewster, C., Wood, G. T., & Goergen, M. (2015). Institutions, unionization and voice: The relative impact of context and actors on firm level practice. *Economic and Industrial Democracy, 36*(2), 195–214.

Brewster, C., Mayrhofer, W., & Sparrow, P. (2018) HRM in Westrrn Europe: Differences without, differences within. In C. Brewster, W. Mayrhofer, & E. Farndale (Eds.), *Handbook of research in comparative human resource management*, 2nd Edn. Cheltenham: Edward Elgar.

Charlwood, A. (2006). What determined employer voice choices in Britain in the 20th century? A critique of the 'sound of silence' model. *Socio-Economic Review, 4*, 301–309.

Croucher, R. (2010). Employee involvement in Ukraine. *International Journal of Human Resource Management, 21*(14), 2659–2676.

Croucher, R. (2016). Employment relations in Europe. In M. Dickmann, C. Brewster, & P. Sparrow (Eds.), *International human resource management: contemporary human resource issues in Europe* (pp. 262–281). London: Routledge.

Croucher, R., & Singe, I. (2004). Co-determination and working time accounts in the German finance industry. *Industrial Relations Journal, 35*(2), 153–168.

Croucher, R., & Brookes, M. (2009). German employers' inputs to vocational education and training. *Industrial Relations: A Journal of Economy and Society, 48*(2), 231–236.

Croucher, R., & Miles, L. (2009). The legal structuring of women's collective voice in the South Korean workplace. *Journal of Contemporary Asia, 39*(2), 231–246.

Croucher, R., & Rizov, M. (2012). Union influence in Eastern Europe. *ILR Review, 65*(3), 630–650.

Croucher, R., Martens, H., & Singe, I. (2007). A German employee network and union renewal: The Siemenskonflikt. *Industrial Relations/Relations Industrielles, 62*(1), 143–169.

Danilovich, H., Croucher, R., & Makovskaya, N. (2015). Compulsory reduced working time in Belarus: Incidence, operation and consequences. *Economic and Industrial Democracy, 38*(4), 723–740.

De Boer, R., Benedictus, H., & Van Der Meer, M. (2005). Broadening without intensification: The added value of the European social and sectoral dialogue. *European Journal of Industrial Relations, 11*(1), 51–70.

European Industrial Relations Observatory (EIRO). (2015, 2016). *Mapping key dimensions of industrial relations*. Luxembourg, European Union.

Eurwork. (2013). Greece: Impact of the crisis on industrial relations. Dublin, European Foundation. Retrieved February 16, 2016.

Falkner, G. (1998). *EU social policy in the 1990s: Towards a corporatist policy community*. London: Routledge.

Guery, L., Stevenot, A., Wood, G., & Brewster, C. (2017). The impact of private equity on employment: The consequences of fund country of origin—New evidence from France. *Industrial Relations: A Journal of Economy and Society, 56*(4), 723–750.

Gold, M., & Schwimbersky, S. (2008). The European company statute: Implications for industrial relations in the European Union. *European Journal of Industrial Relations, 14*(1), 46–64.

Gollan, P. J. (2006). A process of transition—Employer strategies and outcomes of employee voice at Eurotunnel. *Socio-Economic Review, 4*, 337–351.

Gooderham, P., Navreberg, S. E., Olsen, K. M., & Steen, C. R. (2014). The labour market regimes of Denmark and Norway—One Nordic model? *Journal of Industrial Relations, 57*(2), 166–186.

Hall, M., & Purcell, J. (2011). *Information and consultation practice across Europe five years after the EU directive*. Dublin: European Foundation for the Improvement of Living and Working Conditions.

Hall, P., & Soskice, D. (2001). *Varieties of capitalism: The institutional foundations of comparative advantage*. New York: Oxford University Press.

Jackson, G., & Deeg, R. (2008). Comparing capitalisms: Understanding institutional diversity and its implications for international business. *Journal of International Business Studies, 39*(4), 540–561.

Keller, B. (2003). Social dialogues: The state of the art a decade after Maastricht. *Industrial Relations Journal, 34*(5), 411–429.

Kotthoff, H. (1981). *Betriebsräte und betriebliche Herrschaft*. Frankfurt am Main, Campus: Eine Typologie von Partizipationsmustern im Industriebetrieb.

Kotthoff, H. (1994). *Betriebsräte und Bürgerstatus*. Hampp, München: Wandel und Kontinuität betrieblicher Mitbestimmung.

Koukiadaki, A. (2010). The establishment and operation of information and consultation of employees' arrangements in a capability-based framework. *Economic and Industrial Democracy, 31*(3), 365–388.

Larsen, T., & Andersen, S. (2007). Autonomous framework agreements: A new way of regulating Europe. *European Journal of Industrial Relations, 13*(2), 181–198.

Leisink, P. (2002). The European sectoral dialogue and the graphical industry. *European Journal of Industrial Relations, 8*(1), 101–117.

Lewis, D., & Vandekerckhove, W. (2011). Introduction. In W. Vandekerckhove & D. Lewis (Eds.), *Whistleblowing and democratic values*. London: International Whistleblowing Research Network.

Mayrhofer, W., Brewster, C., Morley, M., & Ledolter, J. (2011). Hearing a different drummer? Evidence of convergence in European HRM. *Human Resource Management Review, 21*(1), 50–67.

Meardi, G. (2007). More voice after more exit? Unstable industrial relations in Central and Eastern Europe. *Industrial Relations Journal, 38*(6), 503–523.

Meardi, G. (2014). The (claimed) growing irrelevance of employment relations. *Journal of Industrial Relations, 56*(4), 594–605.

Morrison, C., & Croucher, R. (2010). Moldovan employment relations: Path dependency? *Employee Relations, 32*(3), 227–247.

Ost, D. (2000) Illusory corporatism in Eastern Europe: Neoliberal tripartitism and postcommunist class identities. *Poltics and Society, 28*(4), 503–530.

Pieper, R. (1990). *Human resource management: An international comparison*. Berlin: Walter de Gruyter.

Prosser, T. (2006). Is the "new phase' of the European social dialogue the development of an autonomous and effective form of social dialogue? Warwick Paper in Industrial Relations 82.

Prosser, T. (2011). European social dialogue through 'soft' law? *European Journal of Industrial Relations, 17*(3), 245–260.

Prosser, T. J., & Perin, E. (2015). European tripartism: Chimera or reality? The 'new phase' of the European social dialogue in the light of tripartite theory and practice. *Business History, 57*(3), 376–397.
Ramsay, H. (1997). Fool's gold? European works councils and workplace democracy. *Industrial Relations Journal, 28*(4), 314–322.
Streeck, W. (1997). Neither European nor works councils: A reply to Paul Knutsen. *Economic and Industrial Democracy, 18*(2), 325–337.
Streeck, W. (2010). E Pluribus Unum? Varieties and commonalities of capitalism. MPIfG Discussion Paper 10/12, Cologne.
Thelen, K. (2009). Institutional change in advanced political economies. *British Journal of Industrial Relations, 47*(3), 471–621.
Thelen, K. (2014). *Varieties of liberalization and the new politics of social solidarity*. Cambridge: Cambridge University Press.
Upchurch, M., Richardson, M., Tailby, S., Danford, A., & Stewart, P. (2006). Employee representation and partnership in the non-union sector: A paradox of intention? *Human Resource Management Journal, 16*(4), 393–410.
Upchurch, M., Croucher, R., Danilovich, H., & Morrison, C. (2015). The transformation of work and industrial relations in the post-Soviet bloc: 25 years on from 1989. *Work, Employment & Society, 29*(3), 1–11.
Vernon, G., & Brewster, C. (2012). Structural spoilers or structural supports? Unionism and the strategic integration of HR functions. *International Journal of Human Resource Management, 24*(6), 1113–1130.
Waddington, J., & Conchon, A. (2015). *Board-level representation in Europe*. Brussels: European Trade Union Institute.
Welz, C. (2008). *The European social dialogue under Articles 138 and 139 of the EC treaty: Actors, processes, outcomes*. Alphen aan den Rijn: Kluwer Law International.
Western, B. (2000). *Between class and market*. Mass: Princeton University Press Cambridge.
Whitley, R. (1999) *Divergent capitalisms*. Oxford: Oxford University Press.
Willman, P., Bryson, A., & Gomez, R. (2006). The sound of silence: Which employers choose no employee voice and why? *Socio-Economic Review, 4*, 283–299.
Wood, G. T., Brewster, C., Brookes, M., Cunha y Campos, R., & Dibben, P. (2016 forthcoming). Institutional legacies and capabilities: Work practices and employment relations in Portugal and Mozambique. *International Journal of Human Resource Management*.

Dr. Chris Brewster is now a part-time Professor of International Human Resource Management at Vaasa University in Finland; Henley Business School, University of Reading in the UK; and Radboud University in the Netherlands, specialising in international and comparative HRM. He had substantial industrial experience and got his doctorate from the London School of Economics before becoming an academic. He has been involved as author or editor in the publication of more than 30 books, more than 100 chapters in other books and well over 200 articles.

Dr. Richard Croucher is Professor of Comparative Employment Relations and was formerly Director of Research, Middlesex University Business School, London. He is Visiting Professor at Cranfield School of Management. He is the author of Engineers at War (1982), We Refuse to Starve in Silence (1987), (with Elizabeth Cotton) Global Unions, Global Business and Global Union Federations and International Business (2010; 2nd edition 2011). He has published over 100 articles in leading journals which include Journal of Management, Human Relations and Industrial Relations. A Journal of Economy and Society. He has carried out research funded by the International Labour Organisation, the UK Low Pay Commission, the Leverhulme Trust, the Economic and Social Research Council, the Nuffield Trust and other bodies.

Dr. Thomas Prosser is a Senior Lecturer in European Social Policy at Cardiff University. He specialises in European social dialogue and labour market dualization, and has conducted primary research in a range of European countries. His work has been published in journals such as Journal of Common Market Studies, British Journal of Industrial Relations and Journal of European Social Policy, and he has conducted expert consultancy for organisations like the European Commission and International Labour Organization. In the summer of 2018, Dr. Prosser will publish a book on the reaction of European labour movements to the economic crisis.

Part II
Contemporary Dimensions of Employee Voice

Chapter 4
Social Media at Work: A New Form of Employee Voice?

Peter Holland, Brian Cooper and Rob Hecker

Abstract In the workplace of the twenty-first century, social media cuts two ways. Increasingly there is evidence of the ways in which employers use it as a recruitment tool and use it as part of the process of selecting employees. However, employees can use it to discuss issues at work out of the control of management. Specifically, increasingly savvy employers are building internal social media sites to connect with the immediacy and focus of employee voices on emerging workplace issues. The other major use of social media is where this breakdown in trust between employer and employee which often leads to employees to vent their anger through public social media channels which, in turn, can damage brand image and reputation.

Keywords Digital Platforms · Control · Real time · Trust · Global Reach

4.1 Introduction

> If any company thinks that social media doesn't apply to them they are seriously mistaken. We're in a digital revolution, digital technology is fundamentality changing the way we do business (Mennie 2015: 4).

The above quote illustrates the changing nature and impact of social media from its beginnings as an electronic platform designed for friends to keep in touch to one of the most powerful communication tools both inside and outside the workplace. Social media is now being seen as an alternative, emerging form of 'voice' in the context of declining union density, particularly in Advanced Market Economies (AMEs)

P. Holland (✉)
Department of Management and Marketing, Swinburne Business School, Swinburne University of Technology, Melbourne, VIC, Australia
e-mail: peter.holland@monash.edu

B. Cooper
Department of Management, Monash University, Clayton, Australia

R. Hecker
Tasmanian School of Business and Economics, University of Tasmania, Hobart, Australia

P. Holland et al. (eds.), *Employee Voice at Work*, Work, Organization, and Employment, https://doi.org/10.1007/978-981-13-2820-6_4

and especially among the younger generations. Examples of the impact of social media are already well documented. From the HMV case, where live tweets where emanating from inside the workplace as retrenchments were taking place (see below), disparaging comments about the workplace that have seen employees sacked and organisations going into damage control (Dowling 2015; Broughton et al. 2010), to employees voicing through social media to take a socially responsible stand against their employer (Miles and Mangold 2014). Both employers and the law have often had to take a reactive stance to the impact of this new medium as they attempt to develop appropriate policies and practices. Whilst much of the focus has been on the potential negative and destructive aspects of social media and accompanying prevention and protection measures against employees (Jacobsen and Howle-Tufts 2013; Richards 2008), less attention has been given to the harnessing of social media in a constructive manner. As Miles and Mangold (2014) point out, social media can be an untapped resource if developed properly and in conjunction with employees. Effective use of this resource can only begin where management understands how the resource can facilitate better understanding of issues at work and contribute to decision-making and ultimately competitive advantage of the organisation; meaning management getting messages that they may or may not want to receive (Miles and Mangold 2014).

This chapter explores the issues and opportunities social media provides in the development of employee voice, through its properties of immediacy and range of connections. These have the potential to flatten the organisational hierarchy of voice channels at work as it gives everyone the connected opportunity to have equal input and provides management with an immediate understanding of workplace issues and an opportunity to address them in 'real' time. For those who do not embrace it, it will remain an untapped resource. The chapter also highlights the key values and culture that need to be put in place for such a voice system to operate effectively. The discussion of voice also highlights the issue of silence as an ongoing workplace issue.

4.2 The New Paradigm of Social Media in the Workplace

What is Social Media? At first, this might seem a logical and straightforward question. However, the relative newness and rapid evolution of social media mean that it has come to mean different things to different people. Whilst most people will see social media through the spectrum of Facebook, LinkedIn and Twitter, it is in fact, best described as all digital platforms where people connect and share information. Thus, organisations' interactive websites (with customers and other stakeholders) can be seen as social media (Mennie 2015).

Considering, therefore, the ubiquitous nature of social media and its potential to influence the workplace, and calls for contemporary research on employee voice to push the boundaries, to deepen our knowledge and understanding of voice in the workplace (see Budd 2014), it is surprising the paucity of research on the use of social media and its impact in the workplace and in particular on employee voice (see excellent example—Martin Parry and Flowers 2015). More generally, as Andreassen et al. (2014) note, presently there is not much known about factors influencing attitudes towards and the actual use of electronic communication during work time.

As Miles and Mangold (2014) and Budd (2014: 485) note, the changes in voice brought about by the rapid evolution in technologies has also provided employees with unprecedented power in and outside the workplace, and should prompt a re-evaluation of our approach to voice as traditional approaches fail to fully account for social media. Those studies that have been undertaken have shown a variety of findings on the impact of social media at work (Holland et al. 2016; Miles and Mangold 2014). This chapter looks to explore these issues and add to the body of literature from employee relations and human resource management perspective.

As social media emerges as a relatively new form of voice, it is most likely to be generated externally to the organisation, and initially, there is no guarantee that managers will see them, so in some ways electronic forms can provide voice but no ears. However, this context was arguably changed by the HMV case noted below which highlighted the need for organisations to monitor external communication about their organisation. In the HMV case—ironically, HMV stands for His Master's Voice and the company has a history in communications—it was the live tweets from a termination process that framed an understanding of the impact of social media in and on the workplace as 70,000 followers received the following tweets (and may others) and then re-tweeted them as

> We're tweeting live from HR where we're all being fired! Exciting!!

This was followed by details and descriptions of the 'mass execution' of loyal workers, gross mismanagement and unpaid illegal interns. As Holmes (2013) notes by the time HMV had regained control of the account and deleted the messages, the damage was done as the tweets went viral.

What the HMV case provides is an understanding as to how, as Miles and Mangold (2014) note, the power and potential impact of this new medium of social media voice can bring attention to issues of public interest into the public domain, especially if the employee(s) feels their voice is not being heard. Another high-profile example of this was a staff member who posted pictures of raw food stored outside his restaurant in the US next to a bin swarming with flies. This was posted after the staff got no responses from management or the local health authority over the issue. This example also highlights what Budd et al. (2010) described as the broader use of employee voice on moral, ethical or pragmatic grounds. Such cases provide food for thought for organisations, but also may have resulted in many organisations taking a backward step with social media as they come to fear rather than embrace it. We explore the impact of social media as a potential new form of voice, whilst looking at the positive and negative aspects of social media in the workplace.

4.3 Social Media at Work

Studies that have been carried out in relation to social media and the workplace have found mixed results. Garrett and Danziger (2008), in a study of over 1,000 employees surveyed across a variety of industries in the US, found no significant relationship between social media use and negative aspects of the work environment such as job satisfaction, job stress or perceived injustice. They found that it was higher skilled employees who were the greatest users of the internet for both work and nonwork activities. Lim et al. (2002) found the increasing use of the internet by Singaporean employees was related to increased job demands. A more recent study by Charoensukmongkol (2014) on Thai employees, found that high job demand and co-worker support were positively related to the use of social media. In particular, this study found that social media use did not negatively affect job outcomes and was a way to mitigate demanding jobs. In line with the findings of Garrett and Danziger (2008), these studies suggest that the use of the internet during working hours should not be seen as a negative aspect of the workplace but rather embraced as part of the electronic communication network that is the contemporary workplace (p. 953).

In contrast, a number of studies have focused on social media during working hours for personal use and found it impacting negatively. For example, Liberman et al. (2011) found that work-related factors such as job involvement and intrinsic involvement (which is an employee's perceived ability to make an important contribution to the work) were key job attitudes predicting counterproductive workplace behaviours such as 'cyber-loafing' for those employees with lower levels of job and intrinsic involvement. Cyber-loafing refers to the use of internet/social media for nonwork-related or personal activities during working hours (see Vitak et al. 2011). The culture (and climate) of the organisation in terms of attitudes to cyber-loafing were considered important factors on the incident, amount and acceptance of cyber-loafing. Andreassen et al. (2014) also support these findings and in their study of over 11,000 employees, using social media for work purposes during working hours, also found support from senior managers to Garrett and Danziger (2008) claim that a positive challenging work environment was a factor in reducing cyber-loafing. What was of particular interest was the use of social networking being more prevalent amongst younger workers. Whilst on its own this may not seem surprising; however, the fact that across AMEs younger workers are the least represented by traditional forms of employee voice such as trade unions which is a theme we shall return to later in this chapter.

As noted, cyber-loafing has been linked to a negative work environment characterised by perceived injustice, disengagement and stress (Richards 2008). Hence, the use of social media during working hours may be viewed as a way to alleviate and/or 'voice' personal disaffection (Garrett and Danziger 2008). By contrast, the work of Moqbel et al. (2013) points to the use of social media at work as having a positive effect on job satisfaction and performance, which is also supported by Charoensukmongkol's (2014) work. Malik et al. (2010) identify a positive effect of job satisfaction through enabling better work–life balance. Other research has shown that the use of social media at work has a positive effect on morale (Bennett et al. 2010; Petal and Jasani 2010), productivity (Nucleus 2009; Shepherd 2011), retention, commitment, job performance (Ali-Hassan 2011) and job satisfaction (Kock et al. 2012). As Moqbel et al. (2013) conclude, the use of social media at work could have benefits to both the employee and the organisation. These findings support the idea that the use of social media is linked to anticipated subjective outcomes of the user, be they positive or negative (Garrett and Danziger 2008; Moqbel et al. 2013).

4.4 Employee Voice and Social Media

As noted, whilst the initial research of social media at work has focused on nonproductive and counterproductive behaviours (see Mastrangelo et al. 2006), more recent research has started to explore the key communication implications of social media as it becomes ubiquitous both inside and outside the workplace, in particular, the important aspects of voice at the workplace. As Martin et al. (2015) argue, management can use social media to encourage individuals to exercise direct voice because all employees are likely to have access at work to the technology.

With the weakening in traditional (union) voice in many AMEs through declining trade union membership, increased deregulation of the labour market and the rise of human resource management with its focus of direct communication in the workplace between management and employees, increased research around how management and the workforce communicate has emerged. This issue of performance has been the focus of the literature in HRM, where open channels of comminution are perceived to create more efficient and effective decision-making and has been linked to research on high-performance work systems and employee engagement (Wilkinson and Fay 2011; Boxall and Purcell 2016), ultimately leading to increased competition in the organisation.

As we know, voice arrangements are practices that facilitate two-way dialogue between management and employees. From an employee perspective, voice describes how employees raise concerns, express and advance interests, solve problems and contribute and participate in workplace decision-making with management (Pyman et al. 2010; Martin et al. 2015), thus giving employees the opportunity to (potentially) influence managerial thinking and organisational decisions (Bryson et al. 2007; Dundon and Gollan 2007). From a management perspective, voice arrangements also provide management with the opportunity to discuss issues, provide feedback and gain insight into employees' concerns (Bryson 2004). Employee voice arrangements, therefore, play a central role in employee involvement, participation and managerial communication (Tzafrir et al. 2004). However, with the advent of social media as a form of voice and its reach beyond the traditional managerial structures and hierarchies, an extension of this definition is required. In this context, Miles and Mangold (2014: 403) have suggested that voice is

> …an employee's attempt to use sanctioned or unsanctioned media or methods for the purpose of articulating organizational experiences or issues or influencing the organization, its members, or other stakeholders.

In a strategic HRM context, Budd et al. (2010) note that the HRM literature focuses on the importance of participation and voice to improve organisational effectiveness and these concepts are embedded in the notion of organisational citizenship and organisational democracy. Employee voice is seen as a key aspect of the workplace which includes and facilitates high-performance work systems, high-involvement and high-commitment management approaches (Bryson et al. 2007; Wood and Wall 2007), and has been linked with

- Both increased organisational performance and positive industrial relations climate (Boxall and Purcell 2016; Pyman et al. 2010; Dundon et al. 2004),
- Employee satisfaction, employee commitment and also increased organisational citizenship behaviours (Holland et al. 2011; Boxall et al. 2007; Wood and Wall 2007) and
- A positive supervisor–subordinate relationships, as voice builds awareness of issues from both the employee and employer perspective and can facilitate increased fairness in the employment relationship (Marchington 2007).

Significantly, it is the senior management who creates the conditions and structures that foster voice (Beugre 2010) and middle and supervisory management who maintain it, be it union, nonunion, direct, indirect or hybrid (Holland et al. 2011). As such, management shapes the conditions and structures that foster communication, and therefore employee engagement on workplace issues (Beugre 2010; Donaghey et al. 2011). However, social media communications are more complex and provide a potential paradigm shift, in that they can be set up without management involvement and/or control (Balnave et al. 2014). As such, social media has the potential to recast the nature of workplace communications and employee voice. Further aspects that set social media apart from traditional forms of workplace communication channels are its reach and immediacy. Working in 'real-time', information can be shared with anyone who is able to connect both inside and outside the organisation, with people responding and discussing issues as they emerge.

Given the dynamic reciprocal nature of the employment relationship, the responses and actions of management are continually evaluated and assessed by employees and their representatives (Holland et al. 2012, 2015; Costigan et al. 1998). Employees are, therefore, continually appraising multiple sources of information to inform their impression of the overall relationship with all levels of management (Dietz and Fortin 2007). Social media provides a new immediacy to this relationship and management can view this either in the context of negative or deviant behaviour or embrace this new form of communication and harness its immediacy on workplace issues and opinions. Social media is additionally an opportunity for greater communication in the workplace in view of the increasing evidence of the decline or stagnation of traditional voice forms (Budd 2014), decreasing response rates to organisational climate surveys and employee silence (Donaghey et al. 2011). These factors pose a problem for conventional approaches to employee–employer communications and interactions in the workplace and the quality of information flowing within the employment relationship (Silverman et al. 2013; Broughton et al. 2010), particularly with the rise of technology-based forms of voice (Budd 2014).

Employee silence is where employees deliberately withhold opinions, ideas or information about work-related issues (Van Dyne et al. 2003). Employee silence may be associated with a variety of variables, including fear of retribution for being critical of management, lack of support or a belief that the employee view(s) will not be valued (Milliken et al. 2003; Pinder and Harlos 2001). Donaghey et al. (2011) also point to the role of management in building a culture of employee silence through agenda and institutional structures with deliberate or perceived threats. The deliberate managing out of employee communication or voice can have serious implications for management. Firstly, it can distort and undermine the quality of the information flows upon which management relies for quality decision-making and secondly, it can undermine the employment relationship (Milliken et al. 2003) and lead to increased employee conflict, resistance and turnover (Macdonald and Thompson 2015). Social media has the capacity to cut through this silence and can be a positive or negative experience for management depending on how they relate to and manage this new and dynamic aspect of the employment relationship (Edmonson 2003). A key factor in this is that it is very difficult for management, intolerant of critical feedback, to negate the reach and immediacy of the real-time nature of social media.

Much of the discussion around social media has focused on the negative aspects associated with controlling it (Jacobson and Howle-Tufts 2013), described as the 'dark' side (Holland and Bardoel 2016). Despite, generally, positive findings regarding the use of social media as a form of voice, Martin et al. (2015), did find issues associated with power, control and social voice being perceived to be used to suppress employee voice in the large organisation they studied. We would argue management needs to see the opportunities such a media provides to have an engaged and authentic dialogue with the workforce in real time—or the 'smart' side of managing social media voice (Holland and Bardoel 2016). This latter approach has already been adopted by major organisations such as HP, IBM, SAP Deloitte and Microsoft (Moqbel et al. 2013). As Martin et al. (2015) note, IBM claims that over 300,000 employees have used its internal social media system 'Jams' since 2001 with brainstorming and problem-solving key activities. Dell has also trained 10,000 employees to use social media to augment their jobs (Miles and Mangold 2014). These expressions of voice can provide key insights and strategic advantage to the organisation who take an organisation learning approach to social media (Holland et al. 2016) and, when provided with the proper context and support, can enhance strategic advantage for the organisation (Miles and Mangold 2014). What these examples convey to employees is managements' perceived willingness to engage openly in real time and on issues important to the workforce and allow for critical discussion of issues with employees (Evans 2015). Undertaking this approach also addresses the immediate key emerging issues in the workplace and is supported by research based on the concept of the wisdom of crowds. The immediacy of aggregation of individual communications on workplace issue(s) could provide new forms of collaboration and evolution of employer–employee communications when considered in the context of the 'wisdom of crowds'. Mannes et al. (2014), researching in social psychology, point out that the power of groups has long been recognised, where individual judgements about facts are averaged resulting in the common opinion typically being more accurate than most individual estimates (see Surowiecki 2004). In the same context as the emergence of quality circles and high-performance work teams in the late twentieth century, the capturing of employee knowledge, experience and opinions in real time, through the twenty-first century phenomena of social media, has the potential to enhance management knowledge, responses and decision-making (Silverman et al. 2013) and increases employees' sense of involvement. However, as Martin et al. (2015) in their in-depth case study show, this needs genuine management support, as this is seen as significant in the use and impact of social media as employee voice. In other words, greater access to voice needs the relevant contextual factors to be in place (Martin et al. 2010).

4.5 Social Media, Voice, Trust and Job Satisfaction

A key issue recurring in the research on social media use at work is the link to employee's satisfaction with their working conditions. Within the HRM literature, researchers have advocated for employee communication or voice as a means to enhance organisational performance and competitiveness (e.g. Boxall et al. 2007; Wood and Wall 2007). However, as Marchington (2007) reflects

> Voice is probably the area in HRM where tensions between the organisation and workers' goals and between shareholders' and stakeholders' views are the most apparent, because it connects with the question of managerial prerogatives and social legitimacy (p 142).

From a social media perspective, this point is reinforced by Barry and Wilkinson (2015), who argue that in the context of voice, tension between the aspirations of an independent employee voice and the desire of management to control it as part of the HRM agenda needs to be negotiated. As Budd (2014) also notes the decline in trade unions as a counterbalance is a concern and social media may provide some form of control or a balance in the employment relationship as a complement or substitute for traditional voice channels. Unlike conventional employee voice, which is one way or two way and hierarchical (management to and from employees/unions), social media voice is inherently multidirectional (Silverman et al. 2013) and as Friedman (2005) argues, it has the capacity to flatten the organisation as it enables anyone to add their 'voice' and to target beyond management control. From a management perspective, social media channels have the potential to play a central role in facilitating and enhancing employee involvement, participation and managerial communication in real time, and therefore satisfaction with their job and work. Social media also has the capacity to facilitate organisational learning for both sides of the employment relationship (Martin et al. 2015), is linked to improved relational engagement

(Heikkila 2010) and is an antecedent to voice if it is perceived by employees that they have a degree of control over it (Martin et al. 2015).

In reality, the degree of influence or power attached to each communication or voice arrangement varies significantly (Cox et al. 2006), while social media may provide an immediacy that enriches the communication flow, it requires the target (e.g. management) to respond if such a communication or voice is to be effective (Boxall and Purcell 2016; Hoste et al. 2006; Wood and Wall 2007). Otherwise, it could be problematic and simply become a channel for frustrated employees to vent in response to dissatisfaction at work (Richards 2008).

4.5.1 The Role of Trust in Management

Budd (2014), and Marchington (2007) both indicate trust as a key factor in the development of an employment relationship in which social media can be effective, while trust has been researched extensively (Nichols et al. 2009; Innocenti et al. 2010), particularly, from an economic perspective (Tyler 2003) and psychological perspective (Rousseau et al. 1998). A key theme through these perspectives is that trust is the basis for quality relationships, cooperation and stability (Gould-Williams 2003) and enables and engages employees in some form of cooperation (Creed and Miles 1996). In focusing on trust through management support and employee voice arrangements we see Korczynski's (2000) definition of trust as the most useful, given its focus on an ongoing relationship and economic activity. Trust is, therefore, defined and contextualised as the confidence that one party to the exchange will not exploit the other's vulnerabilities. This definition is more reflective of the ongoing nature and a reliance upon exchange, within the employment relationship.

With respect to the explanations of the role played by trust, Dirks and Ferrin (2002) identified transformational leadership, perceived organisational support and interactional justice as key determinants in the development of trust. They argue that although trust in leadership will be related to behaviours and performance outcomes, it will be most strongly connected with attitudes.

Supervisors play a pivotal role in the development of employee perceptions of trust (Whitener et al. 1998). Indeed, Dirks and Ferrin (2002) and Zhang et al. (2008) identified trust in the direct leader as having the strongest effect of outcomes, with supervisory support for employees seen as a critical factor in the development of trust between supervisors and employees. These important findings were extended by the research of Martin et al. (2015) on the use of social media in the workplace which found that 'signals' from management and the level of trust were key issues. In fact, the lack of support of middle management was seen as a factor in the lack of impact of social media in parts of the organisation studied.

A key aspect in all this is the perception of psychological safety and the assessment of whether management (at all its levels) is considered ethical, open and supportive of genuine voice (Walumbwa and Schaubroeck 2009; Detert and Treviño 2010) and perceived influence (Tangiralia and Ramanujam 2008). Drawing on social exchange theory (SET) (Blau 1964), the argument is that employees consider such support as a gauge of the quality of the exchange relationship between employees and supervisors. Supervisor support involves expressions of concern for employee well-being, career development and signals to employees about the value of their work. In return, employees feel the need to expend effort and demonstrate trust in supervisors. Interesting research by Si et al. (2008) found that where managers perceived a breach in the 'firms' (being senior management) psychological contract, they too were far less likely to practice pro-social or informal voice of which social media can be seen as one form.

The development of the trust relationship between the employee and the supervisor in turn allows employees to make further emotional investments because they have developed the understanding, based on the social exchange experience, that such investments will be reciprocated. Consistent with Dirks and Ferrin's (2002) argument of a mediation effect of trust on attitude and behaviours one such outcome may be more employee engagement and performance. As Alfes et al. (2013) argue employees who perceive the opportunity to effectively communicate with management, be they concerns or advice, are likely to be more positive and achieve higher levels of performance.

The second key exchange relationship for an employee at work, as identified by Masterson et al. (2000), is with the organisation. Unlike the relationship with the supervisor that is characterised by frequent and direct contact about daily work issues (Zhang et al. 2008), the relationship between the employee and the organisation, operationalised primarily through the relationship with senior management, is more distal and less interactive (Dirks and Ferrin 2002). From a social exchange perspective, compared to the development of trust with a supervisor with whom the employee has ongoing opportunities to gauge levels of support and to adjust their reciprocal responses, development of trust in senior management does not have the benefit of such regular interaction and it is here that the direct voice may add particular value. Martin and colleagues' (2015) study found that whilst the support of senior management for social media voice was welcomed, there was a sense that it was seen in some quarters as a 'box ticking exercise' rather than a genuine attempt to develop voice. Alfes et al. (2013), using SET, explain that organisational HRM practices (such as voice) send implicit signals to employees about the extent to which they are valued and this influences levels of trust and employee engagement.

4.5.2 Job Satisfaction

Job satisfaction is an important attitudinal variable that describes the extent to which people like or dislike their work (Locke 1976; Saari and Judge 2004; Spector 1997). Research has shown that the organisational variables are more strongly related to job satisfaction than are personal attributes (Blegan 1993). In examining the relationship between social media use at work as an organisational variable and job satisfaction, research on the motivation to voice suggests that employees can utilise voice mechanisms to express dissatisfaction (Morrison 2014; Mowbray et al. 2014). Martin et al. (2015) also found that levels of satisfaction/dissatisfaction appeared to be factors in the use of social media. Hence, we with others (see Charoensukmongkol 2014 and Budd 2013) argue that in the context of the paucity of social media channels in the contemporary workplace to facilitate discussion, dissatisfied workers are more likely to use social media at work, although, as noted, the evidence is mixed (Liberman et al. 2011; Holland et al 2016). Social media may be seen as a communication channel to discuss or vent about issues at a workplace that frustrates employees.

We also argue that this negative relationship between social media use and job satisfaction is likely to be influenced by age. In our own research (Holland et al. 2016), we found that younger employees (e.g. Generation 'Y' 1977–1996, see Mackay 1997) will be more likely to use social media at work in response to job dissatisfaction. Generation Y employees, who have been brought up in the age of the internet, are also less unionised in most AMEs, and are likely to be more motivated to view social media as a form of employee voice to express dissatisfaction at work. In contrast, older workers who are generally more unionised would be less likely to turn to social media regarding work dissatisfaction.

In our study, we found that the majority of respondents reported using social media or social networking sites, with nearly a third using the media during working hours. Younger people were more likely to report using social media at work for solely personal activities than their older counterparts. Just under half of all employees reported using social media for both work and personal activities. This also highlights the blurring of work and private boundaries in the use of social media (particularly at work). The distribution of reported social media use at work found that Generation Y employees were generally more likely to use social media at work than their older counterparts. What was significant in the findings was that the use of social media at work increased with lower job satisfaction. In comparing social media use between age groups, specifically Generation Y versus older workers, our research found Generation Y employees' use of social media at work increased with lower job satisfaction but no statistically significant relationship was found between job satisfaction and the use of social media for older workers (Holland et al. 2016).

4.6 Social Media and the Workplace

The understanding and management of social media at work are not well developed. Most studies that have examined social media in a work context only looked at nonwork-related use of social media and the incidence of cyber-loafing (cf. Andreassen et al. 2014). With the decline in union voice, not least in the younger workforce, social media is increasingly seen by forward-thinking organisations as a key aspect of voice emerging in the twenty-first century workplace. As such, we would argue that it is an area of employee communication that HR managers should become increasingly aware of and familiar with social media to harness the potential in terms of its immediacy and impact. We suggest that social media has the potential to challenge the hierarchy of existing forms of employee–employer communications. This implies that management must consider relinquishing aspects of this hierarchy that come with conventional voice channels, in order to gain the full benefits of this new form of voice; a point also supported by Martin et al. (2015) in their research. Management's responding efficiently and effectively to this source of information in real time could lead to positive organisational outcomes. However, despite its increasing use, most organisations have not formally developed social media as a form of employee voice at work. Whilst more research into the relationship between job satisfaction and social media at work needs to be undertaken, the evidence from our research is that this voice medium appears to be a form of venting on workplace issues associated with dissatisfaction, limited to younger employees and may be described as 'justice retaliation' voice (Klass et al. 2008; Holland et al. 2016).

From a practitioner perspective, the findings of this chapter have several implications. The relatively low reported use of social media as a form of voice at work suggests that this media is an untapped voice channel. The challenge for management, then, is whether to embrace this new (real time) form of voice to harness the ability to increase knowledge and understanding of workplace issues. Alternatively, management can ignore these developments and allow social media to become a focus for negative issues in the workplace and about the organisation (Gerber and Jackson 2013; Nucleus 2009). Whilst it is acknowledged that setting up a formal system of employee voice around social media could be time consuming and requires resource allocation to manage, there appear to be clear benefits from the development of such a system as an increasing number of larger organisations undertaking such a process are demonstrating (Moqbel et al. 2013). Such an approach conveys to employees that the management is willing to engage openly in real time and on issues important to the workforce and allows for critical discussion of issues with employees (Evans 2015).

4.7 Conclusion

This chapter has examined the increasing impact of social media on and inside the workplace to make contributions to this emerging debate which can be linked to the chapters on employee silence, bullying and whistleblowing and e-unionism in this book. Whilst we see the use of social media during working hours as an untapped resource, it should be considered in the context of issues of poor response rates to climate surveys and employee silence. Social media may be developed to increase employee voice and engagement but this may not be the outcome, particularly if the contextual parameters are not developed and maintained. In the 'e-workplace', digital era leadership is required and management, therefore, needs to be open to these new experiences by demonstrating honesty in communications, transparency and the ability to have frank conversations (Silverman et al. 2013; Silverman and Newhouse 2010).

We believe social media is a resource that has the potential to flatten the organisational hierarchy of voice channels at work. Such a media gives everyone connected the opportunity to have equal input and provides the management an immediate understanding of workplace issues. The reach and immediacy of social media as a form of voice are likely to become key variables in the employment relationship in terms of the degree of genuine employee participation in organisational decisions. As such, management should look to embrace the potential of social media (smart side) in enhancing employee–employer communication rather than fear its 'dark-side' or as Miles and Mangold (2014: 410) note, if this new voice is ignored it can become a time bomb waiting to detonate.

References

Alfes, K., Truss, C., Sone, E. C., & Gatenby, M. (2013). The relationship between line managers behavior, perceived HRM practices, and individual performance: examining the mediating role of engagement. *Human Resource Management, 52*(6), 839–859.

Ali-Hassan, H., Nev D., Kim H., & Perelgut, S. (2011). Organizational social computing and employee job performance: The knowledge access route. In *System Sciences 44th International Conference* 1–10

Andreassen, C., Torsheim, T., & Pallesen, S. (2014). Predictors of use of social networking sites at work: A specific type of cyberloafing. *Journal of Computer-Mediated Communication, 19*(4), 906–921.

Barry, M., Wilkinson, A. (2015). Pro-social or pro-management? A critique of the conception of employee voice as a pro-social behaviour. *British Journal of Industrial Relations*. https://doi.org/10.1111/bjir12114.

Blau, P. M. (1964). *Exchange and power in social life*. New York: Wiley.

Balnave, N., Barnes, A., MacMillan, C., & Thornwaite, L. (2014). E-voice: How network and media technologies are shaping employee voice. In A. Wilkinson, J. Donaghey, T. Dundon, & R. Freeman (Eds.), *The handbook of research on employee voice* (pp. 439–454). Cheltenham: Edward Elgar.

Bennett, J., Owers, M., Pitt, M., & Tucker, M. (2010). Workplace impact of social networking. *Property Management, 28*(3), 138–148.

Beugre, C. D. (2010). Organizational conditions fostering employee engagement: The role of "voice". In S. Albrecht (Ed.), *Handbook of employee engagement: Perspectives, issues, research and practice* (pp. 174–181). UK: Edward Elgar.

Blegan, M. (1993). Nurses' job satisfaction: A meta-analysis of related variables. *Nursing Research, 42,* 36–41.

Boxall, P., & Purcell, J. (2016). *Strategy and human resource management* (4th ed.). London: Palgrave Macmillan.

Boxall, P., Purcell, J., & Wright, P. (2007). *The Oxford handbook of human resource management*. Oxford: Oxford University Press.

Broughton, A., Higgins, T., Hicks, B., & Cox A. (2010). *Workplaces and social networking: The implications for employment relations*. Brighton, UK: ACAS/IES.

Bryson, A. (2004). Managerial responsiveness to union and non-union worker voice in Britain. *Industrial Relations, 43*(1), 213–241.

Bryson, A., Gomez, R., Kretschmer, T., & Willman, P. (2007). The diffusion of workplace voice and high-commitment human resource management practices in Britain, 1984–1998. *Industrial and Corporate Change, 16*(3), 394–426.

Budd, J. (2014). The future of employee voice. In A. Wilkinson, J. Donaghey, T. Dundon, & R. Freeman (Eds.), *The handbook of research on employee voice* (pp. 477–488). Cheltenham: Edward Elgar.
Budd, J., Gollan, P., & Wilkinson, A. (2010). New approaches to employee voice and participation in organizations. *Human Relations, 63*(3), 303–310.
Charoensukmongkol, P. (2014). Effects of support and job demands on social media use and work. *Computers in Human Behavior, 36,* 340–349.
Costigan, R., Iiter, S., & Berman, J. (1998). A multi-dimensional study of trust in organizations. *Journal of Managerial Issues, 10,* 303–317.
Cox, A., Zagelmeyer, S., & Marchington, M. (2006). Embedding employee involvement and participation at work. *Human Resource Management Journal, 16*(3), 250–267.
Creed, W., & Miles, R. (1996). Trust in organizations: A conceptual framework linking organizational forms, managerial philosophies and opportunity cost of control. In R. Kramer & T. Tyler (Eds.), *Trust in organisations* (pp. 16–38). CA: Sage, Thousand Oaks.
Detert, J. R., & Treviño, L. K. (2010). Speaking up to higher-ups: How supervisors and skip-level leaders influence employee voice. *Organization Science*, 21(1), 249–270.
Dietz, G., & Fortin, M. (2007). Trust and justice in the formation of joint consultation committees. *Journal of International Human Resource Management, 18*(7), 1159–1181.
Dirks, K., & Ferrin, D. (2002). Trust in leadership: Meta-analytic findings and implications for research and practice. *Journal of Applied Psychology, 87*(4), 611–628.
Donaghey, J., Cullinane, N., Dundon, T., & Wilkinson, A. (2011). Reconceptualising employee silence: Problems and prognosis. *Work, Employment & Society, 25*(10), 51–67.
Dowling, J. (2015). *The tweets hereafter* (p. 6). Fairfax Media: The Sunday Age.
Dundon, T., & Gollan, P. (2007). Re-conceptualising voice in the non-union workplace. *International Journal of Human Resource Management, 18*(7), 1182–1198.
Dundon, T. A., Wilkinson, A., Marchington, M., & Ackers, P. (2004). The meaning and purpose of employee voice. *International Journal of Human Resource Management, 15*(6), 1149–1170.
Edmonson, A. (2003). Speaking up in the operating room. *Journal of Management Studies, 40*(6), 1419–1452.
Evans, T. (2015). Bad mouth. HR Monthly, August 26–29
Friedman, T. (2005). *The world is flat: A brief history of the globalized world in the 21st Century*. London: Penguin Books.
Garrett, R., & Danziger, J. (2008). Disaffection or expected outcomes: Understanding personal internet use during work. *Journal of Computer-Mediated Communications, 19,* 937–958.
Gerber, M., & Jackson, J. (2013). Retribution as revenge and retribution as just desert. *Social Justice Research, 26*(1), 61–80.
Gould-Williams, J. (2003). The importance of HR practices and workplace trust in achieving superior performance: A study of public-sector organizations. *International Journal of Human Resource Management, 14*(1), 28–54.
Heikkila, J. (2010). A Delphi study on e-HRM future directions. In *Proceedings of the 3rd European Academic Workshop on e-Hrm*, Bamberg, German, p 229–249.
Holland, P., & Bardoel, A. (2016). The impact of technology on work in the twenty-first century: Exploring the smart and dark side. *International Journal of Human Resource Management, 27*(21), 2579–2581.
Holland, P., Pyman, A., Teicher, J., & Cooper, B. (2011). Employee voice and job satisfaction in Australia: The centrality of direct voice. *Human Resource Management, 50*(1), 95–111.
Holland, P., Cooper, B., Pyman, A., & Teicher, J. (2012). Trust in management: The role of employee voice arrangements and perceived managerial opposition to unions. *Human Resource Management Journal, 22*(4), 377–391.
Holland, P., Cooper, B., & Hecker, R. (2015). Electronic monitoring and surveillance in the workplace: The effects on trust in management, and the moderating role of occupational type. *Personnel Review, 44*(1), 161–175.

Holland, P., Cooper, B., & Hecker, R. (2016). Use of Social Media at Work: A New Form of Employee Voice? *International Journal of Human Resource Management, 27*(21), 2621–2634.
Holmes, P. (2013). Inside HMV's twitter disaster: What went wrong (and how to keep your company safe). www.LikedIn.com/pulse. Accessed 14 February
Hoste, P., Sevatos, P., & Cooper, C. (2006). *Happy-performing managers: the impact of affective wellbeing and intrinsic job satisfaction in the workplace*. Cheltenham: Edward Elgar.
Innocenti, L., Pilati, M., & Peluso, A. (2010). Trust as moderator in the relationship between HRM practices and employee attitudes. *Human Resource Management Journal, 21*(3), 303–317.
Jacobson, W., & Howle-Tufts, S. (2013). To post or not to post: Employee rights and social media. *Review of Personnel Administration, 33*(1), 84–107.
Klass, B., Olsen-Buchannan, J., & Ward, A. (2008). The determinants of alternate forms of voice: An integrative perspective. *Journal of Management, 38*(1), 314–345.
Kock, H., Gonzalez, E., & Leidner, D. (2012). Bridging the work/social divide: The emotional response to organizational social networking sites. *European Journal of Information Systems, 21*(6), 699–717.
Korczynski, M. (2000). The political economy of trust. *Journal of Management Studies, 37*(1), 1–23.
Liberman, B., Seidman, G., McKenna, K., & Buffardi, L. (2011). Employee job attitudes and organizational characteristics as predictors of cyberloafing. *Computers in Human Behavior, 27,* 2192–2199.
Lim, V., Teo, T., & Loo, G. (2002). How do I loaf here? Let me count the ways. *Communications of the ACM, 45*(1), 66–70.
Locke, E. A. (1976). The nature and causes of job satisfaction. In M. D. Dunnette (Ed.), *Handbook of industrial and organizational psychology* (pp. 1297–1343). Chicago: Rand and McNally.
Macdonald, P., & Thompson, P. (2015). Social media(tion) and the reshaping of public/private boundaries in employment relations. *International Journal of Management Reviews, 10*(1), 1–16.
MacKay, H. (1997). *Generations*. Melbourne, Australia: Pan-MacMillian.
Malik, M., Saleem, F., & Ahmad, M. (2010). Work-life balance and job satisfaction among doctors in Pakistan. *South African Journal of Management, 17*(2), 112–123.
Mannes, A., Soll, J., & Larrick, R. (2014). The wisdom of select crowds. *Journal of Personality and Social Psychology, 107*(2), 276–299.
Marchington, M. (2007). Employee voice systems. In P. Boxall, J. Purcell, & P. Wright (Eds.), *The Oxford handbook of human resource management* (pp. 231–250). Oxford: OUP.
Martin, L., Buckley, M., & Ketchen, D. (2010). Time banditry: Examining the purloining of time in organizations. *Human Resource Management Review, 20,* 26–34.
Martin, G., Parry, E., & Flowers, P. (2015). Do social media enhance constructive employee voice all the time or just some of the time? *Human Resource Management Journal, 25*(4), 541–562.
Masterson, S. S., Lewis, K., Goldman, B. M., & Taylor, M. S. (2000). Integrating justice and social exchange: The different effects of fair procedures and treatments on work relationships. *Academy of Management Journal, 43,* 738–748.
Mastrangelo, P., Everton, W., & Jolton, J. (2006). Personal use of work computers: Distraction versus distruction. *Cyber-Psychology Behavior, 9*(6), 730–741.
Mennie, P. (2015). *Social media, risk and governance*. UK: Kogan Page.
Milliken, F., Morrison, E., & Hewlin, P. (2003). An exploratory study of employee silence: Issues that employees don't communicate upward and why. *Journal of Management Studies, 40*(6), 1453–1476.
Miles, S., & Mangold, G. (2014). Employee voice: Untapped resource or social media time bomb? *Business Horizons, 57,* 401–411.
Moqbel, M., Nevo, S., & Kock, N. (2013). Organizational members' use of social networking sites and job performance. *Information Technology & People, 26*(3), 240–264.
Morrison, E. W. (2014). Employee voice and silence. *Annual Review of Organizational Psychology and Organizational Behavior, 1,* 173–197.

Mowbray, P., Wilkinson, A., & Tse, H. (2014). An integrative review of employee voice: Identifying a common conceptualization and research agenda. *International Journal of Management Reviews, 17*(3), 382–400.
Nichols, T., Danford, A., & Tasiran, A. (2009). Trust, employer exposure and the employment relations. *Economic and Industrial Democracy, 30*(2), 241–265.
Nucleus, (2009). *Facebook: Measuring the cost to business of social networking*. Boston: Nucleus Research Inc.
Petal, N., & Jasani, H. (2010). Social media security policies: Guidelines for organizations. *Issues in Information Systems, 11*(1), 628–634.
Pinder, C., & Harlos, K. (2001). Employee silence: Quiescence and acquiescence as responses to perceived injustice. *Research in Personnel and Human Resource Management, 20,* 331–369.
Pyman, A., Holland, P., Teicher, J., & Cooper, B. K. (2010). Industrial relations climate, employee voice and managerial attitudes to unions: an Australian study. *British Journal of Industrial Relations, 48*(2), 460–480.
Richards, J. (2008). Because I need somewhere to vent: The expression of conflict through work blogs. *New Technology, Work and Employment, 23*(1–2), 95–110.
Rousseau, D., Sirkin, S., Burt, R., & Camerer, C. (1998). A cross discipline view of trust. *Academy of Management Review, 24,* 485–507.
Saari, L. M., & Judge, T. A. (2004). Employee attitudes and job satisfaction. *Human Resource Management, 43*(4), 395–407.
Shepherd, C. (2011). Does social media have a place in workplace learning. *Strategic Direction, 27*(2), 3–4.
Si, S. X., Wei, F., & Li, Y. (2008). The effect of organizational psychological contract violation on managers' exit, voice, loyalty and neglect in the Chinese context. *The International Journal of Human Resource Management, 19*(5), 932–944.
Silverman. M., Newhouse. P. (2010). The social media garden: A digital era research study into social media at work. www.silvermanresearch.com
Silverman, M., Bakhshalian, E., & Hillman, L. (2013). *Social media and employee voice: The current landscape*. London: CIPD. http://www.cipd.co.uk/hr-resources/research/social-media-employeevoice.aspx.
Spector, P. E. (1997). *Job satisfaction—application, assessment, cause, and consequences*. Thousand Oaks CA: Sage.
Surowiecki, J. (2004). *The wisdom of crowds*. New York: Anchor Books.
Tangiralia, S., & Ramanujam, R. (2008). Employee silence on critical work issues: The cross level effects of procedural justice climate. *Personnel Psychology, 61*(1), 37–68.
Tyler, T. (2003). Trust within organization. *Personnel Review, 32*(5), 556–568.
Tzafrir, S., Harel, G., Baruch, Y., & Dolan, S. (2004). The consequences of emerging HRM practices for employees' trust in their managers. *Personnel Review, 33*(4), 628–646.
Van Dyne, L., Ang, S., & Botero, I. (2003). Conceptualizing employee silence and employee voice as multi-dimensional constructs. *Journal of Management Studies, 40*(6), 1359–1392.
Vitak, J., Crouse, J., & La Rose, R. (2011). Personal internet use at work: Understanding cyberslacking. *Computers in Human Behavior, 21*(1), 1751–1959.
Walumbwa, F., & Schaubroeck, J. (2009). Leader personality traits and employee voice behavior: Mediating the roles of ethical leadership and work group psychological safety. *Journal of Applied Psychology, 94,* 1275–1286.
Whitener, E., Brodt, S., Korsguard, M., & Werner, J. (1998). Managers as initiator of trust: An exchange relationship framework for understanding managerial trustworthy behaviour. *Academy of Management Review, 23*(3), 513–530.
Wilkinson, A., & Fay, C. (2011). New times for employee voice. *Human Resource Management, 50*(1), 65–74.
Wood, S. J., & Wall, T. D. (2007). Work enrichment and employee voice in human resource management-performance studies. *International Journal of Human Resource Management, 18*(7), 1335–1372.

Zhang, A., Tsui, A. S., Song, L. J., Li, C., & Jia, L. (2008). How do I trust thee? The employee-organization relationship, supervisory support, and middle manager trust in the organization. *Human Resource Management, 47,* 111–132.

Peter Holland is Professor of Human Resource Management and Director of the Executive MBA at Swinburne University of Technology, Melbourne, Australia. He has worked in the Australian finance sector and consulted to the private and public sector in a variety of areas related to human resource management and employee relations. His current research interests include employee voice, workplace electronic monitoring and surveillance, and talent management.

Dr. Brian Cooper is an Associate Professor in the Department of Management, Monash University, Australia. His research interests include employee voice, work attitudes and well-being. His research has been published in journals including Human Resource Management, Industrial Relations Journal and the British Journal of Industrial Relations. Brian lectures in research methods and has extensive experience in quantitative business research methods.

Dr. Rob Hecker is an adjunct with the Tasmanian School of Business and Economics at the University of Tasmania. After long careers in business and academia, primarily teaching in organisational behaviour, his research interests continue in the areas of employee voice and extreme work.

Chapter 5
Social Media: Union Communication and Member Voice

Alison Barnes, Nikola Balnave, Louise Thornthwaite and Benjamin Manning

Abstract Trade unions are important avenues for the expression and representation of common social and economic concerns. Despite their significance in civil society, trade unions are currently facing problems maintaining their relevance and membership base. Social media technologies have the capacity to reconfigure dramatically the way in which employees express voice within and through trade unions. This may contribute to the regeneration of unions and, more broadly, the rebuilding of collective participation in civil society. This chapter will explore the results of empirical research on how trade unions are using social media to communicate with and represent members' interests. Trade unions are increasingly active on Facebook, twitter and other social media channels, providing members with a variety of avenues not only to gain information from the union but also to express opinions on industrial issues and to convey their attitudes towards their union and its views and actions. This chapter will provide a pathbreaking analysis on the development of e-voice, how social media is affecting employees' experiences of voice within their trade unions and the implications of this for membership participation and union representation in today's society.

Keywords Trade unions · Social media · E-voice · Union democracy
Member voice

5.1 Introduction

Union democracy is seen by some as central to union health and renewal; for some, a component of union democracy is the strength of member voice within their union (Peetz and Pocock 2009). A number of academics and those working within the labour movement have suggested that contemporary and emerging forms of e-communication, and in particular, social media, might provide an effective means

---

A. Barnes (✉) · N. Balnave · L. Thornthwaite · B. Manning
Macquarie University, Sydney, Australia
e-mail: alison.barnes@mq.edu.au

P. Holland et al. (eds.), *Employee Voice at Work*, Work, Organization, and Employment, https://doi.org/10.1007/978-981-13-2820-6_5

or channel to enhance union democracy and member voice (Diamond and Freeman 2002; Greene et al. 2003; Panagiotopoulos 2012). To date, these views have been largely hypothetical: comparatively little is known about how union members use their union's social media, and whether or not social media enables a form of voice that constitutes participation. The emerging body of research on unions and social media has focused on how trade unions use social media, rather than whether or how members engage with their union's social media (see Panagiotopoulos and Barnett 2015; Hodder and Houghton 2015; Kerr and Waddington 2014).

This chapter looks at how one union's use of social media might facilitate greater member participation in, and engagement with, their union. We explore how members of General Education Union (GEU) regard their union and engage with its use of social media. The chapter assesses how members' use of social media might contribute to member voice and democracy within the union. While providing opportunities for greater member participation, members appear to be largely apathetic in their use of their union's social media and it is not clear whether this varies in times of industrial unrest and bargaining. The findings suggest that, in GEU, social media may contribute to a greater sense of belonging among members but has not led to a significant increase in members using platforms such as Facebook in order to engage with the union. Union members' use of social media is thus more nuanced than accounts that see social media as simply enabling unions to create 'a new form of collective voice that is mobile, organized and intelligent' (CIPD cited in Greene 2015).

5.2 Social Media, Voice and Democracy

Discussion of employee voice, its functions, how it is achieved and who sponsors it have been well traversed (Hirschman 1970; Freeman and Medoff 1984; Addison and Belfield 2004). Barry et al. (2014: 524) note that: 'Within the employment relations (ER) literature, employee voice was traditionally equated with union representation'. This conception of voice as union voice gave way to a broader discussion of how management might sponsor voice. Scholars and practitioners distinguished collective and individual forms of voice, with the latter typically including management-sponsored and management-friendly forms, also referred to as voice-substitution mechanisms (Brewster et al. 2007; Chaison 2002). Much of the voice literature examines the tools that employers and employees use to facilitate voice within employing organisations, such as Joint Consultative Committees, work councils and non-union forms of employee representation such as non-union employee involvement plans, suggestion schemes, meetings, briefings and written forms of communication (Brewster et al. 2007). Wilkinson et al. (2004) (cited in Barry et al. 2014: 523) note that the employer-sponsored perspective 'is typically less concerned with voice per se, and the related issues of social justice and organisational democracy, and is more likely to be focused on the possible business benefits of voice'.

In their research on voice within unions, Buttegieg et al. (2014: 4–5) observe that: 'trade unions have primarily been discussed as *agents* of voice, rather than as the *organization in question*'. Drawing on Hirschman (1970), Leicht (1989) and others, who define voice not simply in terms of the expression of concerns but also the mobilisation of opinion, Buttegieg et al. (2014: 5), use member participation data as the measure for union voice. Greer's (2002) research, focusing on the contribution of voice to union democracy, emphasised the importance of opportunities for members not only to communicate and participate but to express dissent within the union as indicators of voice.

Much has been written about union democracy, with the focus largely on internal characteristics including governance structures, behavioural aspects such as the existence of oppositions, and member participation (Voss 2010). In 2000, Morris and Fosh argued that:

> This debate has now become stale as successive authors have sought to develop the debate by amending or replacing earlier definitions or models with particular conceptions of democracy based on their own strongly held political views. Furthermore, the debate has been characterized by a relatively static perspective, ignoring longer-term changes within unions (p. 95).

Less attention, however, has been paid to the impact that member voice has on union democracy. In their exploration of union power and democracy, Peetz and Pocock (2009: 625) identify two factors as central to union democracy and ultimately to union power. These include members having a voice within their union and that union being responsive to their wishes and interests. Peetz and Pocock observe that:

> Employees cannot have true power in the workplace if they do not have power and effective voice in the union. This suggests that an important part of union renewal is democratization (p. 625).

Le'vesque et al. (2005: 417) note that union democracy is intimately connected to union relevance 'because it reinforces support for the union as an institution and its framing as a set of values and actions'.

However, writers on union democracy have discussed the tension between member participation and apathy. Kaufman (2000: 202–204) notes that early writer John R. Commons provides a number of explanations of why unions move from their democratic origins to greater bureaucracy as membership grows, including member apathy which can work against internal democracy. Apathetic membership has been a perennial feature of unions, with the Webbs commenting that in the 1890s 'only in the crisis of some great dispute do we find the branch meetings crowded, or the votes at all commensurate with the total numbers of members' (1920, cited in Yerbury 1978: 36). Member apathy may stem from various sources including indifference to union affairs or contentment with the way things are run. Autocracy and lack of responsiveness from union leaders may cause, but also be caused by, member apathy (Yerbury 1978). As Anderson (1978) argues, what is the point of creating democratic structures for rank and file participation when the vast majority of members lack commitment and or interest in their union?. An improvement in communications between the union leadership and rank and file is one solution identified by Anderson (1978).

The emergence of e-forms of communication has broadened the range of methods by which trade unions can communicate information, ideas, arguments and campaigns to members (Chaison 2002; Greer 2002), and new channels for members to communicate with the union. An emerging body of research explores how web-based technologies can facilitate union democracy and whether they enable members to have greater or different influence (or voice) over union decisions and activities (Kerr and Waddington 2014; Stevens and Greer 2005; Diamond and Freeman 2002; Aalto-Matturi 2005; Lee 2000; Lucore 2002; Newman 2005). Kerr and Waddington (2014) identified two aspects of union governance and behaviour linked to union democracy which these technologies may influence: first, the adverse effects arising from bureaucratisation and centralisation, particularly in terms of the interests of members and officials diverging; and second, the under-representation of women and minority groups. The tendency towards centralised bureaucracies may have been exacerbated in Australia with the union mergers and amalgamations of the late 1980s and early 1990s.

In terms of reducing leader-member distance, Hogan and Greene (2002: 62) argued that new technologies 'clearly have the potential to refashion union democracy, reducing the distance between the bureaucracy and the rank and file'. Lee (2000) and Lucore (2002) argued along similar lines, highlighting the role of Internet technologies in decentralising union decision making, empowering union members by facilitating communication both between each other and with union officials, and overall making union processes more transparent, thereby enhancing union democracy (see Balnave et al. 2014 for an overview). At the same time, social media technologies provide for an individualistic response to the challenges of democracy, which may work against the collectivity that is at the heart of trade unionism. Greene et al. (2003) noted that the democratising potential of Internet technologies is based not only on broadening the range of communication methods but also reducing leadership control over how communication occurs and increasing the confidence and competence of union members to communicate with and within their union. However, in their study of the introduction of virtual branch websites in UNISON, the largest trade union in the United Kingdom, Kerr and Waddington (2014) found a strong desire remained among members for face-to-face communication and that it was likely that, taking a longer term view, web-based technologies would complement rather than replace existing forms of communication. As Emmott (2015: x) notes, while social media opens 'up a new front in the voice debate', the 'quality of dialogue' may be more doubtful, highlighting the continued need for personal contact.

While web-based technology may have the potential to enhance union democracy by decentralising decision-making and weakening entrenched bureaucracies within unions (Lucore 2002), it can also be used by individual members or factions to push their own agendas. As Greer (2002) notes, e-voice provides union members with a low-cost avenue to air dissent but also an opportunity to establish and maintain blocs through factional websites from which they can project dissident views. It is also the case that the capacity to generate web traffic can misrepresent the strength of opinion expressed on a particular issue. The presence of factions may be viewed as a criterion of union democracy, though, may not be a source of concern for union bureaucracies. Newman (2005) and Shostak (2005) both note that senior union officials were concerned about the capacity of the Internet to splinter union voice, but that their concern may be partly due to the challenges to the status quo that the Internet may facilitate. Upchurch and Grassman (2015: 5) similarly note that 'alternative voices and discourses of struggle conveyed through social media may be equally challenging and subversive of union leadership and its formalised structures of communication'. Such an argument is reminiscent of debates about formal democratic structures versus participation as democracy. As Hodder and Houghton (2015) argue, though, given that unions can largely monitor and control the content of communications on social media platforms, union leaderships can use them to reinforce their power and authority (see also McBride and Stirling 2014).

Greene argues that diversity is at the heart of participatory democracy by 'allowing all employees to have a voice at work' (2015: 67). Social media has the potential to facilitate the engagement of diverse groups with workplace issues. As Kerr and Waddington (2014) note, e-forms of communication enable members to engage with the union without having to be physically present. Further, Greene et al. (2003) argue that these technologies may assist under-represented groups to participate because they provide greater equalities of knowledge, reconfiguring the time-space opportunities for communication, overcoming the physical requirements for participation and enhancing the range of communication methods.

While the democratic potential of web-based communications has been explored theoretically, empirical research suggests that web-based communication methods are used more by those members who are already active in the union, while other members tend to remain passive recipients of communications (Kerr and Waddington 2014). Levels of Internet experience, however, may mediate this factor. In his study of unionism in the Greek banking sector, Panagiotopoulos (2012) found that levels of Internet experience explained much of members' attitudes towards online engagement with their union.

In exploring how social media might facilitate union democracy by enhancing worker voice, we focus on how social media technologies provide a means for members to comment/make judgement on union posts and share information. We also examine how a union's use of social media may influence members' feelings about the union and their engagement in online and offline activity. Following an outline of the research method and GEU members' use of social media, the chapter examines democracy and voice structures at GEU. We then report on the findings of a survey of GEU members on their experiences with social media as a voice mechanism.

5.3 Survey Development, Administration and Respondents

The findings discussed in this chapter are drawn from an online survey of GEU members conducted over two months in 2016. The survey, developed in consultation with the GEU, aimed to explore how members used social media to engage with the union and fellow GEU members. The questionnaire was piloted on both union members and non-union members employed across the sector. The online survey was distributed by email through the GEU state membership list. A total of 553 respondents submitted a questionnaire. After removing invalid or incomplete responses, 519 usable questionnaires remained. Sixteen percent ($n=85$) of these respondents claimed not to use social media at all and were therefore screened out of questions related to social media.

GEU is one national union covering those employed in the education sector in Australia. The union arose from the amalgamation of five unions in 1993. GEU membership is comprised largely of academics (approximately 70% of members) with professional employees making up the remaining 30%. Three-quarters of GEU members are employed on a full-time basis and just over half are female. As shown in Table 5.1, the demographics of the survey responses provide a close representation of the union membership, with the exception of the under-representation of casual employees.

The age profile of the sample (see Table 5.2) is something to consider when looking at the respondents' use of social media. As shown in Table 5.5, national surveys of the Australian population reveal that the age group least likely to use social media are the over 50s. In the national survey (Sensis 2015), 44% of Australians aged 50–64,

Table 5.1 Demographics of survey sample and union membership population

	Survey sample		Union
	N	%	%
Position type			
Academic	301	62.6	71
Non-academic	165	34.3	29
Non-university employer	15	3.1	0.2
Missing	38	7.3	0
Employment status			
Perm full time	334	65.5	75
Perm part time	46	9	10.6
Fixed-term contract	56	11	0
Casual	45	8.8	14
Retired	20	3.9	0
Other	9	1.8	0.04
Missing	9	1.8	0
Gender			
Female	291	56.2	56.5
Male	217	41.9	43.4
Other	4	0.8	0.1
Missing	7	1.1	0

Table 5.2 Age distribution of sample and population

	Survey sample		Total workforce	Academic workforce
	N	%	%	%
18–29	21	4.0	8.6	4.0
30–39	84	16.2	28.1	26.8
40–49	100	19.3	27.0	27.1
50–64	235	45.3	32.2	35.5
> 64	46	8.9	4.2	6.5
Missing	33	6.4	–	–
Total	519	100.0	–	100.0

Source Population data of workforce drawn from based on data published in Department of Education (2016)

and 61% of those aged 65 or over, claimed never to use social networks at all. These two groups represent 54% of the survey sample.

GEU members who completed the survey had higher than average levels of interest in both politics and in trade union activities. Union loyalty or commitment (Gordon et al. 1980; Klandermans 1989; Bolton et al. 2007; Fullagar 1986; Fullagar et al. 1992) and union social identity (Kelly and Kelly 1994) were measured using the established scales and found to be high as were levels of willingness to participate in union activities. In addition to union loyalty, the respondents also recorded high levels of union participation and identification, and satisfaction with their union, with some 62% indicating they were either satisfied or very satisfied. Of the total sample, only 25% of respondents identified themselves as active members, defined as someone who is regularly involved in union activities. Over a quarter of the sample (27%) had at, some time, held a formal or elected position within the union (6% currently; 6% in the past 5 years; and, 15% more than 5 years ago), indicating an unusually high degree of union activity within the survey sample.

The respondents were also asked how likely it is that they would participate in various union activities in the next 12 months. As shown in Fig. 5.1, the activities that respondents were least likely to undertake were to be a delegate at a national meeting or conference; stand as an elected official; and speak at branch meetings. On the other hand, the activities that respondents reported they would be most likely to undertake were voting in elections; discussing union affairs with colleagues; and taking part in union actions. These findings indicate that while most of the respondents are unlikely to undertake formal roles within the union, they are likely to manifest activism and engage in the democratic processes of the organisation.

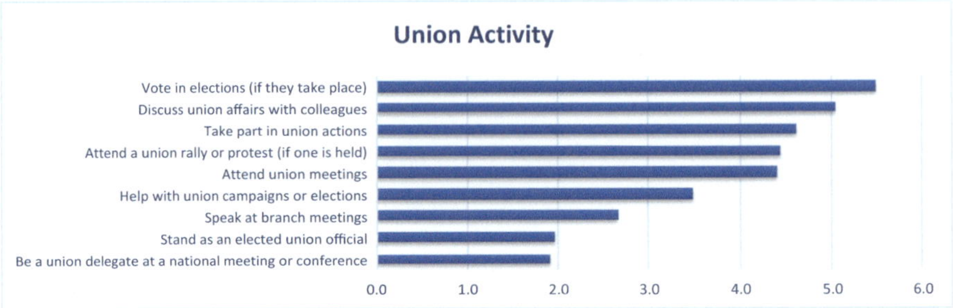

Fig. 5.1 Likelihood of union activity

5.4 GEU Members' Use of Social Media

As a foundation for understanding members' use of the GEU's social media, the survey sought to establish the online presence of respondents in their public and private lives. The survey respondents showed patterns of use that were mostly similar to the Australian population, though with some marked differences. While the proportions of members using the various services resembled those of the general population, more detailed analysis of the data revealed that the survey respondents used social media more often and were more interested in political content than the average Australian.

Internet use in Australia is fairly high by international standards, ranking seventh in the world for Internet penetration on a per capita basis, with 81% of Australians having Internet access at home, and Australia is seventh in the world for social media access (Ernst and Young 2014). Social media represents the largest share of online media penetration, being accessed by 75% of Australian users, compared to news and newspapers sites at 52% (Roy Morgan 2013). Facebook is by far the most popular and most heavily used of all social media services in Australia, followed by YouTube. Different measures indicate different positions in the rankings for other services, but all show far lower levels of market penetration and intensity of use.

When asked about which social media services they use, just 16% of GEU respondents answered that they did not use social media at all, which is half than the national rate of 32%. Facebook is the most popular service, used by 61% of respondents, followed rather distantly by Twitter, which is used by 27%, and Google+ which is used by 23%.

These proportions are roughly in line with the patterns of use by the broader Australian population, as shown in Table 5.3, which compares the survey results with those from a representative national sample (Sensis 2015).

Comparing the kinds of activities and reasons for use of social media with the general Australian population reveals that the respondents are more likely to use social media to get information on news and current events; to connect with people with similar interests; and to co-ordinate events and activities. They are less likely

Table 5.3 Social media accounts

	Survey sample		Australian population	Difference
	N	%	%	%
Facebook	317	61.1	63.2	−2.1
YouTube	252	48.6	*	*
Twitter	142	27.4	11.6	15.8
Google+	117	22.5	15.6	6.9
Instagram	84	16.2	17.7	−1.5
Vimeo	46	8.9	*	*
Flickr	25	4.8	*	*
No Social Media	85	16.4	32	−15.6

Source For general population data, SENSIS (2015)
Note * denotes there is no comparable data available

to use social media to keep up with friends and family (though a vast majority still do); to play games; follow celebrities or meet new friends (see Table 5.4).

The respondents are more likely than the broader Australian population to use social media. This is perhaps unsurprising given the employment sector the union represents, coupled with the fact that this is a self-selecting group responding to an emailed invitation to participate in a web-based survey. On the other hand, the age structure of the sample might be expected to be associated with lower levels of social media use. While there has been a very rapid increase in social media use among those aged over 50 in the past 5 years, there remains a strong correlation between age and social media use, with young adults in Australia (18–29 year olds) the most likely to use social media (90%), compared to the overall average of 69%. As the majority (54%) of the survey respondents are aged over 50, we might have expected the level of social media use among the sample to be much lower than it is. The age structure of the GEU membership is quite different from that of the general population, and analysis of the differences between the sample and the population by age group reveals some interesting differences. As shown in Table 5.5, the pattern of social media account holding within each age group of the survey sample and the Australian population shows that the respondents were more likely to be users of Twitter than the Australian population; less likely to be Facebook users; and more likely to be users of Instagram in the under-50 age groups.

5.5 Democracy and Voice Structures at GEU

The union's structure consists of national, state and workplace levels. GEU encourages worker participation and democracy in a range of ways that are consistent with structural and procedural legal requirements, and also with much of the literature on

Table 5.4 Social media activities

	Survey sample (%)	Australian population (%)
Keep up with family and friends	82	92
Get information on news and current events	59	40
Keep up with local community news and events	46	*
Connect people with the same interests	44	17
Co-ordinate events and shared activities	35	24
Find information about hobbies and interests	35	*
Keep up with work colleagues	32	*
Follow or find out about particular businesses or organisations	23	24
Find out about entertainment events	22	23
Engage with a Government representative or department	10	8
Pressure from family and friends to use them	9	9
Provide reviews/write blogs about products you have bought	8	11
Play games	6	21
Meet new friends	5	14
Follow celebrities	5	12
Find potential dates	4	6

Source For general population data, SENSIS (2015)
Note * denotes that there is no comparable data available

Table 5.5 Age distribution of social media use (Australian population and GEU sample)

Age group	Twitter		Facebook		Google+		Instagram	
	GEU (%)	Aust. (%)	GEU (%)	Aust. (%)	GEU (%)	Aust. (%)	GEU (%)	Aus. (%)
18–29	52	20	86	97	19	20	62	54
30–39	39	28	79	93	19	29	33	21
40–49	30	16	63	95	16	27	18	17
50–64	21	10	56	87	24	20	9	12
65+	11	4	41	88	24	16	2	2

Source For Australian population data: Sensis (2015: 19)

measures of union democracy. For example, elections for representation at the workplace level are held every 2 years, with those elected being unpaid union activists. Members also elect fellow members to represent them at the state and national levels. Each branch elects representatives to both a state and national council, and positions such as President and General Secretary are also elected, with unelected positions including union staff such as organisers, legal officers and administrative support workers.

State councils meet several times a year, with the national council meeting once a year to determine policy and the union's strategic direction. Debate can be heated but is often divided along geographic lines (with one newly elected member wryly remarking that she was surprised that she was expected to caucus with those she lived near rather than those she agreed with). GEU has also been successful in resisting attempts to substitute union with non-union voice (Barnes et al. 2013; Barnes and MacMillan 2015).

Although GEU's structure and functioning facilitate member democracy and participation, worker voice may be inhibited by the exigencies and practicalities of members' working lives such as workload or level of interest in the day-to-day running of the union. GEU branches hold semi-regular workplace meetings to provide members with information and to seek feedback on member concerns and enterprise-bargaining negotiations.

The union's uptake of social media was initially cautious with the GEU's leadership concerned that it was faddish and a misuse of union resources. But attitudes have changed and social media now forms one of a commonly used repertoire of tools that the union draws upon to augment its work (Interview, National Communications Officer 2015). Social media facilitates the work of the union by providing a means to publicise events such as rallies, building a sense of community among members (e.g. sharing photos of members at stalls, rallies or conferences), raising awareness and support among the general public (e.g. around issues such as the deregulation of university fees), sharing information about and generating support for campaigns involving colleagues in other branches, and finally connecting with journalists and bloggers interested in higher education (Interview, National Communications Officer 2015). At a national level, GEU has also used social media in marginal electorates or in regional electorates where universities are located in order to influence voter intentions rather than connect with members per se.

Social media use is not regarded by the union as a panacea for all the problems that beset it: declining density, sustained government attacks on higher education funding, increasing casualisation of the workforce and the emergence of private providers. With the exception of some branches, social media's reach and effectiveness among members is largely untested territory for GEU.

Unlike GEU's traditional approach to communication, such as hardcopy union journals and magazines for staff across the sector, its utilisation of social media has the potential (whether intentional or not) to increase members' voice by allowing members to comment directly on union activities and posts. GEU makes use of six social media technologies, including Facebook, Twitter, Instagram, Vimeo, YouTube and Flickr. Facebook is the chief form used by union officers, both paid and elected/unpaid: both the National Headquarters and State (Division) Offices host Facebook pages linked to their webpages. Social media is also accessible to non-members, thus allowing them, whether they be supporters or critics, to comment on union posts. The union deletes comments by Internet trolls that are racist, sexist or homophobic in nature.

5.6 Social Media and Voice at GEU

Despite relatively high numbers of respondents having social media accounts, very few reported subscribing to the union's social media account. Just 13% of respondents currently subscribe to the union's Facebook page, and a further 1.5% had previously subscribed; 6% subscribe to the union's Twitter account. No other service had a subscription rate of more than 1%. Cross-tabulations between those people holding accounts with a particular service and subscribing to the union's content produced better results, with 40% (n = 67) of Facebook users subscribing to the union's page and 47% (n = 29) of Twitter users subscribing to the union's Twitter feed. Nonetheless, the absolute numbers remain low. Combining all of the services, a total of 17% (n = 88) of respondents reported subscribing to some form of the union's social media.

Written comments by members suggest that concerns about privacy or fear of victimisation are reasons for non-engagement with GEU's social media. One member wrote, 'I also value my personal privacy and prefer face-to-face communications', while others found it time-consuming. While this might suggest that the capacity of social media to enhance member voice is very limited, the majority of respondents (69%) indicated that they would feel comfortable criticising their employer on GEU's social media, while a smaller majority (55%) indicated that they would feel comfortable criticising their union on its social media platform.

There was a strong positive association between comfort with criticising their union and comfort with criticising their employer on GEU's social media ($r = 0.509$, $X^2 = 253.631$, $df = 16$, $p < 0.01$). These findings suggest that social media can enhance the voice of members within the union and also within the sector. Sixty-nine percent of respondents ($n = 219$) appear prepared to speak critically about their wages and conditions or employer actions. However, feeling comfortable about criticising the union or employer does not mean those members actually do raise their voices within the union or workplace (Table 5.6).

There was also a strong association ($r = 0.889$, $p \leq 0.01$) between those who feel that social media made them feel that they belonged to a union community (56%) and the sense they could have their say in union affairs (64%). This suggests that social media may play a role in creating a sense of collective identity which might encourage member voice, should members wish to express it (Table 5.7).

Moreover, 86% of respondents ($n = 173$) disagreed with the statement that 'I would like more opportunity for members to comment on my union's social media content'; and only 8% ($n = 41$) agreed. Seventy-two percent of respondents ($n = 144$) disagreed

Table 5.6 Comment and criticise on union's social media

	Strongly agree (%)	Agree (%)	Neither (%)	Disagree (%)	Strongly disagree (%)	Total
I would like more opportunity to comment on my union's social media content	5	9	29	22	35	303
I would like more opportunity for members to directly contribute to the union's social media content	6	13	34	16	32	302
I would feel comfortable criticising my union on its social media platforms	37	18	28	14	3	318
I would feel comfortable criticising my employer on my union's social media platforms	46	22	20	9	3	319

Table 5.7 Association between sense of community and voice

		Social media makes me feel like I belong to my union community					
Social media has increased my ability to have my say in my union		Strongly agree	Agree	Neither	Disagree	Strongly disagree	Total
	Strongly agree	118	3	8	2	0	131
	Agree	4	43	10	1	1	59
	Neither	4	17	71	16	1	109
	Disagree	0	1	3	9	1	14
	Strongly disagree	0	0	0	0	2	2
	Total	126	64	92	28	5	315

with the statement 'I would like more opportunity for members to directly contribute to my union's social media' and only 28% (n =56) agreed. The vast majority of people who agreed with one statement agreed with the other (83 and 97%), while the majority of those who disagreed with one also disagreed with the other (99 and 95%). This satisfaction with members' ability to comment and contribute might reflect exactly that, as well as the number of avenues members already have within the union to express their views. However, it may also reflect a degree of apathy and indifference amongst members.

While members felt social media provided them with the ability to have their say on union matters, this did not appear to be connected to a desire to actually express voice. Most significantly for advocates of social media as a tool for enhancing voice, its adoption by GEU does appear to enhance the activity of union members beyond the net-sphere. While 69% of respondents acknowledged that their engagement with GEU's social media campaigns led to an increase in online union activities, 67% agreed that their engagement with the union's social media campaigns had led to their increased participation in offline union activities. There was also a strong and statistically significant correlation between all three of these variables, as shown in Table 5.8.

There was no age or gender difference in these results, however, there were differences between employment classifications. Those on fixed-term contracts and casuals were slightly more likely to agree than permanent full-time employees that engagement with union media had increased their offline activity. The number of casuals who answered the question was small and therefore statistically insignificant ($n = 24$), but it is interesting that those casuals who were prepared to join the union (and fill out a survey) appeared to be more engaged in offline activity than their more securely employed counterparts.

Initial reading of these results suggests that social media provide an avenue for worker voice and participation in union activities. However, there is a contradiction between the reported self-perception and reported actions. While respondents claimed that the union's social media campaigns had increased their levels of participation, this was not reflected in their responses to questions about their specific activities. There appeared to be no connection to activities that you might expect them to undertake online. Actions that members were *not* taking included commenting on

Table 5.8 Pearson correlations between voice and participation

	My engagement with my union's social media campaigns has led me to participate more in union online activities	My engagement with my union's social media campaigns has led me to participate more in union offline activities	Social media has increased my ability to have my say in my union
My engagement with my union's social media campaigns has led me to participate more in union online activities	1	0.932**	0.721**
My engagement with my union's social media campaigns has led me to participate more in union offline activities	0.932**	1	0.740**
Social media has increased my ability to have my say in my union	0.721**	0.740**	1

**Correlation is significant at the 0.01 level (2-tailed)

union posts, clicking the 'Like' button on the union Facebook page, inviting friends to the page, tweeting about union issues or campaigns, seeking more information about a particular issue or campaign, participating in an online campaign (e.g. signed petition, online protest), volunteering for offline campaigns, sharing the union webpage on Facebook or tweeting a link to the union webpage. The data reported in Table 5.9 indicates that the absolute numbers of respondents who reported that they had ever participated in such activities were low, below 30% for each of the specific actions and below 50% for the general 'participated in online campaigns'.

On the other hand, more respondents had used the union's social media as a resource to seek information about campaigns, rights and industry events, as shown in Table 5.10.

Table 5.9 Frequency of online union activity

	Frequently (%)	Sometimes (%)	Rarely (%)	Never (%)
Participated in an online campaign (e.g. signed petition, online protest)	9	24	12	54
Clicked the 'Like' button on the union Facebook page	5	12	13	70
Sought more information about a particular union issue or campaign	3	10	16	71
Commented on the union's posts	0	5	13	82
'Tweeted' about union issues or campaigns	1	7	9	82
Volunteered for offline campaigns	2	5	11	82
Shared the union webpage on Facebook	1	8	8	84
'Invited' your friends to the union Facebook page	0	3	9	88
'Tweeted' a link to the union webpage	0	3	8	89

Table 5.10 Frequency of use of union social media for information gathering

	Ever		Never		Total
	n	%	*n*	%	*n*
Gain information about your rights	91	27	248	73	339
Gain information about union campaigns	145	43	192	57	337
Gain information about what is happening in your industry	150	44	188	56	338

Furthermore, as shown in Table 5.11, the association between actively using the union's social media and the subjective sense of community or empowerment is both weak and negative, indicating that the more likely a member is to feel that the union's social media has increased their ability to have a say in their union, the less likely they are to actually report having actively engaged with it.

Those who were politically active appear to be so across the board as well as on the net. When asked about the likelihood that they would engage in the various union activities listed in Fig. 5.1, there were medium to strong positive correlations between the responses to the various items, indicating that people who are active one way are likely to be active in others. Similarly, when asked how frequently they had undertaken various voice activities listed above using the union's social media, there was a high level of intercorrelation, indicating that those respondents who had undertaken one of those activities was likely to have undertaken several. On the other hand, there was little to no correlation between the items measuring propensity to undertake union activities and those measuring frequency of participation in voice activities using the union's social media. So the members who report being most active in union activities are not among the few respondents who report using the union's social media for voice activities.

While few of the respondents had used the union's social media for voice activities, this does not suggest a general disinclination towards the use of the Internet in general nor social media more specifically for political engagement and action. When asked which of 20 online and offline political activities they had undertaken in the previous 12 months, the respondents reported fairly high levels of participation in both. For example, the majority had signed a petition (57%) and an online petition (60%).

Table 5.11 Pearson correlations of frequency of activity and voice

Pearson correlations	Social media has increased my ability to have my say in my union	Social media makes me feel like I belong to my union community
Commented on the union's posts	-0.243^{**}	-0.314^{**}
Clicked the 'Like' button on the union Facebook page	-0.248^{**}	-0.448^{**}
'Invited' your friends to the union Facebook page	-0.211^{**}	-0.347^{**}
'Tweeted' about union issues or campaigns	-0.221^{**}	-0.281^{**}
Sought more information about a particular union issue or campaign	-0.280^{**}	-0.365^{**}
Participated in an online campaign (e.g. Signed petition, online protest)	-0.261^{**}	-0.379^{**}

Thirty-six percent had emailed a politician to express political views, compared to 24% who had telephone, written or spoken to a politician or public servant for the same reason. Large numbers of the participants had also engaged in activities such as product boycotts (48%); demonstrations or street protests (27%); fund raising or donations (34%); and visiting political or advocacy websites (32%). There were less likely to have used social media for political purposes, though the levels of some activities were still high. For example, 35% reported promoting political ideas or news by sharing on social media; 33% had liked, shared or retweeted political stories; 17% had commented on political social media posts; and 12% had contacted a politician via social media to express their views. There was also a high degree of interrelatedness, with strong and high-level medium correlations between all of these activities. However, there was no association between reports of political online or offline activity and the use of the union's social media.

5.7 Discussion and Conclusion

In the early days of the Internet, before the emergence of web 2.0 technologies and social media, Shostak (1999) and Greer (2002) foretold a potential future for unions: riding the Internet wave would dramatically renew the labour movement. Early work on social media and events such as the 'Arab Spring' led many to predict that social media usage would be a key to bringing about change. While this may still be the case in broader political struggles, our study suggests that social media's role in facilitating democracy at a micro level in an education union is limited. For GEU members, social media appears to contribute to a sense of belonging to a union community, rather than inspiring engagement. However, the significance of belonging should not be underestimated. Belonging to a group is intimately related to solidarity and can contribute to a sense of shared purpose, values and collective identity which may grow into mobilisation (Guibernau 2013).

The preliminary research reported here, however, suggests that while social media provides a significant forum for union members to express voice, its use by members remains limited. There may be several reasons why members do not engage with voice mechanisms more actively. GEU's democratic structure provides many avenues for member voice which in part might explain members not using social media to express themselves. Members may be generally satisfied with other voice channels provided by GEU's structure and/or are uninterested in social media as a voice mechanism. Further, many members may not want to be actively involved in their union. Yerbury cites that these 'apathetic members may simply be "exercising their inalienable right to be indifferent"' (Brooks 1960 cited in Yerbury 1978: 36). As noted earlier, such apathy has been a persistent issue for unions, with many members only becoming active in particular periods such as enterprise-bargaining negotiations. The survey results provide a snapshot of a particular point in time; if taken during periods of heightened tension member engagement with the union's social media may increase.

While social media might contribute to a sense of belonging, paradoxically it might also contribute to greater caution on the part of the member. For example, although members who used social media felt confident in being critical of their union and their employer, an increasing body of research suggests that, in many instances, for those who do not define themselves as activists, social media breeds caution and avoidance of political discussion in part because of the individual's enhanced visibility and a desire 'to maintain good relationships' (Miller et al. 2016: 146) and not risk causing offence. Rather, Miller et al. argue, 'social media becomes a space for expressing shared ideas and values' (2016: 146). This might explain the apparent conflict between the sense of community that union members conveyed and the lack of expression of voice. Moreover, GEU does not actively utilise social media to engage member voice, and in many ways, social media does not appear to offer GEU members much that they don't already have.

This does not mean, however, that the union should abandon social media. It has provided an effective way to build support among non-members for higher education and thus has helped to prevent the erosion of conditions across the sector. Furthermore, consistent with the findings of Kerr and Waddington (2014) in the UK, our research suggests that while social media may not replace other methods by which union members express voice, it provides a valuable complement to traditional avenues.

While this chapter presents the first examination of union social media use in Australia and its impact on member voice, the analysis is limited by its focus on one trade union, albeit a union of highly educated workers. Research is needed to investigate trade union use of social media and members' experiences across a range of unions. Further qualitative research is also needed to understand the lived experience of trade union members in relation to the use of social media to express voice. Indeed, in the case of GEU, survey evidence is mixed. Disinterest, distrust and concerns about disruption to work or life were found to have prevented some members from using their union's social media. For others, it has enhanced their feeling of belonging to the union's community, facilitated their ability to contribute to, and comment on, union business, and encouraged greater offline engagement in the union's activities. Qualitative research in the form of interviews and focus groups will allow for a deeper understanding of the complexities surrounding the use of social media by member-based organisations such as trade unions, and its potential to enhance internal democracy into the future.

References

Aalto-Matturi, S. (2005). The Internet: The new workers' hall, the Internet and new opportunities for the Finnish trade union movement. *Working USA: The Journal of Labor and Society, 8*(4), 469–481.

Addison, J., & Belfield, C. (2004). Union voice. *Journal of Labor Research, 25*(4), 563–596.

Anderson, J. C. (1978). A Comparative analysis of local union democracy. *Industrial Relations, 17*(3), 279–280.

Balnave, N., Barnes, A., MacMillan, C., & Thornthwaite, L. (2014). E-voice? How network and media technologies are shaping employee voice. In A. Wilkinson, J. Donaghy, T. Dundon, & R. Freeman (Eds.), *Handbook of research on employee voice* (pp. 439–454). Cheltenham: Edward Elgar.

Barnes, A., MacMillan, C., & Markey, R. (2013). Maintaining union voice in the Australian university sector: Union strategy and non-union forms of employee participation. *Journal of Industrial Relations, 55*(4), 565–582.

Barnes, A., & MacMillan, C. I. (2015). The difficult challenge faced by hybrid employee voice in the Australian university sector. In P. Gollan, B. Kaufman, D. Taras, & A. Wilkinson (Eds.), *Voice and involvement at work: Experience with non-union representation* (pp. 101–126). New York: Routledge.

Barry, M., Wilkinson, A., Gollan, P., & Kalfa, S. (2014). Where are the voices? New direction in voice and engagement across the globe. In A. Wilkinson, G. Wood, & R. Deeg (Eds.), *Oxford handbook of employment relations* (pp. 522–540). Oxford: Oxford University Press.

Bolton, D., Bagraim, J. J., Witten, L., Mohamed, Y., Zvobgo, V., & Khan, M. (2007). Explaining union participation: The effects of union commitment and demographic factors. *S A Journal of Industrial Psychology, 33*(1), 74–79.

Brewster, C., Croucher, R., Wood, G., & Brookes, M. (2007). Collective and individual voice: Convergence in Europe? *The International Journal of Human Resource Management, 18*(7), 1246–1262.

Buttegieg, D., Deery, S., & Iverson, R. (2014). Voices within trade unions? A test of the voice and exit hypothesis. *Journal of Industrial Relations, 56*(1), 3–23.

Chaison, G. (2002). Information technology: The threat to unions. *Journal of Labor Research, 23*(2), 249–259.

Department of Education. (2016, January). *Staff: Selected higher education statistics 2015*. Canberra: Australian Department of Education and Training.

Diamond, W. J., & Freeman, R. B. (2002). Will unionism prosper in cyberspace? The promise of the Internet for employee organization. *British Journal of Industrial Relations, 40*(3), 569–596.

Emmott, M. (2015). Forward. In S. Johnstone, & P. Ackers (Eds.), *Finding a voice at work? New perspectives on employment relations* (pp. vii–xi). Oxford: Oxford University Press.

Ernst & Young. (2014). Digital Australia: State of the Nation 2014. Retrieved from https://digitalaustralia.ey.com.

Freeman, R., & Medoff, J. (1984). *What do unions do?*. New York: Basic Books.

Fullagar, C. (1986). A factor analytic study on the validity of a union commitment scale. *Journal of Applied Psychology, 71*, 129–136.

Fullagar, C., McCoy, D., & Shull, C. (1992). The socialization of union loyalty. *Journal of Organizational Behaviour, 13*(1), 13–26.

Gordon, M. E., Philpot, J. W., Burt, R. E., Thompson, C. A., & Spiller, W. E. (1980). Commitment to the union: Development of a measure and an examination of its correlates. *Journal of Applied Psychology Monograph, 65*(4), 479–499.

Greene, A. (2015). Voice and workforce diversity. In S. Johnstone & P. Ackers (Eds.), *Finding a voice at work? New perspectives on employment relations*. Oxford: Oxford University Press.

Greene, A., Hogan, J., & Grieco, M. (2003). Commentary: E-collectivism and distributed discourse: New opportunities for trade union democracy. *Industrial Relations Journal, 34*(4), 282–289.

Greer, C. (2002). E-voice: How information technology is shaping life within unions. *Journal of Labor Research, 23*(2), 215–235.

Guibernau, M. (2013). *Belonging: Solidarity and division in modern societies*. Cambridge: Polity Press.

Hirschman, A. (1970). *Exit, voice, and loyalty*. Cambridge, Massachusetts: Harvard University Press.

Hodder, A., & Houghton, D. (2015). Use of social media: A study of the university and college union on Twitter. *New Technology, Work and Employment, 30*(3), 173–189.

Hogan, J. & Greene, A. M. (2002). E-Collectivism: On-line action and on-line mobilisation. In L. Holmes and M. Grieco (Eds.), *Organising in the information age: Distributed technology, distributed action, distributed identity, distributed discourse* (pp. 57–79). Aldershot: Ashgate.
Kaufman, B. E. (2000). The early institutionalists on industrial democracy and union democracy. *Journal of Labor Research*, *21*(2), 189–209.
Kelly, C., & Kelly, J. (1994). Who gets involved in collective action? Social psychological determinants of individual participation in trade unions. *Human Relations, 47*(1), 63–88.
Kerr, A., & Waddington, J. (2014). E-Communications: An aspect of union renewal or merely doing things electronically? *British Journal of Industrial Relations, 52*(4), 658–681.
Klandermans, B. (1989). Union commitment: Replications and tests in the Dutch context. *Journal of Applied Psychology, 74*(6), 869–875.
Lee, E. (2000). How the Internet is changing unions. *Working USA: The Journal of Labor and Society, 4*(2), 56–72.
Leicht, K. T. (1989). Unions, plants, jobs and workers: An analysis of union satisfaction and participation. *The Sociological Quarterly*, *30*(2), 331–362.
Lucore, R. E. (2002). Challenges and opportunities: Unions confront the new information technologies. *Journal of Labor Research, 23*(2), 201–214.
Le'vesque, C., Murray, G., & Le Quex, S. (2005). Union disaffection and social identity. *Work and Occupations, 32*(4), 400–422.
McBride, J., & Stirling, J. (2014). Green shoots from the grass roots? The National Shop Stewards Network. *New Technology, Work and Employment, 29*(1), 25–39.
Miller, D., Costa, E., Haynes, N., McDonald, T., Nicolescu, R., Sinanan, J., et al. (2016). *How the world changed social media*. London: UCL Press.
Newman, N. (2005). Is labor missing the Internet third wave? *Working USA: The Journal of Labor and Society, 8*(4), 383–394.
Panagiotopoulos, P. (2012). Towards unions 2.0: Rethinking the audience of social media engagement. *New Technology, Work and Employment*, *27*(3), 178–192.
Panagiotopoulos, P., & Barnett, J. (2015). Social media in union communications: An international study with UNI Global Union Affiliates. *British Journal of Industrial Relations, 53*(3), 508–532.
Peetz, D., & Pocock, B. (2009). An analysis of workplace representatives, union power and democracy in Australia. *British Journal of Industrial Relations, 47*(4), 623–652.
Roy Morgan Research. (2013). Media websites: Who visits what? Article No. 5324, Published Thursday 28 November 2013. Retrieved from roymorgan.com.
Sensis. (2015). How Australian people and businesses are using social media. Sensis social media report, May 2015. Retrieved from http://www.sensis.com.au/socialmediareport.
Shostak, A. B. (1999). Organized labor's best bet? Cyberunions!. *Working USA: The Journal of Labor and Society*, *3*(4), 120–133.
Shostak, A. B. (2005). On the state of cyberunionism: An American progress report. *Working USA: The Journal of Labor and Society*, *8*(4), 403–421.
Stevens, C. D., & Greer, C. R. (2005). E-voice, the Internet, and life within unions: Riding the learning curve. *Working USA: The Journal of Labor and Society, 8,* 439–455.
Upchurch, M., & Grassman, R. (2015). *Striking with social media: The contested (online) terrain of workplace conflict* (pp. 1–18). Organization (first published on August 19).
Voss, K. (2010). Democratic dilemmas: Union democracy and union renewal. *European Journal of Labour and Research, 16*(3), 369–382.
Yerbury, D. (1978). Participation and apathy in trade unions. *Australian Journal of Public Administration*, *37*(1), 33–40.

Dr. Alison Barnes was a Senior Lecturer in the Department of Marketing and Management, Macquarie University, Sydney. She is National President-elect of the National Tertiary Education

Union and will commence in the role in late 2018. Her research interests include trade union strategy, call centres and social media and the workplace.

Dr. Nikola Balnave is a Senior Lecturer in the Department of Management and a member of the Centre for Workforce Futures at Macquarie University. Her main research interests include cooperatives, union renewal strategies and social media @work.

Dr. Louise Thornthwaite is an Associate Professor in the Department of Management at Macquarie University, Sydney, and Co-Chair Employer Association Study Group, ILERA. Louise has published extensively across a range of interrelated and interdisciplinary fields which fall under the broad umbrella of employment relations, public sector management, human resource management and employment law. Her research which has focused on the influence of law and regulation on management policy and the employment relationship includes work on digital technologies, social media policy, privacy and work.

Benjamin Manning is a sociologist with research interests including economic sociology, the sociology of work and professions. He teaches social research methods and management at Macquarie University.

Chapter 6
Managerial Silencing of Employee Voice

Jimmy Donaghey, Tony Dundon, Niall Cullinane, Tony Dobbins and Eugene Hickland

Abstract A growing literature has emerged on employee silence, which is located within the field of organisational behaviour. An alternative reading of silence is offered which focuses on the role of management. Using the non-union employee representation literature for illustrative purposes, the significance of management in structuring employee silence is considered. Highlighted are the ways in which management, through agenda-setting and institutional structures, can perpetuate silence over a range of issues, thereby organising employees out of the voice process. These considerations are redeployed to offer a dialectical interpretation of employee silence in a conceptual framework to assist further research and analysis.

Keywords Silence · Managerial agency · EU legislation
Information and consultation

6.1 Introduction

Employee voice has become an issue of much focus in contemporary industrial relations, human resource management and organisational behaviour literatures. Much of the focus has been concerned with evaluating the different forms and

J. Donaghey (✉)
Warwick Business School, University of Warwick, Coventry, UK
e-mail: jimmy.donaghey@wbs.ac.uk

T. Dundon
Alliance Manchester, Business School, University of Manchester, Manchester, UK

N. Cullinane
Queen's University Management School, Queen's University, Belfast, UK

T. Dobbins
Birmingham Business School, University of Birmingham, Birmingham, UK

E. Hickland
DCU Business School, Dublin City University, Dublin, Ireland

P. Holland et al. (eds.), *Employee Voice at Work*, Work, Organization, and Employment, https://doi.org/10.1007/978-981-13-2820-6_6

processes of voice in terms of their alleged efficacy for worker representation and performance. This chapter, however, will look at what may be regarded as the antithesis of employee voice: worker silence. As will be outlined, the literature to date has been dominated by scholars from organisational behaviour, and to a lesser extent labour process and critical management studies research. This chapter will show that employment relations scholarship can make a valuable contribution to this area by focussing on how management silence workers. To do this, the chapter will review briefly the literature on worker silence to date and highlight some key weaknesses. It will argue how an employment relations perspective can be instructive about worker silence and, in particular, the neglected role of management in silencing worker voice. After outlining the nature of our study's focus on the implementation of the EUs Information and Consultation Directive in the UK and Ireland, the data will show how management responded in three cases to avoid elements of the Directive to prevent worker voice and how management acted in silencing workers. The chapter will close by discussing the implications of the analysis.

6.2 A Review of the Literature on Silence and Relationship to Voice

Worker voice is the latest term which has come into fashion to describe various types of management–worker interaction. While for a period, employee involvement and participation was used to describe worker inclusion around work tasks and the like, the term voice is perceived to be broader and includes direct and indirect participation including issues of representation (Wilkinson et al. 2014). Research into voice has highlighted the myriad meanings associated with the term (Dundon et al. 2004). Without doubt the meaning of voice varies greatly, for example Morrison (2011) associates worker voice with being pro-social, individual and informal in nature. As such, voice is understood as workers directly communicating with management with the aim of improving business operations. This approach has been criticised by Barry and Wilkinson (2016) as being partial as it only considers voice in terms of the extent to which it aligns with what management wants and fails to recognise that competing interests are central to the employment relationship. These distinctions will not be laboured in this chapter. Rather, the point is that the literature to date on silence has been dominated by the more organisational behaviour approach, with rather limited attention from those of a more pluralist and radical orientation. However, this may be due to a methodological issue: how do researchers identify incidents of where workers have not been able to speak up about issues as to their concern? As such, the chapter will put forward the concept of managerial silencing as a method of understanding the voice-silence dynamics of the employment relationship.

6.2.1 *Organisational Behaviour: The Emergence of Worker Silence*

Research into employee silence first emerged from scholars in the area of organisational behaviour where silence has been generally conceptualised as the conscious withholding of information by workers, with an in-built assumption that voicing concerns is an alternative choice. It is, therefore, a communication choice which employees may decide to adopt. Morrison and Milliken (2000) introduced the concept and highlighted silence as a situation when workers consciously decide to withhold information from managers which could be of benefit to the organisation. Two key features are important to highlight from their approach. The first of these is that the information withheld is information which otherwise would be useful to management in pursuit of its interests. Second, the information is intentionally withheld by workers which carries with it an assumption that there is an avenue through which workers could pursue their voice were it not for their choice to withhold. They particularly focussed on an argument that organisations developed 'systematic cultures' of silence where employees do not express their ideas and do not speak the truth due to a fear of negative repercussions and/or to beliefs that their opinions are not valued (see also Pinder and Harlos 2001). A particular issue highlighted was employees were very focused on what they saw as the potential negative outcomes, or risks, of speaking up (Miliken et al. 2003): The desire to avoid negative outcomes influenced significantly their decisions to remain silent. Furthermore, employee silence was seen to stem from a reluctance to convey negative information because of the discomfort associated with being the conveyer of bad news and the effect this may have on a worker's image to management and their peers at work (cf. Morrison and Rothman 2009). These are seen to be powerful norms within the workplace that often prevent employees from saying what they know. In this research, many respondents expressed concerns about damaging relationships or fear of retaliation and punishment such as losing their job or not getting a promotion (cf. Milliken et al. 2003: 1462).

While this approach has been criticised for its overly managerialist approach, it certainly brings attention onto the issue of workers maintaining silence and some sources of such silence. However, the biggest weakness of this approach is that, with the exception of inappropriate actions by individual managers, it fails to examine the role which management may play in creating silence. In fact, Pinder and Harlos (2001) defined employee silence as withholding genuine expressions about behavioural, cognitive, and/or affective evaluations of organisational circumstances to people who seem capable of changing the situation, i.e. there is an assumption that managerial interests and workers interests align in such situations. Indeed, silence tends to be conceptualised in a fashion of withholding ideas, information and opinions with relevance to improvements in work and work organisation (Dyne et al. 2003) and where 'new ideas facilitate continuous improvement' (Van Dyne and Lepine 1998). The position presented in this chapter is based upon an assumption that there will be circumstances in which management wish for employees to be silent.

As such, the mechanisms through which voice is channelled are not neutral: they have highly political consequences. Thus, the design of employee voice systems, who represents and does not represent employees, and the responses to such representation are central issues in silence.

6.2.2 Critical Management/Organisational Studies: The Silent Worker Effort

A second approach to silence is one of the workers who silence themselves based on what are perceived to be the professional and ideological demands of their profession, emerging from the area of critical management studies/organisation studies (CMS). Brown and Coupland (2005) highlight how the training of accountants places a constraint on their speaking out about issues of concern. In contrast to the organisational behaviour approach, the CMS approach recognises that management may actively discourage employee voice and thereby produce silence. This might be achieved through 'normal pressures, ideal types of worker and accounts of overt attempts to quieten them through notional rules and embarrassment' (Brown and Coupland 2005: 1062). Unlike the literature reviewed in the organisational behaviour tradition, silence is seen as dialectically empowering for workers too: in this case of graduate trainees, silence functioned as a resource whereby organisational cultures—discouraging of new ideas from junior personnel—effectively relieving this group from the responsibility to act. That silence might also be a form of power, rather than powerlessness, is evident in Fletcher and Watson (2007) who highlight that silence can actually be an important tool for workers when exercising power as per Lukes' (1974) second and third dimensions of power. In a similar vein, Dean and Greene (2017) highlight how workers in professions where there is a particular ideological vocation associated with the role, such as clergy and actors in their examples, may refrain from speaking out and view their dissatisfaction as part of the sacrifice that is paid as price for their affective commitment to that profession. Within both these papers, the role of ideological constraints whether through managerial type or inter-worker discursive practices are highlighted. While recognising that such ideological tools may be an important part of the armoury of management in issues around the silencing of individual workers, the focus of this chapter is on how management may shape, create and destroy structures through which types and forms of voice may be expressed.

The CMS-based approach to understanding worker silence addresses some of the pitfalls of the micro-dominated OB approach. However, much of the post-modernist strain of CMS argues workers become 'self-disciplined/consenting' subjects who willingly buy into improving customer service and quality (Ashcraft 2005: 69–83). It is then argued that acts such as silence, voice or even resistance function as an 'escape' into work effort (Knights et al. 1999: 19–20). A problem with these interpretations is employee (and union) responses are portrayed as somewhat futile due to organisational hegemony. We argue, in contrast, there are counterarguments which question the extent to which voice is 'allowed' by management, and the factors at play which regulate the positions of power and authority over how much voice (and silence) management either support or withhold (e.g. Ramsey 1977; Marchington et al. 1992). We extend employment relations analysis and labour process theory to argue that voice and silence can be examined through the prism of the 'frontier of control' (Goodrich 1920) in that voice like other areas of the employment relationship plays a key role in terms of workplace struggles (Donaghey et al. 2011; Cullinane and Donaghey 2014). As such, the issue of the extent to which workers and management contest the shape and form of issues over which there is voice or silence is a key issue in the sociology of organisations.

6.2.3 Employment Relations and Labour Process Theory: Identifying and Silencing Workers

As indicated, one of the key issues for employment relations and sociological approaches concerning labour process debates is how to evaluate something which is not readily identifiable (silence). This approach to voice has generally focussed on the identification of mechanisms, processes and institutions of worker voice and evaluating the extent to which these provide for meaningful voice if at all (Dundon et al. 2004; Wilkinson et al. 2014). Methodologically, the organisational behaviour approach has generally focussed on employee surveys and asked workers to identify reasons for not speaking out on various issues. The CMS approach has generally again focussed on individual level analysis, but uses a qualitative approach to linguistic analysis and the reinterpretation of knowledge to evaluate how these organisational dynamics involve workers accepting hegemonic pressures not to speak out and even willingly embrace negative situations. In contrast, there has been some research addressing worker silence from an employment relations and labour process perspective which generally seeks to map the presence or absence of mechanisms in terms of advancing arguments about silence. Willman et al. (2006) in their 'Sounds of Silence' paper, using quantitative data from the UK's Workplace Employment Relations Survey test for the presence or absence of particular voice mechanisms, with the absence being used to extrapolate the presence of worker silence. Using a qualitative case study method, Graham (1993) shows how workers in a car manufacturing plant collectively mobilised against management by refusing to share information about quality and production tasks. In other words, by actively remaining silent worker effectively challenged managements' authority to intensify work effort.

However, these approaches are not entirely satisfactory. While the presence or absence of various features may be a proxy for silence, the argument here is that, from an employment relations perspective, an alternative approach may be insightful. This approach is one of examining where '*management engages in acts of silencing workers*'. As Kaufman (2014: 19) has suggested while 'employees deliberately withdraw their effort or use voice in order to advance their economic position, employers actively discourage voice due to their perception that it is undesirable'. We demonstrate our approach through an example where management were under a legal duty to respond to employee requests for voice and the ways in which they responded to such requests. As will be outlined, even though there was a duty enshrined in law, management actions were such as to, in effect, seek to circumscribe the extent to which worker voice was enacted. In particular, we highlight the role of management 'counter-mobilisation' (Kelly 1998) in silencing workers. Kelly (1998) argues for the use of mobilisation theory as a lens to understand worker collective action: workers have divergent interests from employers, they mobilise around a collectively held grievance attributed to the action of the employer through collective organisation. This mobilisation forms around a particular opportunity to express the grievances with collective action. Kelly highlights that employers will counter-mobilise through ameliorating the source of the grievance or through more punitive tactics. This chapter argues that the mobilisation of workers led to employer responses which carried with it shared features: on the one hand, the employers made some concessions around the substantive issues which drove the grievances about voice; second, employer-driven voice mechanisms were established which fell short of what workers sought but were presented as being a substitute for the form which the workers sought; third, after the initial pressure dissipated, these voice mechanisms were allowed to atrophy. Thus, through a counter-mobilising strategy, management was able to exercise silencing of workers.

6.3 The Experience of Employers Counter-Mobilisation Strategy—The Research

The chapter draws on research on the implementation of the EUs Information and Consultation Directive (2002/14/EC) in the UK and Republic of Ireland. While the project did not specifically focus on silence but on the extent to which the Directive introduced worker voice, the evidence is presented from three cases where management explicitly had to respond to requests or pressure from workers to establish more robust forms of employee representation. In recent years, the European Commission has been prominent in advancing an indirect, collectivist route to employee voice with legislation covering works councils in multinationals, collective redundancies and a general right to information and consultation. The latter was dealt with through European Directive (2002/14/EC) on Employee Information and Consultation which emerged from the shock announcement of 3000 redundancies at the Renault Plant in Vilvoorde, Belgium, in 1997. Summarised simply, the Directive sets out the requirements for a permanent and statutory framework for employee information and consultation. Directive 2002/14/EC marked the introduction of workers' general right to information and consultation for the first time through standing structures across the European Union. While the situation occurred in Belgium, it was always felt that the legislation would particularly affect the voluntarist economies of the Republic of Ireland and the UK (Gollan and Wilkinson 2007; Hall 2005). This was because most other EU member states at the time had mandatory works councils or similar arrangements for representative and collective voice. While the initial draft of the legislation proposed measures including the right for managerial decisions to be overturned where the levels of information and consultation were insufficient, the Directive when finally passed by the EU was much weaker in nature than it had originally been proposed. In addition, the nature of EU Directives is such that a large degree of discretion is afforded to member states in terms of the ways in which they choose to implement them.

Due to pre-existing legislation in most EU member states, many countries had to make little to no changes with the UK and Ireland standing out as the exceptions (Donaghey et al. 2013). While there were differences in the detail, the UK and Ireland implemented the Directive in broadly similar ways. First, in neither state was a positive obligation placed on businesses to establish employee representative bodies. Rather, employers had to respond and establish a body when approximately 10% of workers signed a request for such a body. Second, as such, it was an example of what has been labelled as EU reflexive law as rights are latent unless triggered by individuals rather than existing as part of the national legal framework of rights. Third, within both countries, there is no significant privilege in terms of trade unions as worker representatives. Fourth, in both countries, provisions were established where ‘pre-existing arrangements’ were to be given priority over a default of EU legislated models. Under this provision, companies which had, for example recognised trade unions or a pre-existing Non-Union Employee Representation Scheme could claim that this should be the mechanism for fulfilling the requirements of the Directive.

The Directive states that organisations will have to inform and consult with employee representatives (whether union and/or non-union) on three general areas: the economic situation of the organisation; the structure and probable development of employment (including any threats to employment); and to inform and consult on decisions likely to lead to change in work organisations or contractual relations (Hall et al. 2013). While the transposition of the Directive was relatively unproblematic in most EU member states, where mandatory and more taxing national works council’s legislation existed, it proved more controversial in the anglophone countries of the UK and Ireland, given the absence of a statutory system for involvement and participation and the historical dominance of voluntarist systems of employment relations (Sisson 2002). Potentially, the net effect of the Directive was, for the first time, to allow British and Irish workers a legal right to be informed and consulted on a range of business and employment issues.

On a number of levels, the implementation, or non-implementation, of the Directive in the UK and Ireland is of conceptual relevance to an illumination of our arguments on the role of management in engineering spheres of employee silence. As has been established, the final transposition of the Directive into both the UK and Irish contexts was minimalist (Hall 2005; Dundon et al. 2006, 2014). In both jurisdictions, the nature of the transposed legislation offered a substantial degree of flexibility conducive to management, which could check or minimise the emergence of potentially robust voice regimes. Other noticeable areas in which the full force of the Directive was restricted by the flexibility provided to employers surrounded pre-existing agreements and a recognition that direct involvement schemes would not be compromised by directive. Also, an initial requirement in the draft Directive for enterprises to report on their 'probable economic and financial situation' of enterprises was replaced by 'probable economic situation' reducing the level of financial reporting obligations. Whilst these efforts to reduce employee voice from the remit of strategic management decision-making were largely a product of manoeuvrings at the national-level, the substance of such activities provided the template to replicate this at workplace level also. Employers have considerable flexibility of response to employee requests, including relying on employee ignorance and thereby giving free scope to do nothing. Employees face difficulties when attempting to trigger the procedures and may have to fight to secure information and consultation rights (Cullinane et al. 2015; Roche and Geary 2006). In the main, employers are unlikely to volunteer to introduce such arrangements, unless they perceive a competitive advantage in so doing, and, outside of union strongholds, non-unionised employees may be largely unaware of these new rights. Indeed, given the manner of transposition, employers may simply be able to adopt of a policy of maintaining their existing arrangements where they consider current information and consultation machinery safe from employee challenges to set in motion the legislative process. Management can potentially use the formal protection provided in the regulations by having pre-existing agreements in place which comply with the necessary criteria. These pre-existing agreements could be used as a vehicle to circumvent the likelihood of a potentially more robust statutory model being imposed in the future. How management are responding to this legislation then remains a pertinent one and provides an avenue upon which to explore the conceptual themes around managerial silencing discussed above. The following section draws on three illustrative cases to explore these relationships.

6.4 Research Case Studies

The cases outlined in this chapter all involved companies which explicitly addressed issues involving the implementation of the Information and Consultation Directive. In the first two, one from the UK and one from the Republic of Ireland, management used the provisions of the Directive to establish a voice mechanism instead of recognising a trade union. In the third, an organisation form the Republic of Ireland, management was highly resistant to the establishment of the default provision arising from the implementing legislation in the Republic of Ireland. Thus, the legislated mechanism of voice in all three became a significant contested terrain between management and worker. What unifies all three cases is that within the establishment, workers were seeking the establishment of a more robust form of worker representation than which management was willing to cede.

6.4.1 *Case Study One—Manufacture Co*

Manufacture Co is a family-owned company operating in Belfast, Northern Ireland. At the time of the research, 300 people were employed in its single site with the main concentration being involved in manufacture and assembly of products. The company had expanded rapidly in the first decade after the millennium, going from a small enterprise to a mid-sized manufacturer. Unusually for a medium-sized family-owned firm in manufacturing, it had a well-developed and well-resourced human resources function. The company prided itself on the quality of its people management and high commitment human resource climate. There was extensive communication with shop floor employees using a variety of media. As the company expanded in size and in order to fulfil the requirements of the Investors in People benchmark, the company established a non-union employee representation forum. The company specifically used the default in the Information and Consultation of Employees regulations as its template. Within a year, the forum had atrophied with neither management nor workers showing much interest: being a family firm, many of the workers instead opted to go straight to the owner family to raise concerns.

6.4.1.1 Contesting the Terrain

Disquiet emerged in the firm associated with a new productivity pay system and the suspension of the bonus mechanism. This saw the emergence of what was viewed by management as an aggressive union recognition campaign though estimates put trade union membership never getting much above 10% of the workforce. At this point, management re-initiated the atrophied employee forum as a mechanism to discuss issues of employee concern.

The company was non-union despite recruitment efforts in the mid-2000s by one union. Information and consultation arrangements focussed on an employee forum established under the regulations as a pre-existing agreement (PEA). It had seven employee representatives and five members of management. Notionally, it met each quarter but more frequent meetings were sometimes held. A number of stimuli seemed to be associated with the founding of the forum in 2005. An accreditation body had suggested it to improve communications; some workers interviewed suggested it was an alternative to the union, designed to pre-empt the regulations as a pre-existing arrangement; the growth of the company required more formal communication methods and, most obviously, it was seen as best practice. The forum covered a wide range of topics for information and consultation including probable decisions which would have a substantial impact on aspects of employment and work organisation. Normally, information papers were given to employee representatives 3 weeks prior to the forum meeting to allow for representatives to consult with employees, formulate their opinions and gain a response. A pre-meeting was held to aide this process. Representatives were allocated time before and after meetings to talk with their constituents. Some used time at the end of the supervisors' team briefing to report on forum matters but others did not give this part of their role much priority.

Views on the success of the forum vary. It was highly regarded by management who valued the opportunity, and it gave them to explain the basis of decisions and dispel rumours. However, employees were more sceptical suggesting it was used to legitimise management behaviour. They also highlighted it could get bogged down with housekeeping matters raised by employee representatives. It also proved hard to get employees to stand as representatives and it was rare for an election to be required. That said, the forum was used by employees to debate big issues such as the productivity bonus which did lead to changes in bonus design before it was frozen in economic crisis of 2008–2011. However, this was some years ago and some representatives believe the forum now has no influence over management and has become an irrelevance. One difficulty for representatives was how to find a distinctive role for the forum. Some believed that rather than employees raising matters directly with their supervisor they should ask their representative to deal with the issue. Worker reluctance to do this restricted their role and wider influence of employee representatives. This was because it was not clear whether individual issues are appropriate topics for collective consultation or only collective issues should be raised. These ambiguities may reflect the lack of training given to representatives. Management initiated the process with the goal of reaching active consultation but through non-union means. However, when faced with organisational difficulties, there was a reversion to information/organisational communicator indicating that consultation only developed at a superficial level. As such the process effectively atrophied due to the lack of substantial matters it dealt with and through the way management developed and managed the relationship.

6.4.2 Case Study Two—BritCo

6.4.2.1 Background

BritCo is a former state-owned enterprise from the UK which was privatised by the Thatcher government in the 1980s. Following privatisation, it expanded internationally and began operating in over 80 countries across the world and began operations in Ireland about 2000. In 2005, the company reorganised and merged its operations in Northern Ireland and the Republic of Ireland into one unit 'BritCo Ireland'. The company has high levels of unionisation within its UK operations, including Northern Ireland. However, for its non-UK operations, it pursues a policy of avoiding and not recognising trade unions including in the Republic of Ireland. What was notable about this arrangement was that while the company was operating in business terms as 'BritCo Ireland', workers in the Northern Irish section were covered by an agreement bargained collectively in the UK with the firm operating a 'double-breasting' regime (Cullinane et al. 2012; Dundon et al. 2014).

6.4.2.2 Contesting the Terrain

A divergence occurred in terms and conditions of employment within the same business unit. This divergence was magnified around two issues: redundancies and pay scales. In Northern Ireland, workers were covered by a 'no compulsory redundancy' agreement while there was no such cover for workers in the Republic of Ireland. Second, workers in Northern Ireland were paid according to collectively agreed pay scales, whereas in the Republic of Ireland, staff were effectively on individual salaries with no pay scales, role profiles or other objective rationale to justify salary points. This led to a feeling of resentment amongst some workers in the Republic of Ireland as the more favourable terms in the North were associated with the unionised set up.

In response to this situation, a union organising campaign was initiated by a specific group of workers in the company. The message of the campaign was built around the unequal treatment of workers in the Republic of Ireland, compared to Northern Ireland. Within the Republic of Ireland, a non-Union Employee Representation Scheme had been established pursuant to the requirements of the Provision of Employee (Information and Consultation) Act 2006. However, it was viewed by workers as being very weak and generally ineffective and had become defunct by early 2007. With the commencement of the union recognition campaign, management decided to revamp this forum. In particular, significant effort was put into establishing electoral constituencies with approximately one representative per hundred workers. In addition, while previously the forum had become a forum for management to present information to worker representatives, workers now were given the opportunity to raise issues for inclusion on the agenda.

Two particular issues arose, the redundancy policy and issues around pay transparency. For both issues, management was insistent that the forums were clearly there for information and consultation, and not negotiation. On the issue of redundancy, the forum saw a redrafting of the redundancy policy, with a significant increase in redundancy payments. However, the company insisted on having the ability to pursue compulsory redundancies in the Republic of Ireland, in contrast to Northern Ireland. With regard to pay transparency, there was little movement on the issue of pay scales. The company did introduce a new system where workers were to be told some details of pay determination but the scales remained invisible to workers with no clear criteria as to pay levels. In the short term, the establishment of the forum and the partial addressing of the grievances at the forefront of the union organising campaign were viewed as having settled much of the disquiet. However, following this, employee representatives noted that the utility of the forum diminished and had become reduced to discussing rather mundane issues.

6.4.3 Case Study Three—High-TechCo[1]

High-TechCo is a high-end US-owned manufacturing company based in the Republic of Ireland. A profitable company, at time of the research, it had over 70 sites across 5 continents, employing 25,000 people. The company had 3 sites in Ireland employing over 4000. The focus of the study is its largest plant facility employing close to 3000 mainly in assembly line work, which is also its largest manufacturing site in its global plant network. It has a large, well-resourced personnel department, which has received awards from professional accreditors for its people management practices. The company had no representative voice mechanisms in existence and there were a number of disgruntled staff who was frustrated at the way in which they perceived the company to operate in terms of communicating with staff. This small group of worker activists decided to trigger an employee request for the establishment of an Information and Consultation Forum under the Irish implementing legislation. What is notable is that this group of workers very consciously did not wish to see this as a union organising campaign and did not want to see union involvement in the campaign.

6.4.3.1 Contesting the Terrain

The workers submitted what they believed to be the required number of signatures to the Labour Relations Commission (LRC), the statutory body charged with implementing the legislation in the Republic of Ireland. In response to this, *High-TechCo* claimed that they had a functioning forum under the legislation for the previous four years which they claimed should be treated as a 'Pre-Existing Arrangement' which would take precedence over the EU Directive default mechanism under the terms of Irish law. Despite this claim from the company, there was no substantial evidence produced to verify the claims that the forum had been in existence for any substantial period. *High-TechCo* then circulated a request for new members to this forum with management selecting from workers who would sit on the forum from those who volunteered, rather than carrying out democratic elections of representatives. All those selected were of supervisory grade in the company.

The worker activists persisted in trying to establish a forum under the legislation and a series of exchanges occurred between the workers, the company and the LRC. Eventually, the company decided to hold a worker referendum to allow workers to decide which forum they wished to support. The company also decided to run elections for employee representatives on the forum and this ran concurrently with the referendum. Management encouraged workers to support their preferred option and placed logistical limitations, such as preventing the activists from promoting the alternative in areas other than their own work unit and only circulating material produced by management that prevented the activists from engaging in meaningful canvass-

[1]This is a summary of the full case as presented in Cullinane et al. (2015). Note that the pseudonym has been changed to maintain consistency with the other two cases presented.

ing across the company. In addition, *High-TechCo* provided an FAQ sheet with the referendum that minimised differences in the two alternatives. The company refused to publicise the results of the referendum, except to say that their preferred option had secured a majority. However, two of the activists who had been organising the campaign for the alternative forum were elected as worker representatives. Shortly afterwards, both of the activist members of the forum were dismissed from the company for having claimed undocumented sick leave. Both took cases to employment tribunals for unfair dismissal with the cases settled outside the tribunal. Significantly, after the referendum result and the exit of the two worker activists, the company's attention to maintaining the forum shifted and the initiative has rather unsurprisingly withered.

6.5 Discussion and Conclusion

Two key issues arise in this chapter. The first is that worker silence must be viewed over time and space and in variable macro contexts of broader understandings of the employment relationship. To view silence in terms as outlined in the prevalent organisational behaviour approach misses both the nuances of organisational and wider societal level dynamics where silencing essentially emerges as a managerial tactic to sideline controversial issues within the specific context of the employment relationship. Similarly, the CMS and organisational studies approaches to worker silence risks viewing employee activities and employment structures that shape divergent interests as marginal, or worse still as futile. Within the three cases discussed, a common thread was that the response of management was that any commitment to developing representative voice was done so in a minimalist way and in response to specific pressures in the workplace: once these issues subsided, there was a noticeable reduction in the commitment of management to the voice forums. In terms of responding to employee pushes for greater and more meaningful voice, organisational management adopted multiple and at times uneven approaches. On the one hand, actions over substantive issues were reinvigorated in the short term to deal with worker demands for better quality voice, including in two of the three cases reconstituted non-union employee representation forums. On the other hand, by maintaining, in the medium to long term, an approach which strictly limited the forums once initial grievances dissipated, the structures atrophied. As such, worker silence is more than simply workers exercising a choice over whether or not to speak out: silence is an organisational phenomenon which can be seen, in part at least, to be socially engineered to reinforce the power of employer actors. The recognition that organisations are made up of a plurality of competing interests and that voice is central to the struggle and contested terrain between these voices, encourages the importance of identifying how one party can silence another party.

Second, empirically identifying silence can be a difficult task when silence is seen as the lack of opportunity for workers to voice their concerns. For example, can it be said just because workers don't voice their opinions or have structures through which to voice their opinions that they are silent? In addition, the cases demonstrate that stifled voice can transform into silence. That said, this chapter presents an approach which highlights that silence is an issue of importance for scholars of employment relations and that focussing on cases of when and how management respond to calls for improved worker voice can be instructive in understanding how management silence workers. What makes the contribution of employment relations and wider labour process synthesis important in this area is a deeper understanding of the dynamics and complexities of how interests play a role in shaping mobilisation and counter-mobilisation in terms of voice mechanisms. Worker voice is a key area of employment relations research and by examining the dynamics of the voice and silence extends analysis beyond a narrow dyadic to bring broader valuable light onto the entire area of research into worker voice.

References

Ashcraft, K. L. (2005). Resistance through consent? Occupational identity, organizational form and the maintenance of masculinity among commercial airline pilots. *Management Communication Quarterly, 19,* 67–90.

Barry, M., & Wilkinson, A. (2016). Pro-social or pro-management? A critique of the conception of employee voice as a pro-social behaviour within organizational behaviour. *British Journal of Industrial Relations, 54*(2), 261–284.

Brown, A. D., & Coupland, C. (2005). Sounds of silence: Graduate trainees, hegemony and resistance. *Organization Studies, 26*(7), 1049–1069.

Cullinane, N., & Donaghey, J. (2014). Employee silence. In A. Wilkinson, J. Donaghey, T. Dundon, & R. Freeman (Eds.), *Research handbook of employee voice*. Cheltenham Glos: Edward Elgar.

Cullinane, N., Donaghey, J., Dundon, T., & Dobbins, T. (2012). Different rooms, different voices: Double-breasting, multi-channel representation and the managerial agenda. *The International Journal of Human Resource Management, 23*(2), 368–384.

Cullinane, N., Hickland, E., Dundon, T., Dobbins, T., & Donaghey, J. (2015). Triggering employee voice under the European Information and Consultation Directive: A non-union case study. *Economic and Industrial Democracy*, 0143831X15584085.

Dean, D., & Greene, A. M. (2017). How do we understand worker silence despite poor conditions—As the actress said to the woman bishop. *Human Relations*, 0018726717694371.

Donaghey, J., Carley, M., Purcell, J., & Hall, M. (2013). *National practices of information and consultation in Europe*. Dublin: Eurofound. Retrieved from http://eurofound.europa.eu/sites/default/files/ef_files/pubdocs/2013/29/en/3/EF1329EN.pdf.

Donaghey, J., Cullinane, N., Dundon, T., & Wilkinson, A. (2011). Reconceptualising employee silence: Problems and prognosis. *Work, Employment & Society, 25*(1), 51–67.

Dundon, T., Curran, D., Ryan, P., & Maloney, M. (2006). Conceptualising the dynamics of employee information and consultation: Evidence from the Republic of Ireland. *Industrial Relations Journal, 37*(5), 492–512.

Dundon, T., Dobbins, T., Cullinane, N., Hickland, E., & Donaghey, J. (2014). Employer occupation of regulatory space of the Employee Information and Consultation (I&C) Directive in liberal market economies. *Work, Employment & Society, 28*(1), 21–39.

Dundon, T., Wilkinson, A., Marchington, M., & Ackers, P. (2004). The meanings and purpose of employee voice. *The International Journal of Human Resource Management, 15*(6), 1149–1170.

Dyne, L. V., Ang, S., & Botero, I. C. (2003). Conceptualizing employee silence and employee voice as multidimensional constructs. *Journal of Management Studies, 40*(6), 1359–1392.

Fletcher, D., & Watson, T. (2007). Voice, silence and the business of construction: Loud and quiet voices in the construction of personal, organizational and social realities. *Organization, 14*(2), 155–174.

Geary, J. F., & Roche, W. K. (2006). The future of employee information and consultation in Ireland. In J. Storey (Ed.), *Adding value through information and consultation*. London: Palgrave Macmillan.

Gollan, P. J., & Wilkinson, A. (2007). Contemporary developments in information and consultation. *The International Journal of Human Resource Management, 18*(7), 1133–1144.

Goodrich, C. L. (1920). *Frontier of control: A study in British workshop polities*. Harcourt Brace and Co.

Graham, L. (1993). Inside a Japanese transplant: A critical perspective. *Work and Occupations, 20,* 147–173.

Hall, M. (2005). Assessing the information and consultation of employees regulations. *Industrial Law Journal, 34*(2), 103–126.

Hall, M., Hutchinson, S., Purcell, J., Terry, M., & Parker, J. (2013). Promoting effective consultation? Assessing the impact of the ICE Regulations. *British Journal of Industrial Relations, 51*(2), 355–381.

Kaufman, B. (2014). Theorising determinants of employee voice: An integrative model across disciplines and levels of analysis. *Human Resource Management, 25*(1), 19–40.

Kelly, J. (1998). *Rethinking industrial relations: Mobilisation, collectivism and long waves*. Routledge.

Knights, D., Calvey, D., & Odih, P. (1999). Social managerialism and the time disciplined subject: Quality-quantity conflicts in a call centre. In *Proceedings of the 17th Annual International Labour Process Conference, School of Management*, Royal Holloway, University of London, 29–31 March 1999.

Lukes, S. (1974). *Power: A radical view* (2nd ed.). London: Macmillan.

Marchington, M., Goodman, J., Wilkinson, A., & Ackers, P. (1992). *New developments in employee involvement*. Paper Series No. 2, HMSO. London: Employment Department Research.

Milliken, F. J., Morrison, E. W., & Hewlin, P. F. (2003). An exploratory study of employee silence: Issues that employees don't communicate upward and why. *Journal of Management Studies, 40*(6), 1453–1476.

Morrison, E. W. (2011). Employee voice behavior: Integration and directions for future research. *Academy of Management Annals, 5*(1), 373–412.

Morrison, E. W., & Milliken, F. J. (2000). Organizational silence: A barrier to change and development in a pluralistic world. *Academy of Management Review, 25*(4), 706–725.

Morrison, E. W., & Rothman, N. B. (2009). Silence and the dynamics of power. *Voice and Silence in Organizations, 6,* 111–134.

Pinder, C. C., & Harlos, K. P. (2001). Employee silence: Quiescence and acquiescence as responses to perceived injustice. *Research in Personnel and Human Resources Management*, 331–369.

Ramsay, H. (1977). Cycles of control: Worker participation in sociological and historical perspective. *Sociology, 11,* 481–506.

Sisson, K. (2002). *The information and consultation directive: Unnecessary "regulation" or an opportunity to promote "partnership"?* Industrial Relations Research Unit, Warwick Business School.

Van Dyne, L., & LePine, J. A. (1998). Helping and voice extra-role behaviors: Evidence of construct and predictive validity. *Academy of Management Journal, 41*(1), 108–119.

Wilkinson, A., Dundon, T., Donaghey, J., & Freeman, R. (2014). Employee voice: Charting new terrain. In A. Wilkinson, J. Donaghey, T. Dundon, & R. Freeman (Eds.), *The handbook of research on employee voice: Participation and involvement in the workplace* (pp. 1–16). Cheltenham Glos: Edward Elgar.

Willman, P., Bryson, A., & Gomez, R. (2006). The sound of silence: Which employers choose no employee voice and why? *Socio-Economic Review, 4*(2), 283–299.

Jimmy Donaghey is Professor of Employment Relations at the Industrial Relations Research Unit, Warwick Business School, University of Warwick, UK and Adjunct Professor at Monash University, Melbourne, Australia. His research interests focus on the internationalisation of employment relations and worker voice.

Dr. Tony Dundon is Professor of Human Resource Management and Employment Relations at the Work and Equalities Institute (WEI), Alliance Manchester Business School, The University of Manchester. He is a Fellow of the Academy of Social Sciences (AcSS), the Chartered Institute of Personnel and Development (CIPD) and Honorary Visiting Professor at the School of Management at the University of St Andrews. He has held visiting positions in Sydney University; Deakin University, Melbourne; Queensland University of Technology (QUT); the Centre for Work, Organisation and Wellbeing, Griffith University; and Toulouse Business School.

Dr. Niall Cullinane is a Senior Lecturer at Queen's Management School at the Queen's University Belfast. He specialises in the teaching and research of the employment relations and human resource management field. He has published in several journals in this area as well as contributed chapters to a number of edited collections. He is an author of A Very Short, Fairly Interesting and Reasonably Cheap Book about Employment Relations, published by Sage 2016.

Dr. Tony Dobbins is Professor of Employment Relations and Human Resource Management at Birmingham Business School, University of Birmingham. His research interests include employee voice, silence and industrial democracy; the impact of economic restructuring on labour markets; sociology of work, conflict and cooperation; the living wage and low pay. He has published in journals including British Journal of Industrial Relations, British Journal of Management, Human Relations and Work Employment and Society.

Dr. Eugene Hickland is an Assistant Professor of Employee Relations and Human Resource Management at Dublin City University Business School. Eugene's research interests include workplace innovations, industrial democracy, employee voice, trade union organisations and employment regulation. He has published in top-level peer -review journals including *Human Relations, Work, Employment and Society, Economic and Industrial Democracy, European Journal of Industrial Relations and International Journal of Human Resource Management*. Eugene has also published a number of book chapters and presented his research at a wide range of national and international conferences.

Chapter 7
Workplace Bullying and the Role of Voice and Ethical Leadership

Peter Holland

Abstract Workplace Bullying is increasingly understood as a multilevel phenomenon and in many Advanced Market Economies (AMEs), it is seen as a major issue impacting negatively on the workplace. With a growing understanding of the nature and dimensions of bullying at work, a key aspect to negating such behaviours are increasingly seen as structural and include a central role for employee voice supported by ethical leadership. This chapter explores the role of employee voice or voice in combination with ethical leadership as principles and practices to negate bullying behaviour. A case study is also incorporated to provide context to the role of voice and ethical leadership.

Keywords Bullying · Ethics · Leadership · Toxic work culture

7.1 Introduction

Workplace Bullying is an increasingly pervasive issue in the workplace resulting in damage to the employees and the organisation with evidence linking such work behaviours to mental illness, inability to work and suicide. As such, in many AMEs, it is seen as a major workplace issue impacting negatively on the workplace (Park and Ono 2016). Research into the issues shows it to be better understood as a multi-level phenomenon (Reeves 2013). With a growing understanding of the nature and dimensions of bullying at work (see Appendix), a novel approach is taken in this chapter to negating such behaviours through culture and structural aspects of work, which can include a central role for employee voice supported by ethical leadership. This chapter explores the potential role of employee voice or voice in combination with ethical leadership as principles and practices to negate bullying behaviour. A

P. Holland (✉)
Department of Management and Marketing, Swinburne Business School, Swinburne University of Technology, Melbourne, VIC, Australia
e-mail: pjholland@swin.edu.au; peter.holland@monash.edu

P. Holland et al. (eds.), *Employee Voice at Work*, Work, Organization, and Employment, https://doi.org/10.1007/978-981-13-2820-6_7

case study is also incorporated to provide context to the role of voice and ethical leadership.

7.2 Bullying

Bullying is a form of workplace behaviour that can be defined as a repetitive and persistent activity that can include humiliating, harassing, offending, intimidating, threatening or demeaning behaviour directed at an individual or group of individuals (Einarsen et al. 2003; Workcover NSW 2008). Bullying also includes behaviour that seeks to socially exclude an individual or negatively affect an individual's health and safety (both physical and psychological) as well as their work (Fox and Cowan 2015; O'Rourke and Antioch 2016; Park and Ono 2016; Ritzman 2016; Einarsen et al. 2003). Examples of this include spreading rumours, yelling, harsh criticism, unreasonable workloads and deadlines and removing responsibilities (D'Cruz and Noronha 2013; D'Cruz et al. 2014; Hall and Lewis 2014; Paull et al. 2012; Ritzman 2016). Bullying continues to be identified at increasing rates across all industries in AMEs (Johnson and Rea 2009; Dellasega 2009). The growing seriousness with which bullying and employee mistreatment in the workplace are taken, can be seen with countries such as France and Sweden and the provinces of Canada mandating a safe work environments (Harlos 2010), and is now become a criminal offence with custodial sentence given for such acts in countries such as Australia (Hanley and O'Rourke 2016). A review of workplace bullying across various industries by Zapf et al. (2011) concluded that the healthcare sector has some of the highest incidences of bullying, and an issue we shall return to later in this chapter.

From an organisational perspective, bullying is associated with higher levels of staff turnover, decreased morale, loss of productivity, poor working relationships and an overall toxic work culture (Turney 2003; Hutchinson et al. 2006; Woelfle and McCaffrey 2007). The psychological and physical damage of bullying on individuals is also well documented, with bullied individuals often experiencing headaches, stress, irritability, anxiety, sleep disturbance, impaired social skills, depression, loss of concentration, helplessness and post-traumatic stress disorder and suicidal thoughts (Lewis and Orford 2005; Ramos 2006; Woelfle and McCaffrey 2007). These findings combined with increased awareness and understanding of what is bullying and its implications has led to efforts to find ways in which organisation can create a culture that prevents and/or negates bullying before the need to resort to legal responses.

In this context, the chapter explores two key aspects of organisational structures: first, the development of employee voice and second, the role of leadership and specifically ethical leadership. Voice means providing all employees with the opportunity to 'call-out' bullying behaviour without fear or favour which can be a powerful channel in dealing with this behaviour at the outset or reporting ongoing behaviour done to an individual or group—in effect proactive internal 'whistleblowing' on such behaviours. Underpinning this is the need for ethical leadership. This is because whilst bullying can be upwards or horizontal, most research indicates it is downward and underpinned by a power–distance relationship disparity between the perpetrator and the target(s) (Cowan and Fox 2014; Einarsen et al. 2003; Fox and Cowan 2015; Harrington et al. 2015; Lutgen-Sandvik et al. 2007). As such management must provide clear and ethical leadership, this is easier said than done as the paradox is that as most bullying is downward, it is likely management is the issue or are part of the problem. When dealing with these issues, management may need to reflect on their own behaviour, as rhetoric rather than action and a lack of social support (Einarsen 2000) on such a subject will soon negate any potential change in culture. So, management needs clear and strong lines of communication to facilitate honest and forthright communication.

As Pinder and Harlos (2001) explain, the result of management inaction is employee silence within the organisation which manifests itself through a variety of means. The most likely is withholding information, to people with the power to affect change because of the fear of retribution, in the belief that nothing will be done if they voice concerns on bullying behaviour in the workplace. Further research by Harlos (2010), indicates that a variety of personal and situational factors in particularly power–distance were an important aspect of these decisions. As such, the individual may be confused as to what will and won't be acted upon by management which in itself can lead to silence and self-censoring within the organisation. This can be reinforced at an institutional level, as Donaghey et al. (2011) argue management can build a culture of employee silence through institutional structures with deliberate or perceived threats, pseudo-investigation or lip service. The deliberate managing out of employee voice (and potential misuse of power) can have serious implications. It can undermine the employment relationship (Milliken et al. 2003), leading to increased employee conflict, resistance and turnover (Macdonald and Thompson 2015) and decreased morale and productivity (Fox and Cowan 2015). A key factor in this is that a management, intolerant of critical feedback, will find it difficult to address these issues and close the channels of communication. In these situations, there is required a 'champion of change' which can emanate from human resources (Woodrow and Guest 2014).

An emerging and progressively important aspect of research into bullying which emerged in the OB literature is the bystander effect, due to the impact of their presence as an observer or a witness to bullying incidents (D'Cruz and Noronha 2011). Twemlow et al. (2004) argue that bystanders are more than observers or witnesses because bystanders are actively involved in the bullying processes as a part of social systems. This is because the bystanders have a choice on how they respond to bullying incidents (Tsang et al. 2011). Salmivalli (1999) identified four roles the bystander can take: assistants, who play a role as aiding the bully; reinforcers, who do not directly participate in bullying processes but provide positive feedback by encouraging the bully such as laughing; outsiders, who keep a distance and appear neutral; and defenders, who are against bullying and try to stop or prevent bullying (Salmivalli 1999). Paull et al. (2012) point out that bystander can move between different role categories during the course of bullying or in a different circumstance. This is where the role of voice and ethical leadership provide a frame of reference for first, ensuring those who intervene (such as defender bystanders) and voice on issues such as bullying are supported, by policies, processes and people. Second, those who encourage such behaviour are equally as scrutinised as the perpetrator(s) of the bullying. Third, those who appear neutral are educated in the requirements to report or voice to appropriate staff of witnessing such behaviours.

7.2.1 The Role of Employee Voice

The term employee voice or 'voice' describes two-way communication between employers and employees (Pyman et al. 2006). The contemporary focus takes a proactive approach by lifting voice from simply raising concerns and expressing and advancing interests to facilitating employee engagement, contribution and commitment to and participating in workplace decision-making and solving problems to advance the organisation (Holland et al. 2011). Employee voice is central to how employee and management communicate. Traditionally in AMEs, 'voice' has been channelled through union recognition and representation, but this has never been the exclusive means of communication and influence at the workplace, as the changing landscape of the workplace has markedly transformed the typology and structure of voice arrangements in the last three decades which has seen direct and hybrid channel more prominent (Holland et al. 2011; Bryson et al. 2007). For management, voice can provide a relatively stable structure where information flows between the parties, which increases knowledge and enables better decision-making (Holland et al. 2011). However, for this to be an open and frank form of communication, voice needs to be supported by a high level of trust between the parties (Holland et al. 2012, 2017) and managerial responsiveness (Pyman et al. 2006), to create the appropriate climate. This is especially true when it comes to dealing with sensitive issues such as bullying, which as noted is predominately top (management) down (employees) with significant power–distance relationships.

7.2.2 Trust and Voice

In an employment context, employees' reciprocate the treatment they receive from management as the employment relationship unfolds (Boxall and Purcell 2016; Farndale et al. 2011). Whilst trust has been researched extensively in the wider management literature, the definition of trust remains broad and a source of debate (Nichols 2009; Innocenti et al. 2010). However, in the context of bullying, we take the psychological perspective that trust is a willingness to show vulnerability, through to an imprecise relationship based upon reciprocal cooperation (Rousseau et al. 1998; Mayer et al. 1995). Thus, trust enables management and employees to engage in a mutually cooperative and ongoing relationship. Lewicki et al. (1998) and Gould-Williams (2003) extend the psychological perspective by defining trust as the basis for quality relationships, cooperation and stability. The issue of power is also included in this definition by adding Korczynski's (2000) perspective on trust which contextualises trust in the confidence that one party to the exchange will not exploit the other's vulnerabilities. These perspectives provide a more reflective approach to the ongoing nature of the exchange upon which the employment relationships is based. In the context of voice and in particular, direct or individual voice where the power relationships are potentially significantly unequal, this acknowledges the importance of this relationship when dealing with delicate issues such as bullying (see Harlos 2010).

As noted, from an organisational context, bullying has a negative effect on a variety of productivity indicators from morale to turnover. The concept and development of trust is built upon the need for employee commitment to increase organisational performance (Nichols et al. 2009). As such, there is an obvious economic argument for it to be dealt with in an effective manner by management. Because of the dynamic nature of the employment relationship, this reciprocity has both positives and negatives. As such, the actions of management (or managerial responsiveness) towards employees, in this case, bullying and how it is (or not) dealt with are continually evaluated and assessed by both employees and their representatives (Costigan et al. 1998). Those actions that violate trust can create an atmosphere of distrust and consequently, employees and their representatives may be less willing to develop a committed relationship with management. As Nichols et al. (2009), and Tzafrir et al. (2004) point out, trust is a key outcome variable in the relationship between human resource practices and employee attitudes to management, and is likely to be, in part, influenced by communication channels (voice), and the degree of involvement or participation of employees in organisational decisions (genuine voice) leading to an appropriate organisational climate.

Indeed, the quality of communication between management and employees in an organisation has been shown to be a key indicator of organisational effectiveness and trust in management (Zeffane and Connell 2003). The ability to develop trust within the employment relationship is, therefore, an increasingly critical aspect of the human resource architecture, so as to create a sustainable and productive employment relationship between employees and management (Boxall and Purcell 2016; Guerrero and Herrbach 2008; Whitener 1997), and critical incidents like bullying are litmus test to such a relationship. As Reeves (2013) notes, employee voice can be a critical factor in dealing with and negating workplace bullying.

7.2.3 Ethical Leadership

What do we mean by ethical leadership?

As Monahan (2012) notes, ethical leadership is a complex and relatively new field of study. Avey et al. (2012), argues that ethical leadership includes both traits and behaviours that ethical leaders work by and also encourage employees to follow. Brown and Trevino (2006), review of ethical leaderships provides the most comprehensive assessment of this leadership style, identifying that:

> …ethical leaders are characterized as honest, caring and principled individuals who make fair and balanced decisions. Ethical leaders also frequently communicate with their followers about ethics, set clear ethical standards and use rewards and punishments to see that standards are followed (p. 597).

Developing an organisational climate based upon ethical leadership ensures that moral standards play an important role in organisational decision-making. In this context and by deduction, Brown and Trevino argue that communication and by default, employee voice would be expected to be encouraged and facilitated by (ethical) management (Chen and Hou 2016), underpinned by a trust-based employment relationship. This is because management within this frame of reference would be more willing to engage in open two-way discussion with employees on issues that affect them both and enhance the organisation's performance. Research increasingly indicates that ethical leadership is beneficial to organisations as it has a positive effect on employee behaviour (Piccolo et al. 2010; Walumbwa et al. 2012). This is because employee voice can provide input on a variety of issues and levels including challenging the status quo, which is seen to increase involvement and job satisfaction of employees (Bashshur and Oc 2015; Holland et al. 2011), as well as the quality of management decision-making and responses in an increasingly complex and dynamic environment (Avey et al. 2012).

In the context of ethical leadership, therefore, exploring how this 'plays out' in practice can be addressed through the two major themes of ethical theories—utilitarianism and deontology—a frame of reference can be developed to provide the critical building blocks for ethical leadership and employee voice. This allows for a more nuanced understanding of the ethical leadership frames of reference. Taking a consequentialist or utilitarian perspective first, this contends that the establishment of a holistic framework is by far the most appropriate for all concerned, as it takes account of contextual factors consequently minimising harm and maximising benefits. This is certainly the case in the process of preventing and/or elimination of bullying through policies and practices (Geirsson and Holmgren 2010). This framework can take into account the complex and subtle contextual aspects of workplace bullying such as work overload and social exclusion to identify the bullying behaviour. In addition, this holistic framework would also provide a role for employee voice to 'call out' such behaviour whether by peers or management.

From a deontological perspective, the emphasis on the ethical leader is an obligation and responsibility to the person, and the principle of respect and consistency for rules and respect for the individual's rights are considered and preserved within the frame of rules with which they work (Bowie and Duska 1990) and in this framework, obligation outweigh the potential consequences of any actions. Organisations adopting a rules-based approach are to have zero tolerance for bullying and would encourage the 'calling out' or the use of voice on such behaviour(s). This would need to be underpinned by protecting and supporting those blowing the whistle on perpetrators even in a significant power distant relationship. From these ethical perspectives emerges what Skovira and Harman (2006) describe as an ethical ecology or climate within the organisation to guide both manager and employees, underpinned by the development of educational policy constructs to inform and guide workplace actions, such as codes of conduct.

A code of conduct specifies the ethical and/or professional expectations and consequences of certain actions whilst providing recommendations to management so as to reduce the reliance on individual judgement and morals. In addition, a well structured and carefully devised code of conduct sends a signal to all employees in the organisation (managers and employees) about which practices are acceptable and which are not (such as bullying and the consequences of such behaviours). These building blocks lead to the development and maintenance of what Martin and Kulinna (2004) describe as a quality ethical climate, which frames the development of ethical decision-making and behaviour in response to critical incidents or situations, underpinned by utilitarian (best outcome for the most people) and deontological (within the rules, codes and laws) frames of reference (Bulutlar and Oz 2008). This is important with regard to bullying as research (Cullen et al. 2003; Parboteeah and Kapp 2008; Bulutlar and Oz 2008) has indicated that there is a close link between (un)ethical climate and deviant behaviours such as bullying. As noted, employees and their representatives are continually reviewing management decision-making and behaviours, on critical issues and incidents such as bullying and, while they may not agree on all aspects of the decision-making process, when framed with an ethical landscape and climate the outcomes are likely to be mutually accepted.

7.3 Organisational Climate

What these key factors of voice, ethical leadership, ethical ecology and moral landscape focus on is enhancing the organisational climate. Morrison et al. (2011) define the organisational climate as a shared belief within the workgroup as to the safety (confidence to voice) and efficacy (something will be done). This notion captures what Dastmalchian et al. (1989) describe as a characteristic atmosphere in the organisation; as perceived by organisational members. As noted, management which develops the organisational structures, policies and practices can structure or institutionalise voice or governance mechanisms (genuine not rhetoric) and leadership (genuine open and ethical, not closed and self-serving) to provide such a climate. However, despite the evidence indicating the positive outcomes, as noted, a management intolerant of genuine voice has several avenues to close it down (Pyman et al. 2010). This is because such voice has the potential to challenge the status quo (Frazier 2013), as noted most bullying is top-down and more senior staff (management) to lower level staff. Given the potential risks associated with such behaviour, employees will quickly resolve whether they work in a climate that encourages dialogue in an open and effective way or there is (significant) inherent risk in undertaking such practices (Frazier 2013). In this context, whistleblowing may be the ultimate test of such workplace policies and practices.

7.3.1 Whistleblowing as a Form of Voice

As noted, when considering the nature and structure of voice and ethical leadership, management, as the primary developers of communication channels, has a variety of options as to the way in which they engage with the workforce. Management's choice (or lack of) information-sharing processes, communication channels and employee involvement and participation mechanisms will be a direct reflection of their ideology and style, and ultimately, this influences the level of trust between employees and management (e.g. Lamsa and Pucetaite 2006; Dietz 2004), and also the ethical and organisational climate and the fertility of the ground for bullying to emerge. Indeed, empirical research confirms the importance of 'open' communication in positively influencing trust in the employment relationship (Lamsa and Pucetaite 2006), the role of organisational communication as a predictor of trust (Holland et al. 2012) and the positive influence of a joint problem-solving approach on trust between management and employees (Kessler and Purcell 1996). Employee voice arrangements are associated with governance mechanisms for the employment relationship, and exist where institutions or processes are present to generate two-way communication between managers, employees and/or their representatives (Bryson et al. 2007). With respect to trust and employee voice arrangements, Boxall and Purcell (2016) argue that it is not so much the particular voice practices that matter, but the level of managerial sincerity and the degree of responsiveness that results from them. Where a positive or responsive organisational culture is not developed, or where issues are covered up or suppressed, such as bullying, this can result in these issues being taken out of the institutional process and to be externalised through whistleblowing.

Whistleblowing is the act of disclosure by a current or former organisational member of illegal, negligent or illegitimate practices under the control of the employer, to sources who may be able to effect action (Miceli and Near 2013). As Miceli and Near (2013) indicate, the ethical climate is a factor in employees' willingness to blow the whistle and can be constituted as a form of voice, as it involves the expression of voice on work-related matters. Whilst there is important difference in voice and whistleblowing which will be outlined below an in-depth review of these issues is beyond the scope of this chapter.

First, whistleblowing functions in a much narrower range than contemporary voice in that it focuses on wrongdoing. Second, whistleblowing, is more likely to have an external focus in order for the wrongdoing to be acted upon. Third, voice is internally focused and an ongoing constructive relationship, whereas whistleblowing is more likely to be externally focused and destructive towards the organisation (at least in the short term), as it is likely to not only expose wrongdoing but that in having been identified, it has either been ignored or covered up. However, in an appropriate climate, what Liang et al. (2012) calls prohibitive voice may occur where internal processes may be undertaken in the first instance to correct or deal with the issue(s). Fourth, voice is a process involving current employees where whistleblowing can be current, previous or non-employees (Miceli and Near 2013).

In terms of mapping, the common ground between voice and whistleblowing, Miceli and Near (2013) identify the following: both are seen as pro-social (particularly individual voice), in that the actions challenge, for example questionable activities and deserving of action with an expectation of positive outcomes. Also, the role of evidence appears important in both voice and whistleblowing, it is often the person in less authority (employee) attempting to influence behaviour in those of greater authority (management). As such, the support of evidence is seen as both important (and credible) in seeking change and in protecting the person using voice or whistleblowing—institutional support. Building on this, both voice and whistleblowing are generally seen to be initiated when the employee perceives that in undertaking these activities, they will be the catalyst for action and/or positive change. This also relates to the issue noted earlier in this chapter, the organisational climate or ethical ecology that management develops is a critical aspect of both voice and whistleblowing. As research indicates, in a positive environment, change is perceived to be possible (Ethical Resource Center 2012), rather than be feared for the retribution or negative consequences (Detert and Trevino 2010). This can clearly be seen to provide a framework with which bullying is called out and addressed, be it internally or externally if the internal system fails to support change.

The following section explores these key aspects at play of bullying, silence and finally, whistleblowing as a way to address these issues, in a case study of the Royal College of Surgeons in Australia. Through a series of incidents, an endemic culture of bullying was identified and then addressed.

7.4 Case Study—Surgically Removing Bullying in the Health Sector

In mid-2015, 4 Corners, the Australian Broadcasting Commission's flagship investigative programme reported on endemic bullying by senior surgeons of young doctors in the Australian public health system. The programme focused on a whistleblower who had complained about sexual harassment initially internally (voice), and then as a whistleblower when she was unable to obtain redress (change). The doctor stated that her career had been stifled because of the whistleblowing, a senior (female) surgeon stating on the programme that if she had given sexual favours she might not have had her career stymied. A psychiatrist interviewed in the programme noted and reflected on the significant power difference in the relationship between senior surgeons and trainees. It was also pointed out that the culture of bullying was so entrenched that it was described as a process of teaching by humiliation.

What the programme revealed was the power relationship that existed with senior surgeons in the position of deciding who became a brain surgeon and who doesn't. This was also seen to be linked to the endemic culture dominated by men. Further evidence of this misogynistic culture came from statements to women that they should be at home looking after the children or that they shouldn't wear provocative clothes as this was to blame for the sexual advances. What was clear was that this was a deeply entrenched culture and despite the high-profile whistleblowing, there appeared to be little opportunity to change this culture.

7.4.1 Enter the Royal Australasian College of Surgeons

The whistleblower contacted the Royal Australasian College of Surgeons (RACS)[1] regarding her complaint and was told that it was a matter between her and the hospital and that she should see a psychiatrist, implying she was unstable (according to the whistleblower). However, when 12 further female doctors came forward to complain, RACS acknowledged the problem and that they had to change their own attitude to the incidents, as it was now an issue in the public domain. During this period, the whistleblower had made a formal complaint to the hospital which found the accusation was not proven. Subsequently, in taking the case to court, the judge found in favour of the whistleblower and admonished the surgeon and the hospital for their attitudes. The surgeon was given a first and final warning and remains working at the hospital in question. The whistleblower now works in the private sector in a limited surgical capacity. However, rather than being the end of the issue, this has subsequently seen a dramatic intervention by RACS and a catalyst of change in the context of ethical leadership.

Following the 4 Corners investigation, the RACS set up an expert advisory group (EAG) to address issues of sexual harassment and bullying. The report itself found that:

- 49% of fellows, trainees and international medical graduates reported being subjected to discrimination and/or sexual harassment;
- 54% of trainees reported being subjected to bullying;
- Hospitals identified bullying as the most frequently reported incident;
- Senior surgeons and consultants were identified as the primary cause of these issues.

On accepting the report and recommendations of the EAG, the report was released and the President of RACS made a video apology for the discrimination, bullying and sexual harassment by surgeons. Key elements of the speech noted the loss of trust in RACS itself which needed to be addressed 'through meaningful culture change'. This was followed by the development of an action plan based upon the report.

[1]RACS is the professional association that regulates professional standards among other things and that the people who run RACS are powerful in hospital management. So this is an unusual case as the complaint by the whistlebower could not be addressed satisfactorily by an unreformed RACS.

7.4.2 *The Expert Advisory Group Report to the Royal Australasian College of Surgeons*

In terms of culture change, the EAG reported that it was shocked by the findings regarding bullying, discrimination and sexual harassment and there was a need for the College to lead a culture of positive change. The report found that bullying was endemic, sexual harassment was influenced by a high gender power imbalance that resulted in such behaviour rarely being 'called out', and discrimination being commonplace across cultural, racial and sexual lines (EAG 2015). The key points made by the reports include the need for

- Individual surgeons being held accountable against their legal and professional responsibilities;
- Bystanders to speak up and not to be silent witnesses.

Key policy statement areas to induce this change include:

- Training and education;
- Holding practitioners and employers to account against agreed standards; and
- Lead a culture of change in the health sector against discrimination, bullying and sexual harassment.

What was of particular interest was the real opportunity for change, in that the college accepted that it had shown a lack of leadership on these issues. Part of this culture included a lack of transparency and independent scrutiny. From this, the key recommendation included:

- Cultural change and leadership;
- Surgical education;
- Complaints management.

Whilst this process has only recently been adopted at the time of writing this chapter, it is worth noting the key issues it highlights in relation to bullying, ethical leadership and whistleblowing.

7.5 Discussion

Using the criteria established above, this case study examines the major case of bullying by senior surgeons of junior staff. It was clear that power–distance and gender were factors (Harlos 2010) as well as the institutional culture (Donaghey et al. 2011), of the hospitals and RACS reflected a system that whilst voice mechanisms existed they were structurally weak and ineffective when dealing with issues that challenged the prevailing culture. As such, the alternative became whisltleblowing. As noted within an environment with little ethical leadership or 'ethical ecology' (Skovira and Harman 2006), the whistleblower subsequently had her career damaged.

It was only when a multitude of complaints came forth that RACS felt it needed to act.

Whist the RACS should be commended for its eventual stance and it attempts for root and branch change in the culture of surgeon training. It should never have allowed the situation to have become so endemic, nor attempt to ignore the issue until it became a public issue. Second, simply putting in place a set of procedures will not necessarily change the culture. As noted, a combination of structural and attitudinal change associated with genuine managerial response's to voice and the development of trust are long-term strategies that RACS and the hospitals need to engage in. There is an argument that professional registration should be placed in the hands of the government, as with the Nordic countries as self-regulation appears to have failed. As it stands, it will be interesting to examine how these systems will embed into the culture that has resisted change. It is also worth noting the lack of apparent development of new and effective voice systems and the time required to develop significant culture change at multiple levels within the health system to facilitate a more open transparent and 'ethical ecology or moral landscape'. As Frazier (2013, pp. 217–18) notes in this context of voice climate over time:

> One of the key assumptions inherent in the voice literature is that when employees speak up, the suggestions wind up in the hands of those who can affect change and implement the suggestions.

In such an immature voice climate in the Australian health system, the apparent speed of change implied by RACS within the system is at best appears optimistic.

Appendix 1

What is workplace bullying?

- Workplace bullying is repeated; '*unreasonable behaviour*' directed towards an employee or a group of employees that creates a risk to health and safety. Unreasonable behaviour is behaviour that a reasonable person having regard to all circumstances would expect to victimise, humiliate, undermine or threaten another employee.
- Workplace bullying is often an abuse of power by someone who is stronger either physically, verbally, mentally, socially, electronically, politically or financially.
- Instances of workplace bullying have the deliberate intent of causing physical and psychological distress to another and can include behaviour that intimidates, offends, degrades or humiliates the victim in front of co-workers, clients or customers.
- Bullying can range from managers to workers (downward), a worker to co-workers (sideways) and workers to managers (upwards).
- Indirect bullying is harder to recognise as it's often carried out to harm reputation or cause humiliation, i.e. lying, spreading

rumours, playing nasty jokes, teasing, namecalling, insults, mimicking and encouraging others to socially exclude them.

Examples of workplace bullying?
Bullying in the workplace may include:

- Manipulation and intimidation, making the employee feel less important and undervalued.
- Performing abusive or offensive acts in front or behind their back.
- Unreasonable criticism which is not part of the management performance process.
- Verbal and physical abuse, shouting, making threats and isolation from colleagues.
- Refusing to delegate or withholding information the employee needs to perform duties.
- Making fun of an employee, i.e. comment about their family, sexuality, gender identity, race, culture, education or economic background.
- Deliberately changing work hours or schedules to make it difficult for an employee to function effectively at work.
- Withholding information or tools required to perform role.
- Initiation or hazing—where an employee is made to do humiliating or inappropriate tasks in order to be accepted.
- Intimidation.
- Accusations regarding lack of effort, destructive innuendo and sarcasm.
- Preventing access to opportunities, physical or social isolation.
- Undue pressure and setting impossible deadlines.
- Unnecessary deliberate disruptions.
- Failure to acknowledge good work and destabilisation/undermining behaviours (e.g. failure to give credit, setting people up to fail).
- Allocation of meaningless tasks or removal of responsibility.
- Repeated reminders of blunders and setting up an employee to fail.
- Unjustified criticism or complaints.
- Threats to disestablish or demote.
- Inconsistent and arbitrary enforcement of rules.
- Excessive, unjustified or unreasonable monitoring of tasks.

Workplace bullying definitions

- **Pair bullying**—takes place with two employees, one is active and verbal while the other is watching and listening.
- **Gang bullying or group bullying**—gangs flourish in corporate bullying climates, often called mobbing and usually involve scapegoating and victimisation.
- **Vicarious bullying**—two parties are encouraged to fight, typical 'triangulation' where the aggression gets passed around.
- **Regulation bullying**—a serial bully forces their target to comply with rules, regulations, procedures or laws regardless of their appropriateness, applicability or necessity.

- **Residual bullying**—after the serial bully has left or asked to leave, the behaviour continues and could continue for months and even years.
- **Legal bullying**—bringing of a vexatious legal action to control and punish a person—considered one of the nastiest forms of bullying.
- **Pressure/unwitting bullying**—having to work to unrealistic timescales and or inadequate resources provided to complete task.
- **Corporate bullying**—an employer abuses with impunity, knowing the law is weak and job market is soft.
- **Organisational bullying**—a combination of pressure and corporate bullying occurs when an organisation struggles to adapt to changing markets, reduced income, cuts in budgets, imposed expectations and other extreme pressures.
- **Institutional bullying**—entrenched and is accepted as part of the organisations culture, employees don't challenge the hierarchy.
- **Unwitting bullying**—includes bullying where stressful circumstances, stemming either from the workplace or from personal issues result in a deterioration of office behaviour.

Why don't people report bullying?

- Can't be bothered with the paperwork and red tape, including the written formal complaint.
- Fear of retribution.
- Doubt that the problem can be solved, perceive nothing will be done and thus the behaviour continues to be unaddressed.
- Fear of being regarded as weak or a failure.
- Not being able to deal with it alone.
- Management and staff will label the employee as nuisance.
- Reporting may negatively affect career and impact on advancement or promotion.
- Belief that the behaviour is a normal part of work culture.

Employees are less likely to report bullying if they:

- Don't recognise it.
- Lack knowledge about bullying behaviours and their effects.
- Unsure about procedure.
- Don't know where to seek support.
- Fear retribution from the bully or bullies including losing employment.
- Feel intimidated or embarrassed.
- Believe bullying is part of the workplace culture and feel nothing will change.
- Opportunities for promotion in the organisation may be affected.

References

Australian Broadcasting Commission. (2015). At their mercy: The bullying and bastardisation of young doctors in our hospitals. Monday 25th May.

Avey, J., Wernsing, T., & Palanski, M. (2012). Exploring the process of ethical leadership: The mediating role of employee voice and psychological ownership. *Journal of Business Ethics, 107,* 21–34.

Bashshur, M. R., & Oc, B. (2015). When voice matters: A multi-level review of the impact of voice in organizations. *Journal of Management, 41,* 1530–1554.

Bowie, N., & Duska, R. (1990). *Business ethics* (2nd ed.). New Jersey: Prentice Hall.

Boxall, P., & Purcell, J. (2016). *Strategy and human resource management* (4th ed.). London: Palgrave Macmillan.

Brown, M. E., & Trevino, L. K. (2006). Ethical leadership: A review and future directions. *The Leadership Quarterly, 17*(6), 595–616.

Bryson, A., Gomez, R., Kretschmer, T., & Willman, P. (2007). The diffusion of workplace voice and high-commitment human resource management practices in Britain, 1984–1998. *Industrial and Corporate Change, 16*(3), 394–426.

Bulutlar, F., & Oz, E. (2008). The effects of ethical climates on bullying behaviour in the workplace. *Journal of Business Ethics, 86,* 273–295.

Chen, A., & Hou, A. (2016). The effects of ethical leadership, voice behavior and climates for innovation on creativity: A moderated mediation examination. *The Leadership Quarterly, 27*(1), 1–13.

Costigan, R., Iiter, S., & Berman, J. (1998). A multi-dimensional study of trust in organizations. *Journal of Managerial Issues, 10,* 303–317.

Cowan, R. L., & Fox, S. (2014). Being pushed and pulled: A model of US HR professionals roles in bullying situations. *Personnel Review, 44*(1), 119–139.

Cullen, J., Parboteeah, K., & Victor, B. (2003). The effects of ethical climates on organisational commitment: A two-study analysis. *Journal of Business Ethics, 46*(2), 127–141.

D'Cruz, P., & Noronha, E. (2011). The limits to workplace friendship: Managerialist HRM and bystander behaviour in the context of workplace bullying. *Employee Relations, 33*(3), 269–288.

D'Cruz, P., & Noronha, E. (2013). Workplace bullying in the context of organisational change: the significance of pluralism. *Industrial Relations Journal, 45*(1), 2–21.

D'Cruz, P., Noronha, E., & Beale, D. (2014). The workplace bullying-organizational change interface: Emerging challenges for human resource management. *The International Journal of Human Resource Management, 25*(10), 1434–1459.

Dastmalchian, A., Blyton, P., & Adamson, R. (1989). Industrial relations climate: Testing a construct. *Journal of Occupational Psychology, 62,* 21–32.

Dellasega, C. (2009). Bullying among nurses. *American Journal of Nursing, 109,* 52–58.

Detert, J., & Trevino, L. (2010). Speaking up to higher ups: How supervisors and skip-level leaders influence employee voice. *Organizational Science, 21*(1), 249–270.

Dietz, G. (2004). Partnership and the development of trust in British workplaces. *Human Resource Management, 14*(1), 5–24.

Donaghey, J., Cullinane, N., Dundon, T., & Wilkinson, A. (2011). Reconceptualising employee silence: Problems and prognosis. *Work, Employment & Society, 25*(10), 51–67.

Ethical Resource Center. (2012). National Business Ethics Survey of Fortune 500 Employees.

Einarsen, S., Hoel, H., Zapf, D., & Cooper, C. L. (2003). The concept of bullying at work. In S. Einarsen, H. Hoel, D. Zapf, & C. L. Cooper (Eds.), Bullying and emotional abuse in the workplace: International perspectives in research and practice (pp. 3–30). London UK: Taylor & Francis.

Einarsen, S. (2000). Harassment and bullying at work: A review of the Scandinavian approach. *Aggression and Violent Behavior, 5*(4), 379–401.

Expert Advisory Group (EAG). (2015). Report to RACS on discrimination, bullying and sexual harassment. Advising the Royal Australasian College of Surgeons.

Farndale, E., Hope-Hailey, V., & Kelliher, C. (2011). High commitment performance management: The role of justice and trust. *Personnel Review, 10*(1), 5–23.

Fox, S., & Cowan, R. L. (2015). Revision of the workplace bullying checklist: The importance of human resource management's role in defining and addressing workplace bullying. *Human Resource Management Journal, 25*(1), 116–130.

Frazier, M. L. (2013). Voice climate in organizations: Creating a context for speaking up. In C. Cooper (Ed.), *Burke R* (pp. 205–223). Edward Elgar Cheltenham UK: Voice and whistleblowing in organizations.

Geirsson, H., & Holmgren, S. (2010). *Ethical theory: A concise anthology*. Canada: Broadview Press.

Guerrero, S., & Herrbach, O. (2008). The affective underpinnings of psychological contract fulfilment. *Journal of Managerial Psychology, 23*(1), 4–17.

Gould-Williams, J. (2003). The Importance of HR practices and workplace trust in achieving superior performance: A study of public-sector organizations. *International Journal of Human Resource Management, 14*(1), 28–54.

Hall, R., & Lewis, S. (2014). Managing workplace bullying and social media policy implications for employee engagement. *Academy of Business Research Journal, 1*(1), 128–138.

Hanley, G., & O'Rourke, A. (2016). The race without a finishing line: Legislative means for confronting bullying in the Australian workplace. *Asia Pacific Journal of Human Resources, 54*(3), 352–368.

Harlos, K. (2010). If you build a remedial voice mechanism, will they come? Determinants of voicing interpersonal mistreatment at work. *Human Relations, 63*(3), 311–329.

Harrington, S., Warren, S., & Rayner, C. (2015). Human resource management practitioners' responses to workplace bullying: Cycles of symbolic violence. *Organization, 22*(3), 369–389.

Holland, P., Cooper, B., & Sheehan, C. (2017). Employee voice, supervisor support and engagement: The mediating role of trust. Human Resource Management (US) (forthcoming).

Holland, P., Cooper, B., Pyman, A., & Teicher, J. (2012). Trust in management: The role of employee voice arrangements and perceived managerial opposition to unions. *Human Resource Management Journal, 22*(4), 377–391.

Holland, P., Pyman, A., Teicher, J., & Cooper, B. (2011). Employee voice and job satisfaction in Australia: The centrality of direct voice. *Human Resource Management, 50*(1), 95–111.

Hutchinson, M., Vickers, M., Jackson, D., & Wilkes, L. (2006). Workplace bullying in nursing: Towards a more critical organisational perspective. *Nursing Inquiry, 13,* 118–126.

Innocenti, L., Pilati, M., & Peluso, A. (2010). Trust as moderator in the relationship between HRM practices and employee attitudes. *Human Resource Management Journal, 21*(3), 303–317.

Johnson, S., & Rea, R. (2009). Workplace bullying: Concerns for nurse leaders. *Journal of Nursing Administration, 39,* 84–90.

Kessler, I., & Purcell, J. (1996). The value of joint working parties. *Work, Employment & Society, 10*(4), 663–682.

Korczynski, M. (2000). The political economy of trust. *Journal of Management Studies, 37*(1), 1–23.

Lamsa, A., & Pucetaite, R. (2006). Development of organizational trust among employees from a contextual perspective. *Business Ethics: A European Review, 15*(2), 130–141.

Lewicki, R. J., McAllister, D. J., & Bies, R. (1998). Trust and distrust: New relationships and realities. *The Academy of Management Review, 23*(3), 438–458.

Lewis, S., & Orford, J. (2005). Women's experiences of workplace bullying: Changes in social relationships. *Journal of Community and Applied Social Psychology, 15,* 29–47.

Liang, J., Farh, C., & Farh, J. (2012). Psychological antecedents of promotive and prohibitive voice: A two-wave examination. *Academy of Management Journal, 55*(1), 71–92.

Lutgen-Sandvik, P., Tracy, S. J., & Alberts, J. K. (2007). Burned by bullying in the American workplace: Prevalence, perception, degree and impact. *Journal of Management Studies, 44*(6), 837–862.

Martin, J. J., & Kulinna, P. H. (2004). Self-efficacy theory and the theory of planned behavior: Teaching physically active physical education classes. *Research Quarterly for Exercise and Sport, 75*(3), 288–297.

Macdonald, P., & Thompson, P. (2015). Social media(tion) and the reshaping of public/private boundaries in employment relations. *International Journal of Management Reviews, 10*(1), 1–16.
Mayer, R., Davis, J., & Schoorman, D. (1995). An investigative model of organizational trust. *Academy of Management Review, 20,* 709–734.
Miceli, M., & Near, J. (2013). Some Implications of the voice literature for research on whistleblowing. In R. Burke & C. Cooper (Eds.), *Voice and whistleblowing in organizations* (pp. 182–204). Cheltenham UK: Edward Elgar.
Milliken, F., Morrison, E., & Hewlin, P. (2003). An exploratory study of employee silence: Issues that employees don't communicate upward and why. *Journal of Management Studies, 40*(6), 1453–1476.
Monahan, K. (2012). A review of the literature concerning ethical leadership in organizations. *Emerging Leadership Journeys, 5*(1), 56–66.
Morrison, E., Wheeler-Smith, S., & Kamdar, D. (2011). Speaking up in groups: A cross-level study of group voice climate and voice. *Journal of Applied Psychology, 96*(1), 183–191.
Nichols, T., Danford, A., & Tasiran, A. (2009). Trust, employer exposure and the employment relations. *Economic and Industrial Democracy, 30*(2), 241–265.
O'Rourke, A., & Antioch, S. K. (2016). Workplace bullying laws in Australia: Placebo or panacea? *Common Law World Review, 45*(1), 3–26.
Park, J. U., & Ono, M. (2016). Effects of workplace bullying on work engagement and health: the mediating role of job insecurity. *The International Journal of Human Resource Management, 28*(22), 3202–3225.
Paull, M., Omari, M., & Standen, P. (2012). When is a bystander not a bystander? A typology of the roles of bystanders in workplace bullying. *Asia Pacific Journal of Human Resources, 50*(3), 351–366.
Piccolo, R. F., Greenbaum, R. L., Den Hartog, D. N., & Folger, R. (2010). The relationship between ethical leadership and core job characteristics. *Journal of Organizational Behavior, 31,* 259–278.
Pinder, C. C., & Harlos, K. P. (2001). Employee silence: Quiescence and acquiescence as responses to perceived injustice. In K. M. Rowland & G. R. Ferris (Eds.), *Research in Personnel and Human Resource Management* (pp. 331–369). London: Emerald.
Parboteeah, K., & Kapp, E. (2008). Ethical climates and safety-enhancing behaviours: An empirical test. *Journal of Business Ethics, 80*(3), 515–529.
Pyman, A., Holland, P., Teicher, J., & Cooper, B. (2010). Industrial relations climate, employee voice and managerial attitudes to unions. An Australian study. *British Journal of Industrial Relations, 48*(2), 460–480.
Ramos, M. (2006). Eliminate destructive behaviours through example and evidence. *Nursing Management, 37,* 34–41.
Pyman, A., Cooper, B., Teicher, J., & Holland, P. (2006). A comparison of the effectiveness of employee voice arrangements in Australia. *Industrial Relations Journal, 37*(5), 543–559.
Reeves, M. (2013). Voice as a pivotal force in organizational efforts to curb workplace bullying. In R. Burke & C. Cooper (Eds.), *Voice and whistleblowing in organizations* (pp. 166–181). Cheltenham UK: Edward Elgar.
Ritzman, M. E. (2016). A phenomenon we can't ignore: Performance improvement interventions to address workplace bullying. *International Society for Performance Improvement, 55*(1), 14–22.
Rousseau, D., Sirkin, S., Burt, R., & Camerer, C. (1998). A cross disciple view of trust. *Academy of Management Review, 24,* 485–507.
Salmivalli, C. (1999). Participant role approach to school bullying: Implications for interventions. *Journal of Adolescence, 22*(4), 453–459.
Skovira, R., & Harman, K. (2006). An ethical ecology of a corporate leader: Modeling the ethical frame of corporate leadership. *Interdisciplinary Journal of Information, Knowledge & Management, 1,* 159–170.
Tsang, S. K. M., Hui, E. K. P., & Law, B. C. M. (2011). Bystander position taking in school bullying: The role of positive identity, self-efficacy, and self-determination. *International Journal of Child Health and Human Development, 5*(1), 103–110.

Turney, L. (2003). Mental health and workplace bullying: The role of power, professions and on the job training. *Australian e-Journal for the Advancement of Mental Health, 2,* 1–9.
Twemlow, S. W., Fonagy, P., & Sacco, F. C. (2004). The role of the bystander in the social architecture of bullying and violence in schools and communities. *Annual New York Academy of Sciences, 1036*(1), 215–232.
Tzafrir, S., Harel, G., Baruch, Y., & Dolan, S. (2004). The consequences of emerging HRM practices for employees' trust in their managers. *Personnel Review, 33*(4), 628–646.
Walumbwa, F., Wang, P., Wang, H., Schaubroeck, J., & Avolio, B. (2012). Psychological processes linking authentic leadership to follower behaviors. *The Leadership Quarterly, 21,* 901–914.
Whitener, E. M. (1997). The impact of human resources activities on employees trust. *Human Resource Management Review, 7*(4), 389–404.
Woelfle, C., & McCaffrey, R. (2007). Nurse on nurse. *Nursing Forum, 42,* 123–131.
Woodrow, C., & Guest, D. E. (2014). When good HR gets bad results: Exploring the challenge of HR implementation in the case of workplace bullying. *Human Resource Management Journal, 24*(1), 38–56.
WorkCover, N. S. W. (2008). *Preventing and dealing with workplace bullying: A guide for employers and employees*. Sydney: NSW Government.
Zapf, D., Escartin, J., Einarsen, S., Hoel, H., & Vartia, M. (2011). Empirical findings on prevalence and risk groups of bullying in the workplace. In Einarsen, S., Hoel, H., Zapf, D., & Cooper, C. (Eds.), Bullying and harassment in the workplace: Developments in theory, research and practice (pp. 75–106). Boca Raton FL: Taylor & Francis.
Zeffane, R., & Connell, J. (2003). Trust and HRM in the new millennium. *The International Journal of Human Resource Management, 14*(1), 3–11.

Peter Holland is Professor of Human Resource Management and Director of the Executive MBA at Swinburne University of Technology, Melbourne, Australia. He has worked in the Australian finance sector and consulted to the private and public sector in a variety areas related to human resource management and employee relations. His current research interests include employee voice, workplace electronic monitoring and surveillance, and talent management.

Part III
Employee Voice in Practice

Chapter 8
Employee Voice at the End of the Line at CarCo

Alan McWilliams, Peter Holland and Rob Hecker

Abstract Unlike the dominant discourse in employee voice, this chapter considers voice where the organisation, a subsidiary part of a global corporation, is actually going out of business. So the issue of voice is most important in maintaining employee commitment and engagement and maintaining employee well-being in a unique and difficult situation. This study will draw upon the unusual experience of the closure of motor vehicle manufacturing in Australia.

Keywords Employee Voice · Automotive manufacturing
Industrial relations climate · Australia

8.1 Introduction

This chapter considers the evolution of voice in a major manufacturing organisation, a subsidiary of a global corporation, from its manufacturing 'birth' in 1947 to its 'death' with the closure of this iconic Australian manufacturing company after 70 years of operation in 2017. The organisation is in the international automobile manufacturing sector which has often been at the forefront of workplace innovation and reform. The closure of the Australian operations provides a unique opportunity for reflection, as well as the opportunity to explore new directions in voice, as the 3-year staged shutdown required the maintenance of employee commitment, engagement and well-

A. McWilliams (✉)
Victoria University, Melbourne, Australia
e-mail: Alan.McWilliams@vu.edu.au

P. Holland
Department of Management and Marketing, Swinburne Business School, Swinburne University of Technology, Melbourne, VIC, Australia
e-mail: pjholland@swin.edu.au

R. Hecker
University of Tasmania, Hobart, Australia

P. Holland et al. (eds.), *Employee Voice at Work*, Work, Organization, and Employment, https://doi.org/10.1007/978-981-13-2820-6_8

being in an unusual and difficult situation. The study explores this rare opportunity to analyse voice at the end of the line.

The development of voice is considered through four economic periods. The first period (1947–1982) reflects a post-war period of sustained growth driven by growth in consumer disposable income and increasing demand for consumer goods, albeit with a following decline, under Keynesian models and economic management. This first stage was one of the overall economic stabilities which by the mid-1970s was increasingly coming under pressure. The second stage (1983–1996) explores a period of major microeconomic reform under the Keating–Hawke Labor Government in Australia. These changes included fundamental transformation of both the economy and industrial relations landscape in Australia (Morris 1996). The third stage (1996–2007) explores a period of conservative (Liberal National Party) governments, underpinned by an anti-union and pro-market ideology. The fourth stage (2008–2017) examines the turbulent period following the Global Financial Crises (GFC) and the staged closure of CarCo, and the important role of employee voice in the industrial relations process to achieve an efficient staged closure.

CarCo's origins go back to the mid-nineteenth century as a coach maker and, by the early years of the twentieth century, a manufacturer of car bodies to be married to imported rolling engine/chassis built by international manufacturers. The high tariff protection system in Australia set strict quotas for vehicle importers. These limitations provided the opportunity for the development of an Australian vehicle assembly and car body making industry in which CarCo became a major manufacturer. CarCo as a major carmaker in Australia formally came into existence in 1947 as a subsidiary of the US parent company and manufacturing ceased in late 2017. The chapter explores the development of employee voice patterns and practices over the 70 years of this leading manufacturer in Australia.

8.2 Stage One—Employee Voice in the Golden Years of Employment: 1947–1982

8.2.1 The Economic Landscape

The development of industrial policy in Australia has its origins in Federation in 1901 and the decision to develop 'protectionist' policies for Australia (Costa and Duffy 1991; Kelly 1992). Underpinning the arguments of the protectionists were policies to encourage and develop national economic growth through the defence of fledgling industries (particularly manufacturing), maintaining employment and the development of a balanced, high-wage and self-sufficient economy (Hagan 1981; Costa and Duffy 1991). As Anderson and Garnaut (1986) note 'Tariff protection for manufacturing was advocated as a way to increase the demand for labour' (p. 160). In the post-World War II period, tariff barriers were combined with import licenses to further restrict imports and entrench the 'New Protectionist' philosophy as central to Australian industrial development (Anderson and Garnaut 1986). These policy developments were in contrast to trends developing globally where trade negotiations focused on the reduction of tariff barriers, a process where Australia, through its protectionist philosophy, was clearly out of step.

However, during the post-war period of stable economic conditions and market expansion, these policies were well suited to the structure of the Australian economy (Capling and Galligan 1992). Had protectionism been removed once manufacturing had reached sustainable levels, these policies could have been seen as an integral step in the development of a strong industrial base. However, in the long term, industry (particularly manufacturing) became less competitive as the maintenance of this framework reduced the capacity of Australian industry to react to market conditions. This had the effect of insulating domestic industry from change and competitiveness (Costa and Duffy 1991; Belchamber 1993), while these policies artificially sustained the Australian economy; they left it ill-prepared for any change in economic conditions (Quiggin 1996).

An additional weakness which developed within the highly regulated protectionist system was that both management and trade unions pursued policies, strategies and goals based on a culture and background unimpeded by market force regulation. As Macfarlane (1986) noted

> Management retained a "product orientation" rather than a "market orientation". That is, they produced goods with the expectation - which became for some an entitlement - that they would have a market for those goods. Unions won terms and conditions which would not have been compatible with the more competitive environment, and governments were less inclined than they might have been to consider competitive needs (p. 9).

8.2.2 *Workplace Climate*

The employment relations climate within an organisation is used to describe the environment in which management and workers interact (Guest and Peccei 2001). The employment relations climate can include such things as bargaining structures, the history of employer/employee relations, the nature of competition within the marketplace that the organisation operates in, the current state of the labour market and the prevailing attitudes of employers and management to the employment relationship (Pyman et al. 2010; Drago et al. 1992). Alongside these are the external factors of national industrial relations policy and the broad national and international economic conditions that also impact on the overall performance of the organisation. Together these internal and external factors influence the impact that unions have on organisational productivity; however, the level of trust within an organisation can act to undermine any potentially positive effects of union voice. Belman (1992) argues that in organisations where there is low trust between workers and management

> …there will be little incentive for workers and managers to share information, workers will only produce under compulsion, and the rules of the worksite … will be used to assert or limit control rather than improve output (p. 46).

The industrial relations climate at CarCo in the post-World War II period was one in which trust between management and workers was very low. Levels of union membership were high (nationally union density was 64.9%), while the rate of employee turnover reflected the boom time conditions where workers could confidently expect to have their choice of employment opportunities. Investment in training and retention of skilled workers in Australian industry, in general, were low and the broad expectation was that general factory workers would not stay with the company very long. As one middle manager stated, CarCo had a 'labour turnover of about 45% a year in the 70s, and in the 80s training was seen as not necessary'.

In common with most of the developed western economies of the time, Australia was experiencing a period of growth driven by a population boom and demand for consumer goods. Cars produced by CarCo were in high demand and waiting lists for new cars were long. Early in CarCo's production, demand was so high that the sales managers could report 'that we had a waiting list of at least three years' (Bowden 1989). The emphasis at this time was on production quantity with quality relegated to an 'end of production line' check with many minor quality issues being left to the dealerships to resolve at the time of delivery to the customer.

By the 1990s, about 90% of the motor vehicle manufacturing sector was unionised, the largest membership being with the Australian Manufacturers Workers Union (AMWU) (vehicles division) (Industry Commission 1997). At the time of writing, other unions on site at CarCo included the Communications, Electrical, Electronic, Energy, Information, Postal, Plumbing and Allied Services Union (CEPU), the Australian Workers Union (AWU), the Association of Professional Engineers, Scientists and Managers Australia (APESMA), the National Union of Workers (NUW) and the Australian Municipal, Administrative, Clerical and Services Union (ASU).

Engagement with the workforce by management was through direct communication from management to the workforce through representative voice (trade unions) within the tight framework of industrial awards then existing. The nature of the industrial relations climate fostered an adversarial approach with regard to bargaining around wages and conditions—both of which were being driven well above levels associated with the prevailing economic conditions. Katz et al. (1983, 1985) note that in US organisations a low-trust employment relations climate, protracted negotiations over contracts and high grievance rates were associated with poor plant-level performance.

8.2.3 *The Structure of Voice*

In the immediate post-World War II period of economic growth, labour turnover amongst the assembly line workers was high and investment in employee training for other than the skilled trades was low. The unions representing the skilled trades (fitters, tool makers, electricians, etc.) were able to use their 'voice' to exert considerable pressure on management to ensure favourable wages and conditions during the post-war boom period as demand for skilled labour was high and supply was short

(Costa and Duffy 1991). However, the combination of tariff protection and high levels of unmet demand for motor vehicles and other manufactured goods allowed employers to take the path of least resistance by acceding to union demands and passing the higher costs of production on to consumers.

As a result of the ongoing protectionist structure, and high levels of trade union density, the dominant form of employee voice during this period was union voice, with some limited forms of direct voice for senior professional staff such as engineers. The nature of the relationship between organised labour and the management of CarCo was fiercely adversarial. Disputes quickly escalated beyond the shop floor, and resolution was typically undertaken in government industrial tribunals (State and Federal); the industrial tactic of using wildcat strikes to exert pressure on management was commonplace. The late 1980s saw a lowering in industrial disputes with a drop from 20 disputes to 2 per annum by 1994. From 1989 to 1994 there was a significant decline in the number of days lost to industrial disputes; falling to 36 working days lost per 1000 employees. 1995 marked a departure from this trend with 212 days per 1000 employee lost to industrial disputes, mostly due to a protracted dispute at the Toyota Altona factory in Victoria. Strong union voice at CarCo was sustained as a result of the de jure recognition of trade unions in the Australian industrial relations system and high levels of union density.

8.3 Stage Two—Employee Voice in an Era of Uncertainty: 1983–1996

8.3.1 The Economic Landscape

With the advent of the oil price shocks of the 1970s and the subsequent economic instability that came with them, the structural environment in Australia, both at a macro- and microeconomic level, was exceptionally vulnerable to the new 'post-Keynesian' economic environment. The new environment was characterised by economic instability, deregulation and increasing levels of international competition and stagflation.

The sustained period of protectionism underpinning the economic development of Australia during this period came at the cost of economic and industrial competitiveness (Costa and Duffy 1991). The work patterns and practices developed in Australia under this protectionist economic system were unsuited to the emergence of this post-Keynesian world economy (Gruen and Grattan 1993). What was required for Australia to compete internationally was a complete review and reform of the structures and systems which had characterised Australian industry policy since Federation in 1901 (Sloan 1993).

The Hawke and Keating Federal Labor Governments provided the catalyst for change with a series of extensive microeconomic reforms undertaken during its terms in office (1983–1996), which included more flexible work patterns and practices. The central aspect of these labour market reforms was the policy document named *Australia Reconstructed,* which provided a direction for the fundamental shift in the relationship between labour, capital and productivity in Australia. The focus of reform in the Australia Reconstructed agenda was in moving the emphasis of industrial relations bargaining from the industry-wide level to the enterprise level. Evans (1991) describes this fundamental shift in the relationship between management and labour as a 'New Workplace Culture'. At the centre of these microeconomic reforms was industrial relations (Morris 1996). The major focus was to lessen workplace regulation by industrial tribunals in favour of regulation by enterprise bargaining to focus on efficiency improvements at the 'plant level'. This was a fundamental shift from the policies of macroeconomic adjustment which had characterised the previous seven decades and brought about a fundamental shift in the employment and voice relationships.

8.3.2 Workplace Climate in this New Workplace Culture

8.3.2.1 The Context of Change

This new industrial relations climate was increasingly unfavourable for CarCo and Australian car manufacturing in general. Exchange rates were deregulated. Tariff protection for the industry was being reduced, inflationary pressures led to rapidly rising wages and all of this combined to see increasing import competition erode the market share of the domestic vehicle manufacturers including CarCo. Levels of unionisation in the automobile manufacturing sector remained high compared to the average national levels with around 90% of workers in the sector union members. The level of trust between employees and management also continued to be low; a senior shop steward described the relationship between management and the employees at the time as 'tense' with entrenched positions on both sides:

> … back then … we were never sure what management were up to and we saw every change [in the factory] as being intended to get rid of some of us or to get us to do more work for the same money. The way some of the New Australians [migrant workers] were being treated in particular was shitty … just because they didn't speak good English they were given the worst shifts on the worst jobs … the best way we could look after them was by going to the commission. We spent a lot of time in the commission back then.

Change at CarCo was seen by management as a survival imperative, quality and productivity had to rise if the company was to transition successfully into the new economic conditions and to compete more effectively with the rising Japanese vehicle manufacturers. A new approach was adopted by management at CarCo that was based on the experience of the US parent company in establishing union/management consultation on organisational change.

8.4 Change Born of Consultation Rather Than Confrontation

The management at CarCo described the development of consultative work practices and teams in terms of international competition and changing government policy which was in turn informed by union input in the context of the Accord. The reform of Australian automobile industry set in place by the federal government (known as the Button Plan) in the 1980s was cited by senior managers at CarCo as being a major stimulus for change, as was the associated pressure from international competition. As one senior manager stated:

> … [changing work practices] is part of our survival package, we nearly went out of business in '86, we nearly went bankrupt … we realised then that unless we [changed] we wouldn't survive as an organisation.

A senior union official who worked at CarCo during this period, and who was also part of the company organised overseas fact-finding mission, explained the tense nature of the employee/management relationship as being based on a lack of a willingness on the part of management to hear alternative points of view.

> The culture back in the 1970s and 1980s was one where you had no say as a production worker … where we could see where you could do things differently management wouldn't listen to that.

The relationship of hostility was also more focussed on the conflict between management and the unions than it was on the long-term survival of the business. As a senior union official put it:

> In the 1980s it's probable that the unions wouldn't have accepted [pay or productivity concessions to avoid layoffs] they would have dug their heels in and let the company fold. It was very adversarial back then, everything went to the commission – demarcation, wages, classifications, everything.

The union view of the prevailing culture at CarCo was that it was shaped by the adversarial processes inherent in the Australian industrial relations legislation and the lack of trust between management and the employees. Although it can be argued that the lack of trust was an outcome of the prevailing IR climate rather than an input to it. The senior union official's view was that the procedures mandated by awards and later agreements were taking practical decision-making out of the hands of managers. In his opinion, the legalistic and process-driven focus of constantly taking grievances and minor disputes to the Commission needed a circuit breaker:

> … we didn't trust them [management] and they didn't trust us [unions], it was not a happy time back then. Whatever management told us we didn't believe and they reckoned we were a lazy bunch who were just out for what we could get … every little issue was blown out of proportion and we took every issue to the commission…we were always fighting in the commission about something, but nothing was changing … so the company started working closer with the unions … management got better outcomes more quickly by cooperation with unions.

8.5 Consequences of Consultation

The change from an adversarial, low-trust employment relations climate to a cooperative, higher trust industrial relations climate did not happen quickly, rather it was built over time. However, the early productivity and quality gains surrounding the introduction of manufacturing teams and the establishment of a joint consultative committee were encouraging to both management and employees. Bryson et al. (2007) argue that in high-trust workplaces, where there is a high degree of joint decision-making between unions and management, productivity may be improved through creative integrative bargaining over issues such as technology change, training and upgrading worker skill levels.

Another significant national policy change that coincided with the evolution of employee voice at CarCo was the introduction of the federal government financial initiatives, such as the training guarantee scheme, to provide training which had an immediate effect, as one middle manager explained:

> … quality was top-down and something we inspected for not something we built in.…the support we got from the government to help with training made a big difference … we were looking at giving more quality training to the guys in the factory because we needed to get better at it [quality] if we were going to have any hope of staying competitive…a huge step forward for us…

The view from the production line echoes those of management. The dismissive attitude by management towards the experience and opinions of line workers was also changing to reflect the new status of a better trained and more stable and articulate workforce. As explained by a senior union official:

> …they were educating the unions as well with regard to continuous improvement, our survival [as a company], the next plan and so on … but we were also able to tell management about real issues [e.g. heat stress, water/drinks on the line, breaks, job rotation] as well as how we reckon the job could be done more efficiently.

This shift in training also impacted on productivity and quality, a middle manager stated that the attitude towards line workers changed from:

> … who cares [about training] they will be gone next week, why waste money. The quality of the vehicle in the 60's and 70's left a lot to be desired and then the Japanese came in and suddenly in the 80's quality was the byword [along with] flexibility … the investment in training and the lower rates of turnover were critical to making the changes work.

The unions also noted the changes in attitudes once the company embarked upon formal training and linking promotion and pay seniority to skills acquisition.

> … the company was more interested in keeping workers who they'd paid to get trained up rather than just saying 'there's always someone looking for a job, so why bother trying to keep anyone' … it made a big difference to quality.

These views expressed by CarCo managers and union representatives suggest that CarCo embarked upon a strategy for restructuring the productive system around greater consultation which was intended to meet the challenges of the new national policy environment and international competition. Changes to work practices were not introduced as part of an ideological agenda to move towards an individualised employment relations strategy but as a means of addressing competitive pressures. Rather than seeking to exclude unions, management at CarCo recognised the pivotal role unions have in the survival strategy. As stated by one senior manager:

> …the willingness of the unions to work with us on change was critical … it became fairly obvious not only to the management of [CarCo], but also to the unions that unless we worked in a fairly cooperative way … then we wouldn't survive as an organisation.

The experience of employees and managers at CarCo is consistent with the views expressed by Freeman and Medoff (1984) who argue that the key to unions having a positive impact on productivity is the relationship they have with management. Similarly, a cooperative employment relations climate has been consistently associated with improved employee outcomes and better economic performance (Holland et al. 2009). Loundes (1999) found that good employee/management relations have a positive impact on productivity. Angle and Perry (1986) also point out that a harmonious employment relations climate has been associated with both higher levels of organisational commitment and union loyalty. Organisations with a positive climate also tend to place a strong emphasis on effective communication channels with their employees and tend to avoid an aggressive management style (Webster and Loundes 2002). Pyman et al. (2010) found that where managers have a positive approach towards unions that employees were most likely to describe the employment relations climate as cooperative, and Deery and Walsh (1999) found this was also the case when employees felt their jobs were secure and they believed that they were treated fairly and justly. In similar studies of American manufacturing organisations, it was found that those with employee participation programs jointly administered by management and the union were positively associated with product quality improvements (Cooke 1992a). Cooke (1992b) also found that unionised companies achieved their goal of product quality improvement when union representatives were involved in the administration of participation programs, but not when union leaders were uninvolved. Overall, Cooke (1992b) stressed the importance of joint decision-making:

> …the labour-management climate is a key determinate of whether positive collective voice effects or negative restrictive union effects are dominant. Where the labour-management climate apparently precludes joint decision-making, management seems unable, on average, to tap the full potential of employment input (Cooke 1992b, p. 132).

Deery and Walsh (1999) also found that unions could be influential in improving organisational performance in their study that examined the relationship between the employment relations climate and organisational performance at a large Australian carmaker. The research indicated that employees were more motivated to help the organisation to become more efficient and productive where they believed there was a mutual trust in the relationship between management and the union, they viewed the work environment as fair and believed the union to be effective and influential in the workplace. Deery and Walsh argue that individuals who saw their union as effective in representing and advancing their interests in the workplace were more likely to judge the employment relations climate to be positive and these employees also demonstrated higher levels of commitment to the organisation and loyalty to the union. In addition, they found that employees who perceived their union to be an effective voice in workplace matters had significantly lower levels of absenteeism.

The Australian Workplace Employment Relations Survey (AWERPS) also found that employees' assessment of the industrial relations climate in unionised workplaces was more positive when management was perceived as having a favourable approach to unions (Pyman et al. 2010).

8.6 The Structure of Voice in the New Workplace Culture

The challenge of lowering tariffs and intensifying competition from low-cost and higher quality imported vehicles brought CarCo management to the realisation that the relationship with their workforce needed to change if the necessary improvements to productivity and product quality were to be achieved.

Adoption of team working arrangement, seen in action in the company organised overseas fact-finding mission, was initially raised during industrial relations agreement negotiations around the question of how to improve efficiency (productivity). The negotiations with unions gave rise to significant conflict over how much authority management would give to teams. The details of the introduction of teamwork arrangements proved more difficult, because of differences in the preferred model. Unions proposed a participative group work system, while management favoured a more traditional authoritative model of directed teams formed around specific production line activities. Following a protracted period of debate, the union's preferred approach was ultimately adopted and remained in place until closure. Lansbury et al. (2005) indicate that the union model of 'group-work' has endured as a successful endeavour, despite the difficulty of its initial implementation.

More direct employee voice at CarCo evolved from these earlier forms of employee participation, including the development of semi-autonomous workgroups. The teams at CarCo were formed around specific production line activities and physical location within the manufacturing facility, with teams being clustered around a significant stage of production. The quid pro quo for the unions to accept the change to voice through teamwork was for management to offer a more consultative approach to the management/union relationship. As part of the consultative process in the development of teams, management at CarCo organised a 'fact-finding' trip to the USA, Japan, UK and Europe manufacturing sites. Managers , line workers and union representatives were shown the various team working models within CarCo's US parent company as well at AsianCarCo (a Japanese joint venture partner of the same US parent as CarCo). The AsianCarCo joint venture in Australia gave CarCo access to the Japanese factories that were using the AsianCarCo variant of the Lean Manufacturing approach.

The exposure to international work practices led CarCo to establish a workplace-based consultative mechanism, a Joint Consultative Committee (JCC), which enabled the discussion of a broad array of workplace issues, while originally conceived as a mechanism for discussing and facilitating the introduction of changes to work practices, the establishment of the JCC marked a significant step forward in improving shop floor/management relations. The JCC was important in the development of participative work practices at CarCo and reflected a move to a hybrid type of voice system. The production systems and consultative processes seen at AsianCarCo and European manufacturers were also a strong influence on the change process and evolution of employee voice at CarCo. One middle manager saw the overseas trip as being a turning point in the adoption of team-based work patterns at CarCo:

> The unions at one stage were a bit of a stumbling block, but through the overseas trips and through to the formation stage when we were getting some agreements in place about workgroup leaders … [eventually] we got to an agreement and they [unions] were always very proactive, particularly the leadership of the union and a couple of the senior shop stewards who were extremely supportive.

The organisation of teamwork at CarCo was dictated to a large extent by the conventional production line layout of the plants. As such, a key aspect of the manufacturing teams at CarCo was to enhance communication (lateral voice) between teams and their members, in terms of both quality and productivity, and allow for the exercise of greater procedural flexibility within the team and within the factory (Lansbury et al. 2005). A critical aspect of the change to teamwork at CarCo was the explicit and formal involvement of the trade unions in the design and implementation of the new work arrangements. These new work arrangements gave rise to hybrid voice patterns and systems, where hybrid voice is characterised by the complementary presence of both management-initiated voice arrangements and union representation (Holland et al. 2011; Bryson et al. 2007). As Holland et al. (2009) found, empirical evidence of consultative mechanisms in Australia over the last decades associated with microeconomic reforms indicates this is a durable model of employee voice.

The evolution of employee voice in this period continued to follow a path of hybrid voice with a strong union presence, combined with team-based aspects of direct voice. Union voice at CarCo continued to provide employees with a mechanism through which workplace grievances and productivity suggestions could be channelled. This aligns with the view of Freeman and Medoff (1984) that '… unionism per se is neither a plus nor a minus to productivity. What matters is how unions and management interact in the workplace' (p. 179).

8.7 Stage Three—Employee Voice in the Time of the Global Market: 1996–2007

8.7.1 The Economic Landscape

The election of the Howard Liberal National Party coalition government in 1996 provided further impetus to the decentralisation of labour regulation and workplace reform. As Kramer et al. (1997) note with regard to the objectives of the *Workplace Relations Act (1996)* and the role of voice:

> The objects of the Act reflect the Coalition's wish to entrench the workplace as the focus for industrial relations and provide employers and employees with a choice over the form of agreement to rule in the workplace (p. 115).

The key aims and objectives of the Act include the following:

- a more direct relationship between employers and employees, with a much reduced role for third-party intervention;
- encouragement of international competitiveness through higher productivity and a flexible labour market;
- ensuring the primary responsibility for determining matters affecting the relationship between employers and employees rests with the employers and employees at the workplace or enterprise level (Clark 1997, pp. 31–32).

These changes were predicated on the philosophy that a more dynamic and competitive economic environment can best be enhanced by increasingly decentralising responsibility to the workplace, as it is the management and the workforce that understand the needs and constraints within an enterprise (Fox et al. 1995; Clark 1997). With the main thrust of these changes to shift responsibility for the substance of agreements firmly into the workplace, the need for a more participative voice system was firmly established.

8.7.2 Workplace Climate in a Global Market

The workplace at CarCo from the mid-1990s evolved significantly in relation to the climate of distrust and conflict in the post-war period. The economic policy settings were still placing significant pressure on the industry. However, CarCo had addressed the competitive pressures by responding with investments in equipment and increasing product quality through changing work organisation (teams) and rewarding formal workplace skills acquisition. Linking to the global strategy of their corporate head office in the USA, CarCo integrated engine production with the global supply chain, thus earning valuable export income as well as exporting fully built vehicles globally. The more collaborative culture at CarCo reflected the entrenchment of joint consultative committees, formal recognition of the unions as bargaining agents in enterprise agreements and a more enterprise-level approach to grievance resolution in the workplace.

8.7.3 Employee Voice in this New Global Market

In the articulation of individual grievance, complaints about unfair treatment to be resolved at the lowest organisational level and informally if possible. Consistent with this was the process described by one union senior shop steward as a 'quiet chat' between the shop steward and the frontline manager. Managers typically reported being able to have an informal discussion with shop stewards regarding individual workplace problems and issues, and similarly shop stewards said that they are able to have a 'quiet chat' with line and middle managers when they have an issue to discuss. The informal 'quiet chat' consultation with the line level union representative was consistently reported by management, senior union officials and senior shop stewards as being the desired first step of grievance resolution in contrast to the limited informal voice in the historically more regulated environment.

The expression of collective organisation at CarCo was via the representative trade unions on site and their role being formally recognised in Enterprise Agreements. Senior union members have said that CarCo honoured the spirit of recognising unions in collective bargaining rather than attempting to bypass the unions in favour of individual direct negotiations. Union voice at CarCo acted as a check and balance to management in that it has provided a mechanism for making sure the provisions in the enterprise agreement were followed and facilitating information flows between management and workers. This context continued to shape the nature of the union/management relationship.

The joint consultative committees were illustrative examples of the formal contribution representative collective voices made to management decision-making. CarCo engaged with employees in a variety of ways to solicit contributions to improving work practices, including quality improvement at the team level and suggestion schemes.

Drawing together these aspects of employee voice at CarCo shows that the evolution of systems of Hybrid Voice at CarCo gave rise to a culture of mutual interests being served by cooperative approaches to problem-solving and grievance resolution. Levels of industrial disputation steadily declined from the mid-1990s onwards and one senior HR manager reported that the majority of matters that eventually found their way to the industrial tribunal for formal resolution were to do with individual disputes over unfair dismissal. Larger, collective issues were in the main resolved through discussion and negation. However, one senior manager observed that 'we listen to the unions … but at the end of the day we run the business'.

Employee voice at CarCo includes; shop stewards meetings, senior shop stewards meetings, work area OH&S briefings/meetings, whole of plant OH&S briefings/meetings, union recognition for EBA negotiations and union officials present on consultative forums. Aspects of union instrumentality are, amongst other things, the formal recognition of union representation in collective bargaining and membership of joint consultative committees as well as regular union representative meetings at the workplace level. CarCo gives time to union shop stewards and senior shop stewards to attend regular meetings. The shop stewards and senior shop stewards meetings

Table 8.1 Current consultative forums at CarCo

Forum	Type	Who attends	Comments
Peak committee	Industrial	LS, SSS,[a] organisers, state secretary	Monthly, site focus, SPQRC (safety, people, quality, responsiveness, cost goals) and significant issues (plant committee reports into this)
Plant committee	Industrial	Local management, HRAs, SSS,[a] SS[b]	Monthly, plant focus, SPQRC (safety, people, quality, responsiveness, cost goals) and significant issues (reports into peak committee)
Senior shop stewards	Industrial	SSS, T&NT	Weekly, site focus, SPQRC (what's hot, what's not—temperature check)
SSS,[a] T&NT[c]			
Non-trades	Industrial training	Management reps, SSS, ED representatives	Monthly, site focus (plant training committee reports into this)
Steering committee NTSC			
Quarterly SSS	State of business	RP, JG, organisers, SSS	Quarterly
Organiser update			
Trades training	Industrial training	Management reps, SSS, ED representatives	Monthly site focus (plant training committee reports into this)
Steering committee TTSC			
Plant training committee PTC T&NT	Industrial training	Local management, HRAs, SSS, SS	Bimonthly, site focus (reports into NTSC and TTSC)
Plant shop stewards meeting PSSM T&NT	Industrial	Local management, SSS, SS	Weekly or fortnightly and ad hoc, focus on local issues, not in all plants
Shop stewards meeting SSS T&NT	Industrial union organisers attend	Shop stewards and senior shop stewards—trades	Fortnightly or monthly
		Shop stewards and senior shop stewards—non-trades	
OH&S	Industrial OH&S	JG, RP, organisers	Quarterly, site focus
Plant Safety Review Board PSRB	OH&S	RP, AW, MM, KP, OH&S plant reps, OH&S advisors, area managers	Monthly, site focus
Elected safety	Industrial OH&S	Elected safety reps, nominated union organiser and invited guests	Quarterly, site focussed—chaired by the elected safety representative
Representatives meeting SRM			

[a]Senior shop stewards. [b]Shop stewards. [c]Trades and non-trades (*Source* CarCo company document)

are not required to report to management about the items discussed in them, nor are they attended by management representatives.

Work area and whole of plant OH&S briefings/meetings (workplace health and safety, WHS, is referred to as occupational health and safety at CarCo) require that there is union representation. Workplace safety in the manufacturing setting at CarCo acknowledges that specific and unique hazards exist depending on the work area and the nature of the tasks undertaken in them. As is shown in Table 8.1, CarCo identifies the Plant Safety Review Board, OH&S committee and the Elected Safety Representatives Meeting as being 'industrial' meetings and formally endorses the participation of union representatives as standing members of the committees. Table 8.1 shows a summary of consultative committees at CarCo, who attends each forum and a summary of the types of matters that each committee addresses.

All CarCo enterprise agreements from the 1990s through to the 2015 agreement have included a stated preference of collective bargaining and explicitly nominated the union as formal representative for employees in negotiations. The enterprise agreements also contain formal provision for union meetings (shop stewards and senior shop stewards) as well as standing membership on joint consultative committees. Following the model of Dundon et al. (2004) employee voice at CarCo includes contributions to management decision-making via start of shift meetings, workgroup meetings and supervisor briefings, employees of the month schemes, HR communications, workplace of choice programs (organisational climate surveys) and social media. CarCo has start of shift meetings and supervisor briefings (called 'Talkies' by CarCo staff) for production areas which are focussed on production targets, processes and task allocation as well as workgroup meeting which are focussed more on the team. It is in the smaller workgroup meetings at CarCo that discussions about task allocation and problem-solving take place amongst the staff; however, the scope of these activities is still controlled and limited by 'sign-off' by the supervisor. Tasks are allocated by the supervisor and problem-solving suggestions are taken to the supervisor, not implemented independently.

8.8 Stage Four—Employee Voice During Organisational Close Down: 2007–2017

8.8.1 The Economic Landscape

The Global Financial Crisis (GFC) beginning in 2008 took parts of the world into recession. Australia, through a variety of federal government expenditure policies and the boom in demand for raw materials from China, was one of a small number of advanced market economies not to go into recession. However, the double-edged sword for CarCo was that it was now geared to a global market and the impact of the GFC resulted in a 12-month period of working only one 12 hour shift a day, down from a pre-GFC three shift operation. Reflecting the cooperative nature of the employment relationship, this was achieved with no industrial disputes and by employees taking a variety of leave entitlements to ensure no job was lost.

A key factor in CarCo's survival was the ongoing support and investment in Australian car making by the Federal Government. From the middle 1980s to the 2010s, all sides of Australian politics were producing budgetary policy to support the automotive industry, such as the Automotive Competitiveness and Investment Scheme, to provide an environment for building a sustainable, export-oriented car industry. However, in 2013, this commitment ended for large-scale car making in Australia, pre-empting the findings of an Australian Productivity Commission report.

As a result, between May 2013 and February 2014, the three major car makers in Australia announced the end of car manufacturing. The Australian Productivity Commission (2014) has argued that total manufacturing volumes and export volumes were too small, by global standards, to sustain the industry without the substantial and economically inefficient allocation of government subsidies.

8.8.2 Workplace Climate and Employee Voice at the End of the Line

The impact of the closure announcements on CarCo was widespread and deep. Reports from the managers, union officials and workers interviewed for this research have connected the overarching economic and political circumstances with the lived experience of individuals across the organisation and the new workplace climate. One shop steward told of the four members of one family who were all considering the option of taking a Voluntary Separation Package (VSP) but could not see where they would be able to find work after CarCo. They opted to 'hang on' in the hope that job prospects would improve, and they would still receive a redundancy payment when the factory closed. The relationship with line management seems to have found a new equilibrium. As one senior shop steward put it:

> The [closure] announcement has brought us [work force and management] closer, back to a level playing field … we're all about to lose our jobs.

When asked about employee involvement in committees and their participation in discussions in the workplace, the senior shop steward said that:

> … people who would have been on the sports and social club committee, canteen committee, even shop stewards and OH&S, people are more focussed on their own futures and don't have as much time for those sorts of things …

The view from the shop floor that this senior shop steward provides is a pragmatic analysis of why production output and quality remained consistent following the closure announcement.

> The people on the shop floor are just trying to do a good job, they're probably saying 'we're doing a good job now, let's keep doing it' – I don't think they are worried about being more engaged or anything

The view from the leadership of the union differed little from that from the shop floor. Speaking of the working relationship with management since the closure announcement one senior union official said that:

> … the [union/management] relationship is still strong … they don't open up as much as they used to … but the system is still in place … we can deal with things without [adversarial conflict] before it goes to the commission …

A senior union organiser shared a similar view:

> How are things going now that the factory is going to close? How is the relationship with management? It's still there, it's still working ... they may not see it as important, and we kind of remind them that it is.

From the management perspective, the people management metrics such as productivity, absenteeism and turnover all held steady at pre-closure announcement levels. This is considered as a point of pride for managers at CarCo, with two senior HR Managers both attributing the positive metrics to the culture of communication and participation within the organisation.

The closure was accepted by some managers in similar ways to the factory floor workers. There was an acceptance of the inevitability of change and the end of manufacturing production. When asked about the relationship between management and the workers that existed during this period, a senior HR manager said:

> ...we've learned a lot of lessons about how to get things done without banging heads, we'll probably keep doing what works – why wouldn't we?

The same manager was positive about the opportunities for workers to voice their opinions and make a contribution to productivity, but his views had sharp boundaries.

> ...we don't exactly sit around singing 'kumbaya' but we still talk to each other ... I like to keep the talking [limited] to in the meetings and at the morning [production briefings] ... I'm too busy to have people just pop up with a question at any time ... I'll listen to people I've got time for and that's not always the shop stewards ...I'm here to get a job done, not be a social worker ...

However, older managers viewed the future with less equanimity. Some managers have spent their working life with CarCo, moving from the shop floor through various layers of management to their current positions. Faced with the same choices of taking an early voluntary separation package or waiting until the final closedown, some managers are feeling a closer bond with the line workers. One manager said that:

> ... we're not 'us and them' anymore, we never were really, we're all in the same boat up shit creek together ...we probably talk to each other a lot more now and we probably see each other's point of view differently – maybe a bit better ... we still have our disagreements and we can still sort them out in-house.

It is worth noting that during this period of prolonged closure CarCo also conducted employee experience surveys and developed social media in the final year to a limited extent to reflect that even as the plant drew to a close voice was still evolving.

8.9 Conclusion

CarCo had over 70 years of history in the automobile manufacturing industry in Australia. It is clear that the evolution of the Australian economy, commensurate with workplace climate changes, was facilitating to a great measure by the evolution of employee voice. The adversarial culture was replaced over time by one that was characterised by cooperative trust-based hybrid management/union relations and direct voice through teams. The trade-off for the unions to accept teamwork arrangements was for management to offer a more consultative voice approach to the management/union relationship. The joint consultative committees matured into the main forum for discussion and debate.

Hybrid voice, participative work practices and the acceptance of increasingly flexible work agreements by the unions ensured the CarCO workplace culture was aligned with the productivity and quality goals necessary to be globally competitive. Hybrid voice at CarCo also brought with it a culture of mutual interests being served by cooperative approaches to problem-solving and grievance resolution. Steady declines in the levels of industrial disputes from the mid-1990s onwards point to the effectiveness of hybrid voice in dealing with workplace disputes and deflecting them away from formal resolution processes in favour of in-house resolution.

In the last decade of operations at CarCo, hybrid voice, and the mechanisms supporting it endured the stresses of the global economic shocks of the late 2000s and the decline in demand for exported components that accompanied them. Senior HR managers pointed to productivity figures, quality statistics and low rates of absenteeism as evidence of the consultative processes remaining effective even as the operations were winding down.

The case study of CarCo stands as an example of successful hybrid employee voice despite the decline and collapse of the industry within which it operated. The relentless tide of competition that beset the passenger vehicle manufacturing industry in Australia from the late 1970s shaped the environment within which employee voice proved to be a significant factor in the successful transition of the industry from being domestically focussed and protected to being globally competitive and export oriented. In the end, the economic conditions and government policy settings meant that the industry sector fell into decline and faltered rather than it being the fault of the individual organisations employee relations climate.

References

Anderson, K., & Garnaut, R. (1986). *The political economy of manufacturing protection: Experiences of ASEAN and Australia*. Sydney: Allen and Unwin.

Angle, H. L., & Perry, J. L. (1986). Dual commitment and labor-management relationship climates. *The Academy of Management Journal, 29*(1), 31–50.

Belchamber, G. (1993). *A decade of change: Australian trade unions and global free trade*. Melbourne: ACTU.

Belman, D. (1992). Unions, the quality of labour relations, and firm performance. *Journal of Political Economy, 15*(1), 44–60.

Bowden, T. (1989). *The way my father tells it*. Sydney: ABC Enterprises.

Bryson, A., Gomez, R., Kretschmer, T., & Willman, P. (2007). The diffusion of workplace voice and high commitment management practices in Britain, 1984–1998. *Industrial and Corporate Change, 16*(3), 395–426.

Capling, A., & Galligan, B. (1992). *Beyond the protective state: The political economy of Australia's manufacturing industry policy*. Cambridge: Cambridge University Press.
Clark, D. (1997). *Student economic brief*. Melbourne: AFR Books.
Cooke, W. (1992a). Improving productivity and quality through collaboration. *Industrial Relations, 20*(3), 128–150.
Cooke, W. (1992b). Product quality improvement through employee participation: The effects of unionization and joint union-management administration. *Industry and Labor Relations Review, 46*(1), 299–319.
Costa, M., & Duffy, M. (1991). *Labour, prosperity and the Nineties: Beyond the bonsai economy*. Leichardt NSW: The Federation Press.
Deery, S., & Walsh, J. (1999). The character of individualised employment relations in Australia: a model of "hard" HRM. In S. Deery & R. Mitchell (Eds.), *Employment relations: Individualisation and union exclusion*. Leichardt NSW: The Federation Press.
Drago, R., Wooden, M., & Sloan, J. (1992). Productive relations? Australian industrial relations and workplace performance. *Asia Pacific Journal of Human Resources, 32*(1), 1744–7941.
Dundon, T., Wilkinson, A., Marchington, M., & Ackers, P. (2004). The meanings and purpose of employee voice. *The International Journal of Human Resource Management, 15*(6), 149–1170.
Evans, R. (1991). Introduction. In Costa, M., Easson, M. (Eds.), Australian industry: What policy? (pp. 15–47). Pluto Press Sydney.
Fox, C., Howard, W., & Pittard, M. (1995). *Industrial relations in Australia: Development, law and operations*. Melbourne: Longman.
Freeman, R., & Medoff, J. (1984). *What do unions do?*. New York: Basic Books.
Gruen, F. H., & Grattan, M. (1993). *Managing government: Labours achievements and failures*. Melbourne: Longman-Cheshire.
Guest, D., & Peccei, R. (2001). Partnership at work: Mutuality and the balance of advantage. *British Journal of Industrial Relations, 39*(2), 1467–8543.
Hagan, J. (1981). The history of the A.C.T.U. Melbourne, VIC: Longman Cheshire.
Holland, P., Pyman, A., Cooper, B., & Teicher, J. (2009). The development of alternate voice mechanisms in Australia: The case of joint consultation. *Economics and Industrial Democracy, 30*(1), 67–92.
Holland, P., Pyman, A., Teicher, J., & Cooper, B. (2011). employee voice and job satisfaction in Australian: The centrality of direct voice. *Human Resource Management, 50*(1), 95–111.
Industry Commission. (1997). Report No. 58 The Automotive Industry, Volume II Appendices. AGPS, Canberra.
Katz, H. C., Kochan, T. A., & Gobeille, K. R. (1983). Industrial relations performance, economic performance, and QWL programs: An interplant analysis. *Industrial and Labor Relations Review, 37*(1), 3–17.
Katz, H. C., Kochan, T. A., & Weber, M. R. (1985). Assessing the effects of industrial relations systems and efforts to improve the quality of working life on organizational effectiveness. *Academy of Management Journal, 28*(3), 509–526.
Kelly, P. (1992). *The end of certainty: The story of the 1980s*. Sydney: Allen and Unwin.
Kramer, R., McGraw, P., & Schuler, R. S. (1997). *Human resource management in Australia*. South Melbourne: Addison Wesley Longman.
Lansbury, R. D., Wright, C., Baird. M. (2005). Decentralised bargaining in the Australian automotive assembly industry. In *Proceedings of the 2005 Australian Industrial Relations Association of Australia and New Zealand Conference*.
Loundes, J. (1999). Labour productivity in Australian workplaces: Evidence from the AWIRS. The University of Melbourne, Melbourne Institute Working Paper 19/99.
Macfarlane, R. (1986 April). Business Council of Australia Bulletin.
Morris, R. (1996). The age workplace reform in Australia. In D. Mortimer, P. Leece, & R. Morris (Eds.), *Workplace reform and enterprise bargaining: Issues, cases, trends* (pp. 11–24). Sydney: Harcourt-Brace.

Productivity Commission. (2014). Australia's automotive manufacturing industry: Productivity commission inquiry report, Report No. 70 AusInfo: Canberra.
Pyman, A., Holland, P., Teicher, J., & Cooper, B. (2010). Industrial relations climate, employee voice and managerial attitudes to unions: An Australian study. *British Journal of Industrial Relations, 48*(2), 460–480.
Quiggin, J. (1996). *Great expectations, microeconomic reform and Australia*. Sydney: Allen and Unwin.
Sloan, J. (1993). Wage fixing under Accord Mark VII and the role of national wage principles. *Australian Bulletin of Labour, 19*(3), 218–240.
Webster, E., & Loundes, J. (2002). Factors affecting the industrial relations climate in Australian Enterprises. Melbourne, VIC: Melbourne Institute of Applied Economic and Social Research, University of Melbourne.

Dr. Alan McWilliams is a Senior Lecturer at Victoria University Melbourne, his research interests are in the field of employee voice.

Prof. Peter Holland is Professor of Human Resource Management and Director of the Executive MBA at Swinburne University of Technology, Melbourne, Australia. He has worked in the Australian finance sector and consulted to the private and public sector in a variety areas related to human resource management and employee relations. His current research interests include employee voice, workplace electronic monitoring and surveillance, and talent management.

Dr. Rob Hecker is an adjunct with the Tasmanian School of Business & Economics at the University of Tasmania. After long careers in business and academia, primarily teaching in organisational behaviour, his research interests continue in the areas of employee voice and extreme work.

Chapter 9
Finding Their Voice: Call Centre Employees in a Continuous Service Delivery Context

John Burgess, Julia Connell and Anthony McDonnell

Abstract Much has been written about call centres but not from the perspective of employee voice in an organisational context where work is highly individualised and the work pace is intensive and underpinned by 'churn and burn' HR. The issue is most usefully studied by examining the nature and extent of employee voice in both onshore and offshore contexts.

Keywords Call centres · Churn and burn HR · Employee voice

9.1 Introduction

Call centres have evolved and developed as a consequence of the ICT revolution. Customer-based service delivery has been removed from retail locations to customised locations where specialist operatives are able to link up with customers from around the world. Technology has supported the separation of the consumer and service provider resulting in the development of specialist call centres that service a range of corporate and government clients (Sako 2007). These changes have, in turn, enabled the process of outsourcing and offshoring. Services that were previously provided in-house by employees are now provided at remote locations, by specialist outsourced providers. Multiple call centre hubs can be found in India and the Philippines among other countries (Taylor and Bain 2005). In essence, services that were once provided in person, at a set location and at set times are now provided remotely on a continuous basis. There is also the potential for the complete removal

J. Burgess (✉)
Melbourne, Australia
e-mail: john.burgess@rmit.edu.au

J. Connell
Newcastle, Australia

A. McDonnell
University College Cork, Cork, Ireland
e-mail: anthony.mcdonnell@ucc.ie

P. Holland et al. (eds.), *Employee Voice at Work*, Work, Organization, and Employment, https://doi.org/10.1007/978-981-13-2820-6_9

of service workers and human contact with automated response systems where consumers key numbers into a computer or cell phone to access the services they require (Russell 2008). More recently, we have seen much discussion on the rise of robots and the potential they have to displace a range of jobs into the future (e.g. Ford 2015; Graetz and Michaels 2015).

For call centre, employees work is generally monitored, scripted and subject to forms of close supervisor control. Research has found that call centre work is highly demanding with few opportunities for participation and employee control (Zapf et al. 2003). With extensive pressure to meet performance targets, it is not surprising that call centre work has been found to be associated with poor health and well-being (Holman 2002) and employee burnout (Castanheira and Chambel 2010). Relatedly, the conditions of employment and the nature of the industry do not facilitate formal and indirect voice through collective arrangements. Call centres are individualised, automated work environments and generally located at greenfield sites with employees on contracts who are generally not union members (Korczynski 2001; Russell 2008). In this context, we would expect to find that direct voice predominates, driven by HRM systems that provide voice mechanisms such as staff surveys and suggestion boxes for staff to pass on suggestions and grievances (McDonnell et al. 2014). However, in the call centre environment, research has highlighted the importance of teams as an organisational and motivational process (Kinnie et al. 2000; Hannif et al. 2013). Teams also appear to operate as a quasi-form of collective voice with the team leader having a prominent role in employee attitudes towards their level of voice (McDonnell et al. 2013).

In this chapter, we draw upon studies of voice in call centres that have been conducted in Australia (McDonnell et al. 2014) and the UK (Golan 2004) in order to examine forms of voice mechanisms used and the outcomes emerging in the ICT-driven continuous service delivery context.

9.2 Employee Voice and Call Centres

Definitions and practices related to employee voice include employee participation, involvement, engagement, consultation and empowerment. Employee voice is conceptualised broadly with different meanings being applied across the literature (Dundon et al. 2004; Budd et al. 2010). In spite of the variety of definitions across multiple disciplines (from industrial relations to organisation behaviour), there is consensus that 'voice' is often an inherent element of the employment relationship. Lavelle et al. (2010) define voice as, 'any type of mechanism, structure or practice, which provides for an employee with the opportunity to express an opinion or participate in decision-making within their organisation' (p. 396). Similarly, Wilkinson and Fay (2011, p. 66) propose that employee voice is best viewed as providing staff with 'a say' overwork activities and refer to both direct (for example, meetings between managers and workers) and indirect mechanisms through, for example trade unions. Direct voice channels concern individual staff or groups of employees, being directly involved in workplace decision-making, whereas indirect mechanisms involve 'impacting' establishment level decisions via employee representatives. There is, however, scepticism about the extent to which 'true' influence or voice does occur from direct channels. Consequently, the notion of employee voice, especially through direct mechanisms, has been criticised as being a management-led process where appearance and process, as opposed to effective engagement, dominate the various mechanisms (Strauss 2006). Scholars have argued that the reality of employee voice often falls short of the rhetoric and non-union, direct forms tend to come in for sharp criticism with respect to this (e.g. Donaghey et al. 2012). Direct voice channels are typically central elements to high performance or high commitment work systems which have faced criticism in the call centre context for being more focused on 'distracting employees' attention away from the stultifying effects of an otherwise low discretion environment' (Fleming and Sturdy 2011).

However, there are some questions remaining. For example, is it the voice mechanism itself or the effectiveness of voice that is important? Or is it the appearance that voice counts that really matters? Tangirala and Ramanujam (2008) point out that notions of personal control are perceptual. Allen et al. (2015) argue that employees' perceptions of their work environment can play a key role in relation to how comfortable they feel expressing their voice without fear of negative treatment. Consequently, they are much more likely to communicate their thoughts and ideas when they consider their managers to be open and fair. Voice can be an important form of participation and influence in the workplace (Van Dyne et al. 1995), so when employees perceive they have low personal control, they may be motivated to engage in change-oriented behaviours aimed at improving their situation. Tangirala and Ramanujam (2008) cite a number of studies which indicate that when employees perceive that they have control it is associated with increased job satisfaction, reduced stress, dissonance and improved job performance.

Wilkinson and Fay (2011) outline four schools of thought in the voice literature which are outlined in Table 9.1. We suggest that there is a fifth form of voice, which is resistance since in the context of call centres, the literature suggests that employees may react to extensive control and having limited or no voice through committing acts of sabotage (van der Broek 2002). The first form of voice outlined in the HRM-performance literature concerns informing and involving employees in the workplace and organisational decision-making with the expectation that this can help improve decisions, and facilitate commitment (Wilkinson et al. 2004). The mechanisms of this process include newsletters and suggestion schemes. The process is managerially led and is linked to strategic HRM, that is, improving employee and organisational performance. Although critics suggest that this represents employee voice without authority (Kaufman and Taras 2010).

Second, voice is referred to as a mechanism of industrial democracy where employees have input and participation over organisational decision-making (Huiskamp 1995). In this case, voice is associated with formal representation and participation in decision-making, usually supported by legislation. Processes linked to industrial democracy include works councils and joint consultative committees

Table 9.1 Forms of voice

Forms of voice	Key components	Relevant literature
HRM-performance literature	Informing and involving employees in decision-making—intended to elicit employee commitment	Wilkinson et al. (2004), Wilkinson and Fay (2011)
	Can include newsletters, managerially led—employee voice without authority	Kaufman and Taras (2010)
Industrial democracy	Input and participation associated with formal representation—usually supported by legislation	Huiskamp (1995)
	Can involve works councils/joint consultative committees	Knudsen and Markey (2001)
Collective representation	As a mechanism/channel for employee protection and communication with management	Freeman and Medoff (1984)
Organisational behaviour	Teamwork, particularly self-managed can support high-performance work systems	Wilkinson and Fay (2011)
	Teams may not actually work as teams in call centres however	Van den Broek (2004), Townsend (2004)

(Knudsen and Markey 2001). This model is pertinent to the analysis of voice in the UK call centre researched by Gollan (2003) and reported in this chapter.

Third, from an industrial relations context, indirect voice through collective representation provides a mechanism for employees to 'have a say' (Freeman and Medoff 1984). Through voice, employees can present grievances through collective representation and engage with management over workplace challenges. If voice mechanisms are effective, then reportedly employee engagement improves and employee turnover declines. Union voice mechanisms were created to protect individuals and provide a formal channel of communication with managers.

Fourth, from an organisational behaviour perspective, the use of teams, especially self-managed teams, is said to increase autonomy and provide a source of influence for employees over a range of workplace activities—such as training and the intensity of work. As pointed out by Hannif et al. (2013, p. 129) 'in the absence of trade unions, the team leader represents a source of employee voice'. Specifically, their study indicated that issues could be raised with team leaders who would raise them with the call centre manager and team leaders also worked together with other team leaders to 'bring any issues to the forefront' (Hannif et al. 2013, p. 129). Using this lens, the teams are part of the process of improving workplace performance and are linked to high-performance work systems (Wilkinson and Fay 2011). Teamwork and coordination through teams is widespread in call centres, but whether these teams constitute effective forms of participation, or are just teams in name only, has been questioned in the literature (van den Broek et al. 2004; Townsend 2004). For example they may be referred to as a team only because they report to the same person rather than needing other team members to accomplish their work.

In terms of the call centre context, collective voice through union representation and formal industrial participation mechanisms applies to a minority of workplaces. Given the outsourced, offshore, greenfield site locations and contingent work arrangements (contract work) prevalent for call centres, there are some major challenges in organising union membership. Voice in call centres generally consists of formal arrangements coordinated by HRM departments—including employee surveys and newsletters; communication through teams; and in the absence of any formal or effective voice mechanisms, forms of resistance and disobedience. The literature suggests that call centre employees are concurrently utilising a number of voice channels, excluding collective representation through unions and employee consultative groups (Hannif et al. 2013; Wilkinson and Fay 2011).

9.3 Voice in Australian Call Centres

Although employee voice is an established area of enquiry, Gollan (2003), McDonnell et al. (2014) and Russell (2008) suggest that there has been a paucity of research in the call centre context to date. McDonnell et al. (2014) examined voice mechanisms in Australian call centres using a mixed-method approach that included focus groups of call centre operatives located in 10 call centres as well as a survey of 354 operatives across the 10 call centres. The selected call centres were confined to the south-east coast of Australia and included stand-alone centres which were mainly small call centres (with fewer than 20 operatives) and large call centres (comprising over 100 operatives) with centres in a number of locations. Only 3 of the 10 sites were unionised. The study found that a range of mechanisms appeared to be utilised in providing employees with information on workplace activities and some level of voice in relation to workplace change. Such direct and indirect mechanisms are often utilised by organisations and tended to vary as to whether they are more a communicative/information mechanism rather than a means of providing employees with a real 'voice' over workplace change. In the three unionised workplaces, there was still a reliance on direct voice mechanisms such as quality circles/problem-solving groups and self-directed team working. Across the call centres team-directed activities, including forms of socialisation (Kinnie et al. 2000), were common and were intended to develop team member identity, rivalry between teams around performance and improve the overall performance.

The most commonly reported voice channel within the unionised workplaces, and the remaining six call centres, was direct voice achieved through the team leaders. Over 80% of survey respondents reported that their team leader was the key contact for consultation concerning workplace changes that had occurred in the previous 12 months. The survey findings and focus group results re-affirmed that team leaders were the main conduit for information and grievance resolution. Team leaders were recognised as 'the first port of call' and hence acted as both a form of voice and a conduit between operatives and managers. Clearly, in this role, there is a division in responsibilities, identity and commitment of team leaders—as agents of management and as agents of employee voice. The literature also highlights the key role of team leaders in disseminating HR policy and in affecting employee behaviours and attitudes (Purcell and Hutchinson 2007; McDonnell et al. 2013).

Focus group participants indicated that it was through direct dealings with their respective team leader that most employees considered that they 'had a voice'. The extent to which such mechanisms provide a voice, and the extent to which employees were satisfied with this, and the work environment was also of interest. The qualitative data indicated that there appeared to be widespread satisfaction across all call centres with regard to the opportunities provided to raise concerns and have some influence over workplace decisions. In terms of the typology across the call centres, the voice mechanisms were in accord with HR-directed processes with team leaders and line managers performing a central and crucial function in the process.

In the three unionised call centres, there appeared to be a negative view towards the role of unions in the call centres. It was reported that when issues had arisen, there was little union involvement with call centre employees reporting that the company came to arrangements directly with staff. Across the call centres, there was some acknowledgement of the utility of trade unions; however, this was considered more a form of protection against disciplinary action, dismissal and loss of conditions. However, it was clear that when it came to workplace change and as active agents of employee voice, unions were viewed as having a limited influence.

In this study, the use of direct individual employee voice (the first voice mechanism outlined in Table 9.1) was found to be the most pervasive intervention used in the call centres according to the survey respondents. Employees referred to multiple channels being utilised in their workplace for the purposes of information provision and consultation. Overall, there was supporting evidence for the use of a hybrid system of voice, consisting of a variety of mechanisms whereby employees received information and could contribute to some workplace decisions (Bryson et al. 2010). This was evident in both the unionised and non-unionised call centres. Even in the unionised environments, direct voice channels dominated as the forums for discussing/influencing workplace change and employees were reportedly happy with this situation.

The results of this study align with the first and fourth strands of the employee voice literature summarised by Wilkinson and Fay (2011). The findings imply that the greater the number of voice mechanisms, the more likely that an employee will perceive having their influence on work issues. There is little to suggest that a particularly strong voice was present in any of the call centres with regard to higher order decisions or when it came to actually influencing decision-making. However, it was apparent that the call centre operatives perceived opportunities to express their voice and they saw this as occurring largely through team leaders.

McDonnell et al.'s (2014) study emphasised that the role of the team leader is critically important regarding an employee's perception of their level of voice. In the focus groups, it emerged that employees were confident of their ability to talk to their team leader on an informal basis, perceiving their line manager took issues raised seriously and brought them to the attention of higher levels of management. The importance of team leaders as an informal voice mechanism was also apparent in the large call centres given that the senior managers were remotely located from the call centre environment. Thus, team leaders represented the 'voice' of the team to senior management, and in a sense, they were both agents for management and conduits for employees voice channels to management (Frenkel et al. 2005).

A potential explanation behind the lack of interest in union representation and perceived satisfaction in direct voice channels was the apparent high levels of trust between the call centre operatives and management. Their positive attitude towards management was commonplace across almost all call centres in the study, with the view being that management looked after employee interests, and were open regarding decisions that were taken which affected employees. When there was dissatisfaction with any workplace issue, employees indicated that they could approach their team leader and, if necessary, a higher level manager for consultation. These findings also support Waring's (1999) suggestion that direct communication between management and employees can improve trust and cooperation in the workplace.

There was no evidence of resistance and disobedience being present in the call centre case studies. This is not to say that it was not present, as it is difficult through formal research processes, such as surveys and focus groups, to obtain admission that such practices had taken place. Likewise, the nature of the study excluded exit behaviour. In an industry characterised by stress, burnout and relatively high turnover, it is difficult to identify the reasons for exit and to what extent that limited voice or ineffective voice was potentially one of these reasons.

Overall, the findings suggest that employees were predominantly informed or consulted on lower level workplace issues. For example, the need to change the script used in customer engagements was mentioned in a number of focus groups as well as improving the efficiency of workstations. Consequently, it can be argued that management may only really be interested in employee consultation where they perceive there is likely to be a positive 'pay-off'. This supports the contention of Freeman et al. (2007) that the more management initiates forms of voice, associated with primarily serving organisational goals, the more they meet the desire of employees with respect to being involved in decisions that directly impact on them.

Pyman et al. (2006) argued that the presence of multiple voice mechanisms was perceived by call centre operatives as evidence that their voice has legitimacy within the workplace. In turn, this has resonance with Benson and Brown's (2010) proposal that the existence of voice mechanisms were significantly less important than how employees perceive their level of voice.

9.4 Voice in a UK Call Centre

There are few studies of voice in call centres. One reason is that call centres are a recent phenomenon. Another is that call centres are often located on greenfield sites that were non-unionised. One study that explicitly investigated voice in a call centre context was by Gollan (2003) who presented findings on voice research from a single case study of a UK call centre. His study concerned the Eurotunnel, a joint UK/French private company responsible for the cross tunnel traffic and services. Eurotunnel has a 50 year lease on the operations of the tunnel that connects the UK and France. It is a joint UK–French entity and has a call centre operation based in Folkestone, UK. The call centre employed multinational staff representing the main European language groups using the Eurotunnel services—English, French, Dutch and German. Approximately, 150 staff was employed in the call centre which operates 7 days per week on a team basis with limited hours in the evening. Around 80% of staff was employed on a full-time basis. Compared to the other parts of the organisation, the call centre staff were more feminised and had, on average, much shorter job tenure in the current job.

The context of the call centre is unusual, and very different from the call centres reported in the Australian study. First, it was an in-house call centre. Second, the call centre, though not unionised, operated in a larger organisation that was unionised. Third, the organisation had a formally constituted process of workplace representation and participation that resembled industrial democracy.

The UK operations have a formal council with elected employee representatives which operates as the formal mechanism for employee voice in decision-making. The council has three functions: to represent the views of employees, to manage a social and welfare fund that constitutes around one per cent of payroll and to represent employees in bargaining. Under the constitution of the council, it deals with all matters of interest to employees—including shifts, terms of employment, workplace change, financial and performance data (Gollan 2003, p. 519). The call centre workforce was non-unionised, while in the other sections of the company, the workforce was unionised. The employee council represents a form of industrial democracy to represent employee voice. The council members were elected by employees for a 2-year term and they perform quasi-trade union agency functions in negotiating over-pay and conditions. This is a form of 'soft' industrial democracy to the extent that there was no requirement that employee views had to be considered in developing and implementing the workplace policy and programmes.

Gollan's (2003) study involved the use of documentary analysis, a survey, observation and focus groups. The purpose was to assess the effectiveness of formal partnership arrangements in representing employee voice. His work largely refers to the survey findings and differences between the call centre (non-unionised) workforce and other employees in the organisation (largely unionised). The findings are summarised below according to the major issues addressed in the survey:

Information and consultation—60% of call centre (CC) staff indicated that they were not informed or not well informed about workplace issues; this was close to the 58% reported by other staff. In terms of the workplace issues that they regarded as being very important, compared to other staff, CC staff, stressed job security and relations with line managers, but were not as concerned as other workers about OH&S issues (p. 524).

Consultation methods—CC workers found that notice boards, word of mouth and meetings with council representatives and line managers were the most effective forms of communication (p. 524).

Information supplied—around 75% of CC respondents were dissatisfied with the amount, type and timing of information provided by management (similar results were reported for other staff) (p. 525). On specific issues such as pay, staffing and work practices, CC employees suggested that compared to other Eurotunnel workers, they received little or no information (p. 526).

Consultation with workplace representatives—only 10% of CC workers had regular contact with their council representative (compared to 30% of other workers) (p. 527).

Representation and trade union influence—on a range of issues, all employees (including CC workers) indicated that a trade union would be more effective than the council or individual representation (p. 529). Workers also believed that trade unions would better represent their interests with respect to pay, job security and grievances—only with regard to training did they believe that trade unions would be less effective (p. 532).

Gollan (2003, p. 537) suggested that 'there is widespread dissatisfaction with management, especially their lack of understanding and willingness to make decisions and consider employee concerns' and that the CC staff, in particular, felt that the council had failed 'to fulfil its requirements to represent the interests of employees.' The findings are noteworthy since they provide an example of a formally constituted consultative mechanism that applies across the workforce. In this case, the collective form of voice was found in a non-unionised call centre. The research found widespread dissatisfaction regarding the effectiveness of the council in terms of communication and its overall effectiveness in influencing decision-making within the organisation. It was interesting that employees perceived that trade unions, even in the non-unionised call centres would be more effective than the council in representing and achieving outcomes that were compatible with the interest of employees. Yet, at the same time, the use of direct voice mechanisms was regarded as being important.

9.5 Discussion

The two empirical studies reported here provide examples of the different configurations of voice arrangements that are present in call centres. There are clear contrasts between the UK case study and the Australian findings. In the Australian cases, there was reliance on direct voice mechanisms supporting a strategic HRM approach to supporting and managing voice. The presence of teams in call centres supported the high-performance work system (HPWS) approach, but whether teams in a controlled and monitored workplace context constitute teams in the sense of having autonomy and decision-making powers is debateable (van den Broek et al. 2004). Teams were also associated with forms of socialisation and performance enhancement through contests and games (Kinnie et al. 2000). In the Australian call centre study, the immediate supervisor was regarded as the most effective conduit for employee concerns. This applied for both unionised and non-unionised call centres. This highlights the importance of the line manager within the organisation, both in terms of managing employees and facilitating employee voice (Purcell and Hutchinson 2007). Whether the voice mechanisms were effective in terms of influencing organisational decision-making could not be established, however, but as Allen et al (2015) suggest, it is the perception of voice that counts, not the effectiveness of voice.

The UK call centre study context was unique as it portrays a non-unionised call centre operating within a formalised organisation consultation model. This is along the lines suggested by the industrial democracy approach to voice. The company council was constituted to represent the voice and concerns for all employees across different industries and occupations, both unionised and non-unionised. However, as Gollan (2003) indicated, call centre employees reported widespread dissatisfaction with the quality of the information sharing and consultation process, and with the effectiveness of the council in negotiating with management across a range of issues. In this case, employees, unionised and non-unionised, call centres and other employees suggested that trade unions were likely to be more effective in terms of representation and negotiation.

If we consider the Eurotunnel example as a unique case, the Australian evidence suggests that in call centres, direct voice mechanisms are likely to be prevalent given the low rates of unionisation and the prevalence of greenfield locations and contingent employment arrangements. Employee perceptions of the availability of voice mechanisms does matter (Allen et al. 2015; Tangirala and Ramanujam 2008). However, trust and rapport with line managers, as demonstrated in the Australian case studies, is also a crucial factor in supporting employees' perceptions of the availability of voice mechanisms and associated effectiveness. Teams are another mechanism that helps to develop trust and allow for the collective representation of voice through the team leader/line manager conduit (McDonnell et al. 2013). Ironically, both studies indicated that, even in the unionised Australian call centres, direct voice mechanisms were regarded as being more effective than voice mechanisms available through the unions. In the non-unionised UK call centre with a formalised employee council, indirect voice through trade unions was regarded as the preferred, or more effective, voice mechanism.

This chapter highlights that there are still some areas of research that warrant further investigation. For example, there was an absence of any examination of resistance and misbehaviour as a form of (protest) voice (van der Broek 2002). Although this is an issue that is difficult to research, it is a mechanism that we would expect to find where employees lack effective voice and do not see any formal voice mechanism as being available. Arguably, the extent to which such a protest of voice existed would also be impacted by the nature of the immediate external labour market.

Another area for further research is the examination of the effectiveness of voice mechanisms, namely whether the views of employees are transmitted to those who make decisions, and whether those decisions incorporate suggestions obtained through employee engagement (Doellgast 2010). In the case of the UK case study, even though a formalised voice process was available through the employee council, call centre workers regarded the communication process as inadequate and the council was considered ineffective in influencing organisational decisions.

A final observation regarding the industry and national context is that both technological change and outsourcing are now so extensive that the consolidation of professional services from medical to logistical services means that specialist call centres embody professional employment and highly skilled workers performing critical tasks (Mueller et al. 2008) where voice expectations may be higher. The call centres reported here were largely linked to routine customer service delivery such as billing and inquiries. The technology and outsourcing model means that call centres are not confined to purely routine and standard procedures, but also involve non-routine and professional service delivery, where workers have autonomy and discretion, and in turn have the potential for voice through their professional status and critical functions in organisations. They also have access to voice mechanisms through quasi-union processes such as professional associations (Russell 2008). The Anglo-Saxon context of both studies has established institutions around bargaining and employment conditions. There are clear differences with the institutional arrangements, especially around formal voice, in a European context (Doellgast 2010 and chapter x) and in the emerging call centre industry in offshore locations such as India (Taylor and Bain 2005) which may also warrant further investigation. The institutional context is likely to have a significant impact on employee voice, well-being and satisfaction with countries characterised by very limited employment protection arguably. Organisations in such contexts may well be more able to exercise greater managerial prerogative and control over the employment relations and the terms and conditions of employment workers face. Consequently, voice channels may be particularly limited.

References

Allen, J. A., Yoerger, M. A., Lehmann-Willenbrock, N., & Jones, J. (2015). Would you please stop that!? The relationship between counterproductive meeting behaviors, employee voice, and trust. *Journal of Management Development, 34*(10), 1272–1287.

Benson, J., & Brown, M. (2010). Employee voice: Does union membership matter? *Human Resource Management Journal, 20,* 80–99.

Bryson, A., Gomez, X., & Willman, P. (2010). Voice in the wilderness: The shift from union to non-union voice in Britain. In A. Wilkinson, P. Gollan, M. Marchington, & D. Lewin (Eds.), *The Oxford handbook of participation in organizations*. Oxford: Oxford University Press.

Budd, J. W., Gollan, P. J., & Wilkinson, A. (2010). New approaches to employee voice and participation in organizations. *Human Relations, 63,* 303–310.

Castanheira, F., & Chambel, M. J. (2010). Reducing burnout in call centers through HR practices. *Human Resource Management, 49,* 1047–1065.

Doellgast, V. (2010). Collective voice under decentralized bargaining: A comparative study of work reorganization in US and German call centres. *British Journal of Industrial Relations, 48*(2), 375–399.

Donaghey, J., Cullinane, N., Dundon, T., & Dobbins, T. (2012). Non-union employee representation, union avoidance and the managerial agenda. *Economic and Industrial Democracy, 33,* 163–183.

Dundon, T., Wilkinson, A., Marchington, M., & Ackers, P. (2004). The meanings and purposes of employee voice. *International Journal of Human Resource Management, 15,* 1149–1170.

Fleming, P., & Sturdy, A. (2011). 'Being yourself' in the electronic sweatshop: New forms of normative control. *Human Relations, 64,* 177–200.

Ford, M. R. (2015). *The rise of the robots: Technology and the threat of a jobless future*. Philadelphia: Basic Books.

Freeman, R. B., Boxall, P., & Haynes, P. (2007). *What workers say: Employee voice in the Anglo-American world*. Ithaca, NY: Cornell University Press.

Freeman, R., & Medoff, J. (1984). *What do unions do?*. New York: Basic Books.

Frenkel, S. J., Orlitzky, M., & Wallace, C. M. (2005). Accounting for absence from work in Australian call centres: Re-enter human relations theory? In *International Human Resource Conference Proceedings*, Limerick, Ireland, June.

Gollan, P. (2003). All talk but no voice: Employee voice at the Eurotunnel call centre. *Economic and Industrial Democracy, 24,* 509–541.

Graetz, G., & Michaels, G. (2015). Robots at work. CEPR Discussion Paper No. DP10477 Available at SSRN. Retrieved from January 13, 2017, from http://ssrn.com/abstract.

Hannif, Z., McDonnell, A., Connell, J., & Burgess, J. (2013). Teams in call centres: Does size make a difference? *Labour & Industry: A Journal of the Social and Economic Relations of Work, 23*(2), 121–136.

Holman, D. (2002). Employee wellbeing in call centres. *Human Resource Management Journal, 12,* 35–50.

Huiskamp, R. (1995). Regulating the employment relationship: An analytical framework. In J. van Ruysseveldt (Ed.), *Comparative and employment relations* (pp. 16–36). London: Sage.

Kaufman, B., & Taras, D. (2010). Employee participation through non-union forms of employee representation. In A. Wilkinson, P. Gollan, M. Marchington, & D. Lewin (Eds.), *The Oxford handbook of participation in organizations*. Oxford: Oxford University Press.

Kinnie, N., Hutchinson, S., & Purcell, J. (2000). Fun and surveillance: The paradox of high commitment management in call centres. *International Journal of Human Resources Management, 11*(5), 967–985.

Knudsen, H., & Markey, R. (2001). *Works councils: Lessons from Europe for Australia*. Department of Economics: University of Wollongong.

Korczynski, M. (2001). The contradictions of service work: Call centres as a customer-oriented bureaucracy. In A. Sturdy, I. Grugulis, & H. Wilmott (Eds.), *Customer service: Empowerment and entrapment*. Hampshire: Palgrave.

Lavelle, J., Gunnigle, P., & McDonnell, A. (2010). Patterning employee voice in multinational companies. *Human Relations, 63,* 395–418.

McDonnell, A., Connell, J., Burgess, J., & Hannif, Z. (2013). Climbing the ladder in call centres: Is the view different on the way to the top? *New Technology, Work and Employment, 28*(2), 145–159.

McDonnell, A., Connell, J., Hannif, Z., & Burgess, J. (2014). Having a say: Forms of voice in Australian call centres. *Employee Relations, 36*(3), 214–234.

Mueller, F., Valsecchi, R., Smith, C., Gabe, J., & Elston, M. (2008). We are nurses, we are supposed to care for people: Professional values among nurses in NHS Direct call centres. *New Work, Technology & Employment, 23*(1–2), 2–16.

Purcell, J., & Hutchinson, S. (2007). Front-line managers as agents in the HRM-performance causal chain: Theory, analysis and evidence. *Human Resource Management Journal, 17*(1), 3–20.

Pyman, A., Cooper, B., Teicher, J., & Holland, P. (2006). A comparison of employee voice arrangements in Australia. *Industrial Relations Journal, 37,* 543–559.

Russell, B. (2008). Call centres: A decade of research. *International Journal of Management Reviews, 10,* 195–219.
Sako, M. (2007). Outsourcing and offshoring: Implications for productivity of business services. *Oxford Review of Economic Policy, 22*(4), 499–512.
Strauss, G. (2006). Worker participation—Some under-considered issues. *Industrial Relations, 45,* 778–803.
Tangirala, S., & Ramanujam, R. (2008). Exploring nonlinearity in employee voice: The effects of personal control and organizational identification. *Academy of Management Journal, 51* (6), 1189–1203.
Taylor, P., & Bain, P. (2005). India calling to the far away towns: The call centre labour process and globalization. *Work, Employment & Society, 19*(2), 261–282.
Townsend, K. (2004). When LOST found teams: A consideration of teams within the individualised call centre environment. *Labour and Industry, 14*(3), 111–126.
van den Broek, D. (2002). Monitoring and surveillance in call centres: Some responses from Australian workers. *Labour and Industry, 12*(3), 43–58.
van den Broek, D., Callaghan, G., & Thompson, P. (2004). Teams without teamwork? Explaining the call centre paradox. *Economic and Industrial Democracy, 25,* 197–218.
Van Dyne, L., Cummings, L. L., & McLean Parks, J. (1995). Extra-role behaviors: In pursuit of construct and definitional clarity (a bridge over muddied waters). In L. L. Cummings & B. M. Staw (Eds.), *Research in organizational behavior* (Vol. 17, pp. 215–285)., JAI Press CT: Greenwich.
Waring, P. (1999). The rise of individualism in Australian industrial relations. *New Zealand Journal of Industrial Relations, 24*(3), 291–318.
Wilkinson, A., & Fay, C. (2011). New times for employee voice. *Human Resource Management, 50,* 65–74.
Wilkinson, A., Dundon, T., Marchington, M., & Ackers, P. (2004). Changing patterns of employee voice: Case studies from the UK and Republic of Ireland. *The Journal of Industrial Relations, 46,* 298–322.
Zapf, D., Isic, A., Bechtoldt, M., & Blau, P. (2003). What is typical for call centre jobs? Job characteristics and service interactions in different call centres. *European Journal of Work and Organizational Psychology, 12*(4), 311–340.

Dr. John Burgess is Professor of HRM, RMIT University, Melbourne. He has previous professorial appointments at the University of Newcastle and Curtin University. He is Associate Editor of Personnel Review and on the editorial board of Human Resource Management Journal. His research interests include transitional labour markets; working time and health; HRM practices of multinational enterprises and work in the aged care sector. His latest book publication is Roslyn Cameron, Subas Dhakal and John Burgess eds. Transitions from Education to Work: Workforce Ready Challenges in the Asia Pacific, Routledge, Abingdon.

Dr. Julia Connell is Professor and Assistant Dean, Research Training at Newcastle Business School, University of Newcastle, Australia. She has published numerous refereed journal articles/book chapters, co-edited 16 special issue journal volumes and 8 books. Many publications have focused on employment-related issues, change/people development, industry organisational effectiveness, vulnerable workers/precarious jobs and also issues related to higher education. She is on the Editorial Board for the Springer series in Flexible Systems Management and the Editorial Advisory Board for Personnel Review.

Chapter 10
Employee Voice in Practice: Aged Care in Australia and New Zealand

Sarah Kaine and Katherine Ravenswood

Abstract The centrepiece of this study will be the on examining whether there is a legacy impact on the nature and development of voice arrangements in privacy utilities. In particular, the chapter will traverse the changing pattern of union representation and activity and the development and impact of alternative forms of employee voice.

Keywords Aged care · Employee voice · Silence · Regulation

10.1 Introduction

The aging of the population in most advanced economies has brought with it issues associated with the provision of care for the elderly. These issues relate to an increasing need for aged care employees to provide care to the aging population and a simultaneous decrease in the working population due to its aging. Obviously, governments face difficult decisions over the funding of aged care including funding quality care and quality workplaces. For example, the scale of the situation (UNPF 2012; WHO 2011) and its social and economic implications have seen increasing policy attention being turned to the financial and human capital required to provide adequate levels of care. In both Australia and New Zealand, over the past decade, numerous policy prescriptions have attempted to guide the development of the aged care sector (Kaine and Ravenswood 2014). Given the labour-intensive nature of care work, a key focus has been on attracting and sustaining a suitable workforce to deliver services to the aged, either in their own home or in residential care facilities (Thornton 2015; Productivity Commission 2008, 2011). Improving retention is key to sustaining the aged care workforce and requires the provision of work conditions

S. Kaine (✉)
Business School, University of Technology Sydney, Ultimo, Australia
e-mail: Sarah.Kaine@uts.edu.au

K. Ravenswood
Auckland University of Technology, Auckland, New Zealand

P. Holland et al. (eds.), *Employee Voice at Work*, Work, Organization, and Employment, https://doi.org/10.1007/978-981-13-2820-6_10

(including training to upskill within aged care) that encourage people to work in aged care and develop long-term attachments to it. High labour turnover in the aged care sector has frequently been attributed to low rates of pay (Kaine 2012a; Productivity Commission 2008, 2011), characteristics of the workers and the regulatory environment for aged care in Australasia. These are important contextual matters that should be taken into account when considering how and why different employees will have more or less opportunity for effective voice. The regulatory environment for aged care in New Zealand and Australia provides an interesting context for considering employee voice and other work conditions because aged care is largely publicly funded and therefore the government in each country is arguably the lead employer in a domestic supply chain (Ravenswood and Kaine 2015). The following sections outline the characteristics of the aged care workforce in both countries, followed by the funding models and policy and the regulatory environment. It must be noted that aged care comprises both care provided in residential care homes (or nursing homes) and home and community care. The latter is where older people remain in their own homes and a care worker comes to their place of residence to provide care and support in their home. Those who receive home care usually require less care and are more independent. Home and community care provide its own challenges to the management of people and employment relations as the employees work in multiple locations with little contact with the central office. This chapter focuses predominantly on residential aged care.

This chapter focuses on the growing aged care sector as a case study of voice in the workplace. It begins by outlining the context of residential aged care in both New Zealand and Australia, in particular highlighting the interactions between workforce characteristics on workers and funding. The chapter then considers the different levels at which voice is exercised as a means to analyse different voice channels and their efficacy.

10.1.1 Workforce Characteristics

The main characteristics of the residential aged care workforce in Australia and New Zealand are summarised in Table 10.1.

Anyone familiar with aged care will not be surprised to learn that this is a predominantly female workforce. The same is true of home and community care also (Clarke 2015; Ravenswood et al. 2015). An important comparison to consider when comparing residential and community aged care is that the latter is generally characterised by much more part-time work and less certainty in hours (Ravenswood et al. 2015; Ravenswood and Douglas 2017). A distinction in national contexts is that aged care in Australia relies upon agency workers to fill shortages (King et al. 2017), and New Zealand's labour market is increasingly reliant upon migrant workers to meet the labour shortages. In New Zealand's the use of migrant labour different may be due to an overall labour shortage, compounded by the perception of aged care work as unskilled and low wage (Ravenswood and Harris 2016) that discour-

Table 10.1 Residential aged care (RACS) workforce characteristics: Australia and New Zealand

Australia	New Zealand
216,300 RAC workers[a]	Approx. 25,000 RAC workers[a]
73% in direct care roles	66% in direct care roles (approx)
89% women	93% women
72% working part-time	64% working part-time
56% aged 35–55	56% aged 50 years or older
Increasing use of agency staff	Increasing use of migrant labour
Turnover of approx. 25%	Turnover of approx. 25%

Source Australian Bureau of Statistics (2013a, b), Badkar (2009), Department of Health and Aging (2012), Thornton (2015), King et al. (2012), Martin and King (2008), Meagher (2016), Miller et al. (2008), Ravenswood et al. (2015)

[a]Residential aged care worker: the employees in aged care who provide direct care to the older people, and are not considered professionals. There are few requirements for formal training and the qualifications available are at a sub-degree level. RAC workers comprise the majority of the care workforce

ages New Zealand citizens from the sector. Furthermore, it has been suggested that migrant workers from developing countries may have a more 'family-oriented' attitude towards care (Dodson and Zincavage 2007) and may be willing to work for lower wages as they still compare favourably to wages in their home countries (Thornton 2015).

In 2014 in New Zealand, approximately 31% of the aged care workforce in residential services were born overseas, up from 19% in 1991 (Callister et al. 2014: 7). Among both home and community and residential aged care workers, the figures were 68% European, 15% Maori, 14% Asian and 9% Pacific People (Callister et al. 2014). The number of caregivers born overseas is regionally differentiated: The Auckland region stands out, with almost 60% of caregivers born overseas (Callister et al. 2014: 8). Although nationally the demographics of caregivers' origin and/or ethnicity are broadly similar, in Auckland it may not be. For example, based on 2013 Census data, 39% of all people residing in Auckland were born overseas (MBIE 2016). Caregivers born overseas are also part of a younger age demographic. In the oldest age bracket of caregivers, very few are of Asian ethnicity, whereas 25% of females younger than 30 years are Asians who were born overseas (Callister et al. 2014: 15).

Data from the 2016 National Aged Care Workforce Census and Survey in Australia show that there has been a slight drop in the number of overseas-born residential aged care workers down from 35% in 2012 to 32% in 2016. With a similar decrease occurring among home care workers from 28% in 2012 to 23% in 2016. The largest percentage increase between 2006 and 2011 was among workers from South Asia, whose number increased from 1.6 to 5.3% of the workforce followed by workers from sub-Saharan Africa, who represented 1.9% of the workforce in 2006 and 3.3% in 2011 (Negin et al. 2016: 14). Like New Zealand, the number of caregivers born overseas is regionally differentiated: in Western Australia, the figure stands at 51% in 2011, whereas overseas-born caregivers in the other large states were between 33 and 37%. Nepal, India and Liberia are the three countries that have provided the largest percentage increase, but the Philippines is the largest source country for foreign workers (Negin et al. 2016: 15).

The aggregate rates of unionisation in the aged care sector in both Australia and New Zealand are quite high relative to overall union membership. In Australia, unionisation in 'Residential Care Services' is 32% (ABS 2013a, b, nationally the rate of unionisation is around 16%), but these figures are not specific to aged care. Furthermore, the aggregate obscures the difference between different categories of workers. In New Zealand, 2014 data indicated overall union density to be 18.5% nationally, with density in 'health care and social assistance' at 40.1% (Ryall and Blumenfeld 2015). However, even when unions are present, collective voice mechanisms are rare (Kaine 2012a; Ravenswood 2012; Ravenswood and Markey 2017), and in Australia, where collective agreements have been made, there is little evidence that these have been precipitated by grassroots activity or that it has resulted in substantial improvements in wages and conditions for aged care workers (Kaine 2012b).

10.2 Funding of and Policy on Aged Care

Australian government expenditure on aged care services was $15.8 billion in 2014–2015, of which residential aged care accounted for the largest proportion (68.1%) (Productivity Commission 2016). In 2014, there were 192,834 places in residential care and 1016 care provider organisations (Department of Social Services 2014). The Australian Government's 2016 Budget and Mid-Year Economic and Fiscal Outlook sought to reduce the aged care budget by $1.71 billion over four years. However, the 2017 Federal Budget was seen as more stable with inititvaites including the establishment of $1.9 million taskforce to be established to develop and aged care sector workforce strategy and no funding cuts (Basstian 2017). In New Zealand, 2017 saw an increase in funding (and extra $3.9 billion over 4 years) to District Health Boards to administer across all of their functions. However, nearly half of that is already earmarked to cover the cost of increased wages aged care and also disability workers after an equal pay settlement was agreed to in May 2017.

In both Australia and New Zealand, aged care is predominantly funded by the government although the funding mechanisms between the two countries vary. In New Zealand, public money is distributed to private (i.e. non-governmental) providers of aged care (both for-profit and not-for-profit) through agreements for provisions of service with 'District Health Boards' (DHBs) (Carryer et al. 2010; Kaine and Ravenswood 2014). Providers of residential aged care must be accredited under national legislation to provide healthcare and they must successfully tender for contracts with the DHBs. Accreditation is regulated through the Health and Disability (Services) Act 2001 (Kaine and Ravenswood 2014; Lazonby 2007). The Health and

Disability (Services) Act 2001 outlines key requirements of patient care in respect to consumer rights, and some aspects of organisational management. All providers are regularly audited to ensure that they meet the requirements of the Act, with the threat of being unable to provide the service if they are not accredited.

Whereas in residential aged care there is a national service agreement for providers, there is no standardised agreement for home and community care, and providers may have to contract with several different government agencies, even within one regional area.

To some extent, home and community care is more closely regulated than residential care, with recent legislative changes resulting from legal action that was diverted into tripartite negotiations over payment for travel time and mileage between clients and further ongoing discussions over regularising work hours–in other words, guaranteed minimum hours, for example (Ravenswood and Douglas 2017). The 'travel time' changes were fully implemented from April 2016 through the Home and Community Support (Payment for Travel between Clients) Settlement Act 2016 (Ministry of Health 2017).

Ownership of both residential and community aged care in New Zealand has historically included a significant proportion of not-for-profit providers, but this is changing with profit providers acquiring smaller care providers. Currently, in community care, just over half of providers are not for profit (New Zealand Productivity Commission 2015).

In Australia, the residential aged care market is 'managed' by the federal government through the Aged Care Act 1997 (the Act) (Davidson 2009). A main characteristic of this managed market is that the federal government provides the majority of funding for the provision of services allowing it to constraint the actions of providers by placing conditions on the granting of subsidies (Kaine 2012a). The Aged Care Act 1997 was substantially revised and came into force in July 2014. The revisions to the Aged Care Act (Living Better, Living Longer; LBLL) encased the existing regulatory mechanisms within a consumer choice model and a more 'market-based system'. The Act establishes the funding framework and lists the responsibilities for service providers in receipt of public funding (Nicoll and Jackson 2003). Specifically, the Act details the regulatory mechanisms with which the government controls the allocation of beds, limits service prices and accommodation bond charges, allocates funding and assesses the clients' eligibility to attract subsidies.

The LBLL reforms aim to shift the balance of care offered towards home care over residential care and increase the level of contribution that aged care consumers make. The move towards 'consumer-directed care' in the LBLL reforms has several impacts on the provision of care and work within the aged care sector. The idea of consumer-directed care orients care around resident preferences. This means, for example, self-service breakfast bars or longer meal-times, both of which have effects on staffing levels and service delivery (Somerville and Greene 2016: 26). In keeping with the idea of consumer-directed care, the LBLL reforms prioritise the individualisation of care provision, specifically in the home. The LBLL reforms aim to double the amount of in-home care offered as a ratio of population by 2022, from 27 to 45 places for every 1000 people aged 70 years and over (ACFA 2016: xii).

In Australia, owners of residential care places are composed of a mixture of religious (25.1%), private for-profit (37.5%), community-based (13.6%), charitable (17.6%), state and territory government (5.5%) and local government (0.8%) entities (Productivity Commission 2015, Table 13A.14). The main growth in the sector has been in private for-profit and charitable operators rising from 25.5% of operators in June 2006 to 32.5% in June 2015. In New Zealand in 2010, 61% of homes were privately owned, 20% owned by a charitable, religious or welfare organisation, and 19% were publicly listed (Thornton 2015).

10.3 'Voice' in Aged Care

Research on employee voice emanates from a variety of disciplines, with much of the contemporary literature being found in the areas of organisational psychology, organisation studies and human resource management (Budd 2014), with an emphasis on individual voice behaviours (albeit with differing assumptions and motivations). According to Dundon et al. (2004), voice can be taken to mean one or all of the following: the 'articulation of individual dissatisfaction', 'the expression of collective organisation', 'contribution to management decision-making' or a 'demonstration of mutuality and cooperative relations' (1152), with each of these meanings being associated with particular practices and potential outcomes (Kaine 2012b). In industrial relations scholarship, voice research traditionally focused on the institutional mechanisms of collective voice. This largely focused on union voice but also built on concepts of industrial democracy and worker participation in decisions around how they do their work, as well as the strategic direction of their workplace. In response to the demise of union voice since the 1980s, more recent scholarship has questioned the utility of confining voice to only unions and collective voice owing to the 'representation gap' caused by low unionisation rates (Heery 2009a; Freeman and Rogers 1993). This chapter clearly situates itself within the industrial relations scholarship that focuses not only on organisational and individual voice but also on the role of institutions and regulation in forming both the opportunities for and outcomes of voice. We refer to a variety of voice mechanisms, such as those described by Dundon et al. (2004).

Voice may be expressed at a number of levels and through a variety of mechanisms (Kaine 2014). The concept of levels is one that researchers have debated, for example, Wilkinson et al. (2010) refer to a 'staircase of voice' which, rather than being an organisational locus of voice, refers to the strategic importance of the decisions that employees can influence through voice mechanisms. As Kaine (2014) illustrates in residential aged care, levels can also refer to the level of voice in terms of workplace, sector or industry, national and international. Kaine's (2014) explanation of levels of voice provides a means to exam the interaction between individuals, organisations/workplaces and national and international institutions that interact to regulate employee voice. This is a fruitful avenue of research, as it enables analysis of the complex power relationships between employees and employers (Marchington 2015)—and acknowledges the research on individual and organisational voice.

Much of the literature on voice that is not focused on unions consider company-specific methods of non-union employee representation (NER) (Dobbins and Dundon 2014; Taras and Kaufman 2006). Some key features of NERs include the following: they are generally limited to employees within an organisation; they have no links to external organisations such as unions; they are commonly resourced by the employer; they provide 'indirect' representation rather than individual mechanisms; and often they cover all employees within a workplace (Gollan (2000) in Dobbins and Dundon 2014).

It has also been suggested that limiting consideration of worker dissatisfaction to observable 'voicing' of concerns obscures the phenomenon of 'silence' in the workplace and what such silence means (Donaghey et al. 2011; Josserand and Kaine 2016). Therefore, in some cases, 'voice' may not prove the most appropriate explanatory idea, and indeed 'silence' may better convey how workers choose or have to navigate the vagaries of their workplace. However, much of the literature on silence is predicated on managerialist assumptions and its ideological lexicon, in that overcoming employee silence matters because such silence is representative of missed opportunities to improve productivity (or at least avoid problems) through employees' input (Cullinane and Donaghey 2014). However, 'silencing' is the mechanism by which workers' voices may also be ignored in such managerialist discourse and is a strategy that is frequently enacted to marginalise workers' voices, for example, migrant women, who are exiled by schemas that locate authority and legitimacy elsewhere. Frazer's observation that 'institutionalized patterns of cultural value recognise some categories of social actors as normative and others as deficient or inferior' (cited by Sarikakis 2012: 802) gives some explanation as to why the voice of some groups of workers (Frazer's 'social actors') might be ignored. This has implications for employee voice in a feminised industry with an increasing proportion of migrant workers, as is the case of aged care.

Extant research has emphasised the impact of various modes of regulation (both 'hard' and 'soft' regulation) on the expression of voice by aged care employees in Australia (Kaine 2012a). Specifically, the historical development of the sector and its intersection with what was the centralised system of wage setting in Australia (Kaine 2012b) shaped the nature of voice. Under that centralised system, workplace-level negotiations (collective or individual) around pay were negligible, and while pay is not the only issue on which employees might wish to express voice, it is the most obvious concern (Butler 2005) as it is at the heart of the employment relationship (Forth and Millward 2004). The legacy of this arrangement is a culture within which collective voice is not readily accessed or demanded. In New Zealand, there has not been the same continuation of centralised wage setting since the Employment Contracts Act 1991 saw the end of arbitration and compulsory unionism. New Zealand has, in the last 15 years, emerged from a decade of limited regulatory protection of unions' right to organise and limited ability to create workplace collective agreements in the 1990s under the Employment Contracts Act. Since 2001 The Employment Relations Act (with various amendments) has encouraged collective

Table 10.2 Levels[a] and channels of voice in aged care

Level of voice	Example
Individual	Feedback/suggestion form Staff surveys
Workplace	Collective agreements, consultative committees, Staff surveys 'Working parties'/taskforces
Industry	Equal pay cases
National	Equal pay cases National inquiries Union campaigns Legislation prohibiting or allowing voice mechanisms
Transnational	Campaigns in MNCs

[a]Based on Kaine (2014)

bargaining and allowed for multi-union and multi-enterprise collective agreements. These rights have been eroded somewhat since 2008 under a government that has step by step reduced protections for employees (Le Queux et al. 2016). Since 2002 the Health and Safety in Employment Act, and its successor the Health and Safety at Work Act 2015, have required participatory systems in health and safety, which often manifests in representative health and safety committees (Ravenswood et al. 2013).

An important aspect of regulation is that of 'soft regulation'—the ways in which social norms, for example, influence work (Kaine 2012a). A key regulatory impact to consider in voice in aged care is, therefore, the well-established gender norms that influence not only how the work is 'valued' but how employees in aged care are viewed. For example, Ravenswood and Harris (2016) argue that gender and class intersect to confine aged care employees to stereotyped workers who are low-skilled, lacking in agency, and independence. Ravenswood and Markey (2017) argue that these same gender norms limit employee voice opportunities and outcomes for aged care employees.

The following sections consider voice mechanisms in aged care and are organised according to 'level of voice' (see Table 10.2), and in some places overlap in levels. When considering these 'levels', it is important to understand how they interact, and to what extent employee voice enables meaningful participation in decisions that affect employees' work both in the short term and long term (i.e. strategic decisions).

10.3.1 Transnational Voice

The aged care markets in Australia and New Zealand are becoming increasingly penetrated by large multinational organisations that have identified a strategic benefit in investing in a growing sector that is assisted by a significant amount of public subsidy. For example, BUPA now has the largest share of the Australian market, with 3% (Lie 2015). These companies are significant players in New Zealand also—where major providers such as Ryman Healthcare are buying out smaller, often single-site, facilities and expanding across the Tasman (Aged Care 101 2016). The recent rapid growth of these large, for-profit providers has been changing the composition of the sector, which (in Australia) was previously dominated by not-for-profit providers that have consistently outperformed for-profit and public providers in terms of revenue (ACFA 2016). The ‘marketisation of care’ evident in residential aged care has been the focus of research, with concerns being raised about its implications for the quality of care received by residents (King and Meagher 2009) and the working conditions and voice opportunities available to aged care workers (Kaine 2012a; Ravenswood and Markey 2017). However, unlike in other industries where unions have been able to mount international campaigns for international framework agreements (IFAs), and despite forming a global steering committee focusing on care work, the global union representing care workers (UNI Global Union) has yet to negotiate an IFA in the care sector (UNI Global Union 2016). This lack of voice mechanisms at an international level reflects the paradox that has been noted with regard to transnational labour agreements. Such agreements have been found to be ‘effective locally only in cases where unions are already strong’, with the observation being made that ‘in the absence of local workers’ voice, new regulatory mechanisms [such as IFAs]’ are difficult to implement and monitor (Josserand and Kaine 2016). The institutions of voice at an international level are yet underdeveloped—perhaps because the proportion of international and multinational companies is small compared to other industries. Opportunities for voice may also be affected by increasing flows of migrant care workers—workers who are mostly women and are also ‘vulnerable’ due to their migrant status, and shaped by experiences in their countries of origin (Josserand and Kaine 2016). Another factor in the lack of development in international voice is that aged care, in Australia and New Zealand, is largely funded by national governments, keeping the focus and conditions specific to each country.

10.3.2 National Voice

Voice at a national level is often expressed through ‘test’ cases that seek to change the overarching regulatory framework and lobbying that aims to influence policy-makers and broad community campaigns that attempt to shape social conditions (Kaine 2014). In both Australia and New Zealand, unions in the aged care sector have engaged in actions at a national level, although in New Zealand, the unitary nature of the political system has often led to the national level being conflated with the industry level. For example, in Australia, the Nurses and Midwifery Association, (the union that represents Nurses and Midwives) is currently running campaigns to address education and professional development leave, a process to address short staffing, and for an independent commission to decide on disputes. Their submission to the Federal Senate's inquiry 'The Future of Australia's aged care sector workfroce', recommended that the government mandate minimum staffing levels and skills mix requirements, the wages gap be closed, licensing requirements be increased a minimum standard of care for nursing/personal care workers be brought in and a mandated requirement for a 24-hour registered nurse for all high-care residents in aged care facilities be established (ANMA 2016).

In New Zealand, multiple unions had campaigned together on 'fair share for aged care' before, in 2012, the Service and Food Workers Union supported aged care worker Kristine Bartlett to take legal action against her employer Terranova Care Homes Ltd under the Equal Pay Act 1972 (Ravenswood and Harris 2016). While an individual complaint was taken under the Act, several interested parties took part in the case, with the New Zealand Nurses Organisation supporting ongoing work with members along with the Public Service Association so that approximately 3,000 individual complaints of gender discrimination in pay had been lodged by the end of 2014. While this is an individual taking legal action, the individual was encouraged and supported by her union as the 'claim' was one experienced by all across the sector and industry. This is one example of how union voice has begun to change and adapt in how they organise and provide voice (Bailey et al. 2014) The legal action by law had to be taken by an individual, but the legal representation was Union provided and supported by a multi-union social campaign. Reflection on connections between institutions—although the fight for equal pay is actually a minimum legal work entitlement, it has not been an issue explicitly addressed by unions in previous decades when protecting the full-time jobs of men was often an unspoken objective in the award system in the middle part of 20th Century New Zealand (Williamson 2017). The legal action went through several appeals and ultimately came before the Supreme Court, where the case was put on hold to allow tripartite negotiations to (1) determine principles for determining gender discrimination in pay for employees and employers to use and (2) conduct separate negotiations to determine increased funding for increased wages in residential aged care. The pay negotiations were only possible because aged care is government funded, outsourced to private providers. The pay increases have also been granted to home and community aged care and also the disability workforce, so what started off in residential aged care sector on a national level has resulted in positive outcomes of voice across several sectors. The Judgement in the legal case also overturned previous interpretations of the Equal Pay Act 1972 to allow industry based claims (not just individual), thus having a broader impact on both union and non-union women in any industry. This one use of union voice has resulted in sector and ind.

10.4 Industry Voice

With the expansion of the 'representation gap' (as explained above: if unions are the key form of collective voice, yet unionisation rates are relatively low). exacerbated by the continued downward trajectory of levels of unionisation in both Australia and New Zealand over the past 30 years, workplace-based collective bargaining has become increasingly difficult (see next section). However, recent history around collective voice at the industry level in residential aged care in Australia has proven interesting (Kaine 2012b). The Fair Work Act 2009 (FWA 2009) contains provisions designed to assist workers in low-paid industries, who have historically had difficulties bargaining, (those industries characterised by low levels of collective voice due to being feminised, low-paid and poorly unionised) by giving them access to a centralised system of bargaining allowing multiple employers to be involved (FWA 2009, Division 9, s. 241). The development and inclusion of this 'Low-Paid Bargaining Stream' (LPBS) in the FWA 2009 represented political and institutional acknowledgement that traditional channels of collective voice such as collective bargaining (Doellgast and Benassi 2014) are not universally or uniformly accessible.

In 2011, two unions representing (non-nurse) aged care workers (United Voice and the Australian Workers Union's Queensland branch) made an application under the LPBS provisions to access industry-level bargaining and involve the major funder of the sector: the Commonwealth government. The outcome of the application was mixed for the unions. The decision was handed down by Fair Work Australia (the predecessor of the Fair Work Commission) to apply a low-paid bargaining authorisation to only those aged care employees who had their wages and conditions determined by the award (Fair Work Australia 2011). This excluded those aged care workers who had previously engaged in any collective bargaining (even of a defensive nature with minimal pay increases; Kaine 2012b), thereby limiting this mechanism's potential to provide a sector-wide solution to low pay.

If successful, this channel of industry-wide collective voice may have begun to address issues of power imbalance during the bargaining process. However, it would not have dealt with problems associated with the enforcement of any bargained outcomes, itself reflective of the capacity to voice concerns. Nor would it have necessarily led to the development of appropriate voice mechanisms for aged care workers. The result does suggest that institutional support is not enough to mitigate the vulnerability of some workers and that it is not nuanced enough to allow for the sub-sections of the workforce and how different categories of workers might experience voice and silence.

In New Zealand, unionisation in aged care has quite likely been helped by the 'fair share for aged care' and equal pay campaigns that the three main unions have led. These campaigns have worked hard to gain attention in society and have used multiple communication platforms including, Twitter, Facebook and hard copy campaign material such as postcards to sign and send to members of parliament. Media attention through press and television has also been gained, with unions aiming to highlight the importance of aged care work, including having aged care clients speak up in support. The broader campaign has been based on a discourse of unfairness and disempowerment against which workers have to fight to get what they deserve. The campaign has also 'politicised' union members, in that the campaign has legitimised the value of their work, and claims that it is paid unfairly. It has also activated members, approximately 3,000 of whom filed individual claims under the Equal Pay Action 1972. The unions' campaign has also been supported by greater civil society support through revitalising equal pay coalitions and groups such as the Auckland Equal Pay Coalition. This example of a change in organising to campaigning on issues of equality may also buffer legislative attacks on union power since 2008, such as changes to the Employment Relations Act to allow employers to refuse unions permission to enter the workplace. Ravenswood and Markey (2017) argue that the national context bears on both workplace and individual voice. In New Zealand, this is apparent from both union voice and the role that informal regulation such as social norms have on voice. The examples given here of union voice supporting legal action at a sectoral national level have resulted in changes enforced on the workplace. These changes were what employees were (perhaps) unable to achieve through workplace-level voice. Social norms and also employer power at a national level, have also considerably constrained employee voice at both the workplace and the individual levels (Ravenswood and Harris 2016; Ravenswood and Markey 2017).

10.5 Workplace Voice

The lack of union collective voice (as in other industries) should not be taken to mean the absence of voice altogether. NER has become a standard feature in the voice literature and extant research on voice in the aged care sector has demonstrated its prevalence in that context as well (Kaine 2012a; Ravenswood 2012). In essence, it refers to mechanisms for collective voice in the workplace not facilitated by unions—that is, 'a company-specific forum of some sort that provides opportunities for non-union employee representative voice' (Dobbins and Dundon 2014: 343). While there has been debate about the authenticity of NER and its capacity to deliver benefits to employees, it has certainly gained in prominence, and there has been a proliferation of indirect channels such as 'works councils, joint consultative committees, staff associations, partnership forums, health and safety committees, quality and productivity committees, or employee representatives on company boards' (Dobbins and Dundon 2014: 344).

Marchington and Wilkinson's (2012) three categories of voice—direct communication, upward problem-solving and representative participation—are evident to varying degrees in residential aged care workplaces. Representative participation takes place at the workplace level, commonly in the form of consultative and health and safety committees, although these tend to be skewed towards quality-of-care issues or identifying efficiency improvements (Kaine 2012a; Ravenswood 2012; Ravenswood and Markey 2017). While collective agreements are negotiated in the aged care sector, in the Australian context, collective agreement making cannot be equated with evidence of voice, collective or otherwise. Bray and Stewart (2013) make the distinction between agreement making under the Fair Work Act and the promotion of bargaining in which unions potentially compete with other 'bargaining agents' to represent workers. Furthermore, there is 'no guarantee of collective voice for employees in determining the content of the agreement. An employer can validly make an agreement simply by informing the relevant group of employees of their right to be represented, showing them a copy of a draft agreement and explaining its effect, and then persuading a majority to vote in favour' (Bray and Stewart 2013: 36) Union strength has been largely exercised through legal action as outlined above In New Zealand, collective voice in relation to collective agreements has largely been confined to enterprise-level bargaining. However, in residential care, there have been efforts between more than one union to bargain together, as is allowed under the Employment Relations Act 2000 In New Zealand, the three main unions representing aged care employees are E Tū Union, the New Zealand Nurses Organisation and the Public Service Association where more than one of these unions represent employees in the same provider, they have attempted to form a multi-union collective employment agreement. A further consideration around voice in New Zealand is through a required opportunity for employee participation in health and safety, guaranteed in the Health and Safety at Work Act 2015. To what extent OHS committees consider day to day working decisions and hazard identification versus more strategic decisions relating to the work environment and OHS varies considerably and is often dependent on managerial initiative and encouragement (Ravenswood 2012). It could be that the revised legislation of 2015, which specifically identifies stress and fatigue as OHS issues, may over time result in OHS committees considering issues such as staffing levels and workload and the psycho-social environment of OHS which has been largely unexamined in care work (Kurowski et al. 2015).

10.6 Individual Voice

In addition to the health and safety committees and quality circles, direct communication and upward problem-solving are also seen in aged care; in particular, climate or engagement surveys and feedback/suggestion forms. These have the potential to result in tangible change. Kaine (2012a) describes how the results of the employee survey in one larger charitable aged care provider in Australia prompted the organisation to adopt more family-friendly work practices, including paid maternity leave, prior to such a scheme's becoming mandatory. However, a care manager in the same organisation admitted that she actively discouraged union membership because it was 'very undermining'. Similarly, in New Zealand, managers sometimes try to discourage unions owing to an impression that they are necessary only if management is bad (Ravenswood and Markey 2017). Furthermore, direct voice does not recognise the impact of culture and class in organisations in which some employees may not feel comfortable dealing directly with managers, particularly senior managers (Ravenswood and Markey 2017). For example, in aged care an employee may feel that as an 'unskilled' worker, they are not in a position to raise issues with a manager on site, or a regional or national manager in their workplace. There are also potential issues around culture and attitudes towards hierarchy: depending, of course, on the country a recent migrant originates from, they may come from work cultures that expect employees to respect the status of their manager and not question their management in anyway. This could be inconsistent with concepts of employee voice that expect individuals to raise issues that they consider need improvement, for example. There is clearly a diversity of approaches within a single organisation and between organisations that reinforces the impact that local or line managers can have on voice. In New Zealand, the role of HR has been in meeting the demand for employees, but also focussing on employee training in relation to regulatory requirement and also to improve customer service. Specifically, this supports Townsend's (2014) assertion that: '… while the HR department may play a vital role in developing the formal and informal mechanisms for voice, it is the managers who are closest to the employees who will play the critical role of facilitating voice in the organization' (p. 156).

10.7 Conclusion

Ravenswood and Kaine (2015) suggested that an increased institutional response was required in order to address low wages and other sub-optimal conditions in aged care. To date, in both Australia and New Zealand government has played a key role as a funder of aged care, and could regulate working conditions through this role. However, as mentioned above, there is a shift towards home care and consumer-directed care. While this is still couched in rhetoric of subsidised funding, with increasing demand for care on government budgets, it would not be surprising to see governments incrementally remove themselves from this relationship. With unions acting on an industry and national level through existing employment law, a shift towards private aged care may not be a threat to voice at that level. However, when aged care workers are employed by their 'client' and work in private homes, it is difficult to foresee how those workers will be able to voice dissatisfaction with wages and other work conditions when they are effectively contractors (Macdonald and Charlesworth 2016). The market has not yet provided fair wages for these workers, even when they have the protections of employment law. This signals a key concern for those investigating voice in aged care, and of course any other industry: how do our models of voice accommodate not just decreased unionisation but also an increasingly deteriorating employment relationship where an employee becomes their own boss as a contractor?

References

Aged Care 101. (2016). *Ryman sets sights on fifth retirement village and nursing home*. Retrieved October 25, from https://www.agedcare101.com.au/articles/ryman-sets-sights-fifth-retirement-village-and-nursing-home.

Aged Care Financing Authority. (2016). *Fourth report on the funding and financing of the aged care sector*. Canberra: Australian Government.

Australian Bureau of Statistics (ABS). (2013). *Employee earnings, benefits and trade union membership*. Canberra: ABS, Cat. no. 63100TS001.

Australian Bureau of Statistics (ABS). (2013). *Forms of employment.* Canberra: ABS, Cat. no. 6359.0.

Australian Nurses and Midwifery Association (ANMA). (2016). *Submission to senate inquiry: The future of Australia's aged care sector workforce*. Kingston ACT: ANMA.

Badkar, J. (2009). *Demographic shift. The future demand for paid caregivers in a rapidly ageing society*. Wellington, New Zealand: Department of Labour.

Bailey, J., Robertson, M., & Hulme, L. (2014). Challenging the "care penalty": The Queensland pay equity campaign for community services workers. *Journal of Industrial Relations, 56*(1), 43–61. https://doi.org/10.1177/0022185613503537.

Basttian, D. (2017). Federal budget 2017–2018: The sector reacts. *Aged Care Insite*. Retrieved August 16, 2017, from https://www.agedcareinsite.com.au/2017/05/federal-budget-2017-18-the-sector-reacts/.

Bray, M., & Stewart, A. (2013). What is distinctive about the Fair Work regime? *Australian Journal of Labour Law, 26*(1), 20–49.

Budd, J. (2014). The future of employee voice. In A. Wilkinson, J. Donaghey, T. Dundon, & R. B. Freeman (Eds.), *Handbook of research on employee voice* (pp. 170–188). Cheshire: Edward Elgar.

Butler, P. (2005). Non-union employee representation: exploring the efficacy of the voice process. *Employee Relations, 27*(3), 272–288.

Callister, P., Didham, R., & Badkar, J. (2014). *Reliance on migrant caregivers, a 2014 update*. Wellington, New Zealand: Callister & Associates. Retrieved from www.callister.co.nz.

Carryer, J., Hansen, C., & Blakey, J. (2010). Experiences of nursing in older care facilities in New Zealand. *Australian Health Review, 34,* 11–17.

Clarke, M. A. (2015). To what extent a "bad" job? Employee perceptions of job quality in community aged care. *Employee Relations, 37*(2), 192–208. https://doi.org/10.1108/ER-11-2013-0169.

Cullinane, N., & Donaghey, J. (2014). Employee Silence. In A. Wilkinson, J. Donaghey, T. Dundon, & R. B. Freeman (Eds.), *Handbook of Research on Employee Voice* (pp. 398–409). Cheltenham: Edward Elgar.

Davidson, B. (2009). For-profit organisation in managed markets for human services. In D. King & G. Meagher (Eds.), *Paid care in Australia: Politics, profits and practices*. Sydney: Sydney University Press.

Department of Health and Aging. (2012). *Aged care workforce, 2012—final report*. Canberra: Australian Government.

Department of Social Services. (2014). *2013-13 Concise facts and figures in aged care*. Canberra: Australian Government.

Department of Social Services. (2016). *Subsidies and Supplements* (p. 20). Canberra, March: Australian Government.

Dobbins, T., & Dundon, T. (2014). Non-union employee representation. In J. Donaghey, T. Dundon, & A. Wilkinson (Eds.), *Handbook of employee voice* (pp. 342–362). Cheltenham: Edward Elgar.

Dodson, L., & Zincavage, R. M. (2007). 'It's like a family': Caring labor, exploitation, and race in nursing homes. *Gender and Society, 21*(6), 905–928.

Doellgast, V., & Benassi, C. (2014). Collective bargaining. In J. Donaghey, T. Dundon, & A. Wilkinson (Eds.), *Handbook of employee voice* (pp. 227–247). Cheltenham: Edward Elgar.

Donaghey, J., Cullinane, N., Dundon, T., & Wilkinson, A. (2011). Reconceptualising employee silence: Problems and prognosis. *Work, Employment & Society, 25,* 51–67.

Dundon, T., Wilkinson, A., Marchington, M., & Ackers, P. (2004). The meanings and purpose of employee voice. *International Journal of Human Resource Management, 15,* 1149–1170.

Fair Work Australia. (2011). United Voice and Australian Workers' Union Queensland, s. 242—Application for a low paid bargaining authorisation—Decision FWAFB 2633.

Forth, J., & Millward, N. (2004). High-involvement management and pay in Britain. *Industrial Relations, 43*(1), 98–119.

Freeman, R., & Rogers, J. (1993). Who speaks for Us? Employee representation in a non-union labor market. In B. Kaufman & M. Kleiner (Eds.), *Employee representation: Alternatives and future directions* (pp. 13–80). Madison: Industrial Relations Research Association.

Gollan, P. (2000). Non-union in the United Kingdom and Australia. In B. E. Kaufman, & D.G. Taras (Eds.), *Non-union Employee Representation: History, Contemporary Practice, and Policy*. (pp. 410–449). New York: M.E. Sharpe.

Heery, E. (2009). The representation gap and the future of worker representation. *Industrial Relations Journal, 40*(4), 324–336.

Josserand, E., & Kaine, S. (2016). Labour standards in global value chains: Disentangling workers' voice, vicarious voice, power relations, and regulation. *Relations Industrielles, 71*(4), 741.

Kaine, S. J. (2012a). Collective regulation of wages and conditions in aged care—Beyond labour law. *Journal of Industrial Relations, 54*(2), 100–116.

Kaine, SJ. (2012b). Employee voice and regulation in the residential aged care sector. *Human Resource Management Journal*, *22*(3), 316–331.

Kaine, S. J. (2014). Union voice. In A. Wilkinson, J. Donaghey, T. Dundon, & R. B. Freeman (Eds.), *Handbook of research on employee voice* (pp. 170–188). Cheshire: Edward Elgar.

Kaine, S., & Ravenswood, K. (2014). Working in residential aged care: A trans-tasman comparison. *New Zealand Journal of Employment Relations (Online), 38*(2), 33–46.

King, D., & Meagher, G. (Eds.). (2009). *Paid care in Australia: Politics, profits, practices*. Sydney: Sydney University Press.

King, D., Mavromaras, K., Zhang, W., Smith, L., Macaitis, K., Moskos, M., & Smith, L. (2012). *The aged care workforce—Final report*. Adelaide: National Institute of Labour Studies (NILS) Flinders University.

King, D., Svensson, S., & Wei, Z. (2017). Not always a quick fix: The impact of employing temporary agency workers on retention in the Australian aged care workforce. *Journal of Industrial Relations, 59*(1), 85–103.

Kurowski, A., Boyer, J., & Punnett, L. (2015). The health hazards of health care: Physical and psychosocial stressors in paid care work. In M. Duffy, A. Armenia, & C. L. Stacey (Eds.), *Caring on the Clock. The complexities and contradictions of paid care work* (pp. 83–93). New Brunswick, USA: Rutgers University Press.

Lazonby, A. (2007). *The changing face of the aged care sector in New Zealand*. Retirement Policy and Research Centre Working Paper 2007–1, University of Auckland, New Zealand.

Le Queux, S., Rasmussen, E., Lamm, F., & Ravenswood, K. (2016). Nouvelle-Zélande—Steady as she goes, l'austérité du politique. La Revue de L'IRES (Institut de Recherches Economiques et Sociales), 154:49–60, (June).

Lie, R. (2015). *Profit from ageing population*. www.asx.com.au/education/investor-update-newsletter/201504-profit-from-ageing-population.htm. Accessed February 1, 2017.

Macdonald, F., & Charlesworth, S. (2016). Cash for care under the NDIS: Shaping care workers' working conditions? *Journal of Industrial Relations, 58*(5), 627–646.

Macquarie Bank. (2014). *Understanding the living longer, living better, aged care reforms*. Macquarie Bank. Retrieved May 22, from http://macquarie.com.au/dafiles/Internet/mgl/au/docs/noindex/mastech/Understanding-the-LLLB-aged-care-reforms.pdf. Accessed January 27, 2017.

Marchington, M. (2015). Analysing the forces shaping employee involvement and participation (EIP) at organisation level in liberal market economies (LMEs) *Human Resource Management Journal*, *25*(1), 1–18. https://doi.org/10.1111/1748-8583.12065.

Marchington, M., & Wilkinson, A. (2012). *Human resource management at work* (5th ed.). London: Chartered Institute of Personnel and Development.

Martin, B., & King, D. (2008). *Who cares for older australians?*. Adelaide: National Institute of Labour Studies.

Meagher, G. (2016). *Research report: Valuing care work and care workers: Workforce and equal pay issues in NZ aged residential care*. Sydney: Macquarie University.

Miller, E. A., Booth, M., & Mor, V. (2008). Meeting the demographic challenges ahead: Toward culture change in an ageing New Zealand. *Australia and New Zealand Health Policy*, *5*(5) https://doi.org/10.1186/1743-8462-5-5.

Ministry of Health. (2017). *In-between Travel Settlement*. Retrieved from https://www.health.govt.nz/new-zealand-health-system/claims-provider-payments-and-entitlements/between-travel-settlement.

Negin, J., Coffman, J., Connell, J., & Short, S. (2016). Foreign-born aged care workers in Australia: A growing trend. *Australasian Journal on Aging, 35*(4), E13–E17.

New Zealand Productivity Commission. (2015). *More effective social services*. Wellington: NZPC.

Nicoll, P., Jackson, D., Then, E-L., & O'Hanlon, B. (2003). *Managing residential aged care accreditation: The Aged Care Standards and Accreditation Agency Ltd* (Audit report No.42, 2002–2003). Canberra: Australian National Audit Office.

Productivity Commission. (2008). *Trends in aged care services: Some implications*. Canberra: Commission Research Paper

Productivity Commission. (2011). *Caring for older Australians*. Report no. 53. Canberra: Final Inquiry Report

Productivity Commission. (2015). *Report on Government Services 2015*. Canberra: Aged Care Services, Australian Government.

Productivity Commission. (2016). *Report on Government Services 2016*. Australian Government. Canberra: Aged Care Services.

Ravenswood, K. (2012). *Productivity, Participation and Employee Wellbeing in the Residential Aged Care Sector. Doctoral Thesis*. AUT University.

Ravenswood, K., & Douglas, J. (2017). *The New Zealand Aged care workforce survey 2016 report*. Auckland: New Zealand Work Research Institute. Retrieved from www.workresearch.aut.ac.nz.

Ravenswood, K., & Harris, C. (2016). Doing gender, paying low: gender, class and work-life balance in aged care. *Gender, Work & Organisation, 23*(6), 614–628.

Ravenswood, K., & Kaine, S. (2015). The role of government in influencing labour conditions through the procurement of services: Some political challenges. *Journal of Industrial Relations, 57*(4), 544–562.

Ravenswood, K., & Markey, R. (2017). Gender and voice in aged care: Embeddedness and institutional forces. *International Journal of Human Resource Management*, https://doi.org/10.1080/9585192.2016.1277367.

Ravenswood, K., Harris, C., Williamson, D., & Markey, R. (2013). Missing in action: Building a case for culturally diverse OHS committees in New Zealand hotels. *Policy and Practice in Health and Safety, 11*(1), 45–60.

Ravenswood, K., Douglas, J., & Teo, S. (2015). *The New Zealand Aged Care Workforce Survey 2014 report*. Auckland: New Zealand Work Research Institute. Retrieved from www.workresearch.aut.ac.nz.

Ryall, S., & Blumenfeld, S. (2015). The state of New Zealand union membership in 2014. Centre for Labour, Employment & Work, Victoria University of Wellington.

Sarikakis, K. (2012). Access denied: The anatomy of silence, immobilization and the gendered migrant. *Ethnic and Racial Studies, 35*(5), 800–816.

Somerville, F., & Greene, L. (2016). *CDC in residential: Writing's on the wall* (pp. 26–27). Mar/Apr: Australian Ageing Agenda.

Taras, D., & Kaufman, B. (2006). Non-union employee representation in North America: Diversity, controversy and uncertain future. *Industrial Relations Journal, 37,* 513–542.

Townsend, K. (2014). The role of line managers in employee voice systems. In A. Wilkinson, J. Donaghey, T. Dundon & R. B. Freeman (Eds.), *Handbook of research and employee voice* (Chapter 10, pp. 155–169). Cheshire: Edward Elgar.

Thornton, G. (2015). *Growing with aged: Dealtracker for the aged care sector.* Grant Thornton Retrieved March 2015, from http://www.grantthornton.com.au/globalassets/1.-member-firms/australian-website/industry/hac/pdfs/gtal_2015_growing-with-age_-aged-care-dealtracker.pdf, Accessed 27/01/2017.

UNI Global Union. (2016). *UNICARE: Breaking through for care workers*. Retrieved from www.uniglobalunion.org/news/unicare-breaking-through-care-workers. Accessed 1 Feb 2017.
United Nations Population Fund. (2012). *Population ageing: A larger and older population*. Retrieved March 5, 2012, from www.unfpa.org/pds/ageing.html.
Wilkinson, A., Gollan, P. J., Marchington, M., & Lewin, D. (2010). Conceptualizing employee participation in organizations. In A. Wilkinson, P. J. Gollan, M. Marchington, & D. Lewin (Eds.), *The Oxford handbook of participation in organizations* (pp. 3–25). New York: Oxford University Press.
Williamson, D. (2017). *In search of consensus: A history of Employment Relations in the New Zealand Hotel Sector – 1955–2000 (Doctoral thesis, AUT, Auckland, New Zealand)*. Retrieved from http://aut.researchgateway.ac.nz/handle/10292/10412.
World Health Organisation. (2011). *What are the public health implications of global aging*? Retrieved 22 February 2017, from www.who.int/features/qa/42/en/index.html.

Dr. Sarah Kaine is an Associate Professor in HRM and ER in the University of Technology Sydney (UTS) Business School. Her research focuses on several broad themes: the transformation of employee relations in the digital economy, the development and exercise of employee voice, the formal and informal regulation of employment relations and HRM and CSR. Specifically, Sarah is interested in innovation of employment relations and regulation–beyond the bounds of traditional labour law, corporate social responsibility and its link to industrial relations and the role of leadership in promoting ethical innovation in the management of work.

Dr. Katherine Ravenswood is an Associate Professor in Employment Relations at Auckland University of Technology (AUT) Business School. She focuses on high-quality research that has strong links with the community and industry and, as just one example, leads the New Zealand Aged Care Workforce Survey. Her research focuses on the examination of power, gender and diversity in the employment relationship in three key areas: Care/work regimes; gender and employee well-being; and inequality, power and voice at work.

Chapter 11
Scenarios and Strategies for Social Media in Engaging and Giving Voice to Employees

Emma Parry, Graeme Martin and Joe Dromey

Abstract Social media have become ubiquitous in non-work lives, however, evidence suggests that organizations are much less likely to use social media for these purposes, despite the positive claims made by many advocates for these media in employee relations (Dromey in Going digital? Harnessing social media for employee voice? Research paper, ACAS, 2016). This evidence gives rise to two questions that require further research. The first is: why have some organizations and some employees been less enthusiastic about the typically positive case for using social media to help them collaborate, share their knowledge and give voice to their views about issues over which they are most concerned in their organizations? Second, and following on from this first question, what options are best for organizations seeking to engage employees in using social media for employee collaboration, knowledge sharing and voice through social media? This chapter attempts to answer both questions.

Keywords Employee voice · Social media · Collaboration · Technology
Communication

11.1 Introduction

Social media have become ubiquitous in the non-work lives of many people who frequently use these media to express their thoughts and ideas, share matters of common interest with friends and colleagues and collaborate for socially useful ends. However, evidence suggests that organizations are much less likely to use social

E. Parry (✉)
Cranfield, England
e-mail: emma.parry@cranfield.ac.uk

G. Martin
University of Dundee, Dundee, Scotland

J. Dromey
IPPR, Coventry, England

P. Holland et al. (eds.), *Employee Voice at Work*, Work, Organization, and Employment, https://doi.org/10.1007/978-981-13-2820-6_11

media for these purposes, despite the positive claims made by many advocates for these media in employee relations (Dromey 2016). This evidence gives rise to two questions that require further research. The first is: why have some organizations and some employees been less enthusiastic about the typically positive case for using social media to help them collaborate, share their knowledge and give voice to their views about issues over which they are most concerned in their organizations? Second, and following on from this first question, what options are best for organizations seeking to engage employees in using social media for employee collaboration, knowledge sharing and voice through social media? In this chapter, we attempt to answer both questions by identifying two dimensions of technology—technological engagement and organizational control—to offer a framework suggesting possible answers to these questions. Based on our framework, we analyze data from six cases, which we use to shed further light on these questions. Our analysis focuses on how power is used in organizations to control social media, generate positive and negative patterns of trust dynamics and encourage employee voice and collaboration.

11.2 Social Media, Employee Engagement and Voice: A Framework for Analysis

Potentially powerful social media are increasingly widely used by the HR function (Martin et al. 2015; Parry and Solidaro 2013) to enable incremental and transformational change in organizations. Such change focuses on (a) encouraging collaboration and engagement among key stakeholders, (b) sharing knowledge and facilitating organizational learning, (c) helping organizations communicate with social media 'savvy' employees, (d) helping organizations, employees and potential employees learn more about each other and (e) giving employees and other key stakeholders, such as customers, more powerful 'voice' over key features of their working lives. As can be seen from this list, employee voice and how is it exercised have become central concerns of organizations: but what exactly do we mean by employee voice?

Most research on the topic begins with reference to Hirschman's (1970) perspective of voice as a human tendency to express discontent by 'kicking up a fuss' (p. 30), which he saw as a positive alternative to existing organizations. More recently, Budd (2014, p. 477) has defined employee voice as 'expressing opinions and having meaningful input into work-related decision-making', which includes 'individual and collective voice, union and non-union voice, and voice mechanisms that cover employment terms, work autonomy and wider strategic and business issues'. In previous work (Martin et al. 2015) we have defined the exercise of voice as (a) whether employees choose to 'speak up' or remain silent, (b) whether they use their voice in a pro-social manner to share knowledge with each other and with managers, and collaborate to improve decision-making, or use it as a form of revenge, and (c) the extent to which employees enjoy the freedom to exercise voice as a democratic input into decision-making and to control their work situations (Wilkinson and Fay 2011).

One way of framing the relationship between social media and employee voice, and answering the two research questions we posed in the opening paragraph, is to draw on the concepts of technological engagement and organizational control (Martin et al. 2009; Martin and Siebert 2016). We define these concepts in the following paragraphs.

Technological Engagement. Since all technologies have to be designed and implemented by people, technologies such as social media can be more or less engaging because they mediate between people and the objects of their engagement. This idea draws on socio-technical systems thinking, in which organizational design is based on the interaction between people, work organization and technical systems for its effectiveness. By technology, we mean hardware, software and the knowledge and social forms of work organization which typically accompany any given form of technology (Martin and Siebert 2016). So, we define technological engagement to express the extent of employees' attachment to particular forms of technology. This attachment has three components:

employees' social identification (Brown 2015) with a particular form of technology (to what extent does it help them express their personal identity – who am I and who am I not?),

employees' internalization of a given technology's built-in values (does the technology embody values that employees hold?); and

employees' psychological ownership of a technology (to what extent do they believe the technology is their own and no-one else's?).

It might help to think in terms of a music genre analogy. Jazz and Skiffle in the 1950s, rock music, soul and punk in the 1960s and 1970s, followed by new romantic, hip-hop, rap and house music can all be seen as socio-technical systems that helped different generations express their identities of who they were (and who they definitely were not, e.g. their class), their values (guitar bands versus electronically generated music) and their sense of psychological ownership over a technology of music (e.g. jazz and improvisation).

Thus, we can think of technological engagement in terms of a continus answering the question: how easy is it for employees to identify and engage with a particular technology to collaborate, share knowledge and express their voice in their organizations? At one end of the scale, technologies can be highly engaging for certain groups of employees and facilitate their voice and collaboration; on the other end of the scale, some technologies can disengage employees and inhibit voice and collaboration.

Organizational Control. A second way of thinking about technology is the extent to which it facilitates organizational control—one of the core issues in the academic and practitioner literature on organizational analysis. Organizations are sometimes defined as control mechanisms, designed to ensure predictability by aligning stakeholders such as employees with their vision and values and to ensure they comply with these. Control, however, can be seen in a positive and negative light since it is manifested in the use and abuse of power in organizations, and how these generate low and high trust dynamics between managers and employees (Siebert et al. 2015). Trust dynamics refer to the extent to which employees and managers regard each other as trustworthy, in terms of their competence (skills and ability), benevolence (wishing to do well by the other) and integrity (adhering to principles that the other regards as important or acceptable) (Mayer et al. 1995). Power can be articulated in distinctions made by sociologists and philosophers such as Stephen Lukes (2005) and Ricouer (1992). The first distinction is to think of power in the sense of '*power-over*', which, according to Lukes, manifests itself in (a) the power to win, (b) the power to set the agenda, and (c) ideological power, often covertly, to influence or manipulate people's wishes and interests. This use of power-over is widespread in organizations and is usually likened to a zero-sum game—the more power-over the organization has to determine what is done and 'how things are done around here', the less power stakeholders, for example, employees, enjoy to further their interests or ways of working. Often, as Fox (1974) argued in his classic work on power and trust relations, power exercised as power-over generates a low trust response among employees because they see it as a low trust initiative.

A second distinction is to see power in terms of '*power-to-do*' (Ricouer 1992), which is a positive-sum game, whereby two or more people or groups can share their power to collaborate to achieve something collectively they cannot achieve individually. This use of power underlies the pluralist theory of integrative bargaining and partnership agreements in HRM and the Wisdom of Crowds thesis, which refers to the power of crowds to generate better ideas and innovation than individuals. Collaboration often means that managers and employees agree to follow the classic dictum that to (re)gain control, you have to share control, which is a concept at the heart of the debate over authentic voice. According to researchers such as Fox (1974), this use of power-to-do is associated with generating high trust dynamics in organizations, with high trust initiatives by managers much more likely to be met by high trust employee responses.

A third distinction has its origins in Ricouer's notion of '*power in common*', which he saw as a property of collectives working together to ensure 'we live well as a community'. While this third use of power is sometimes seen as somewhat idealistic, we can perhaps think about it as embracing a system whereby managers and employees come together to articulate an organization's aims as being equally concerned with ethics and morality as with economic outcomes, and with ensuring well-being at work for all. We shall return to this aspect of control and power in our conclusions.

Thus, organizational control can be thought of as the extent to which technologies are put into the hands of employees for expressing authentic voice and collaborating over the means and ends of their working lives in organizations. At one end of this continuum, employees enjoy maximum autonomy and high trust from managers; at the other end, employees enjoy minimum autonomy and experience low trust from managers in how they use technologies.

We can relate these two variables in the form of a two-by-two matrix to set out four scenarios of employees likely use of enterprise-based social media to express authentic voice and collaborate with one another for the purposes of learning and sharing knowledge (see Fig. 11.1). By enterprise social media, we mean social media introduced by the organization for specific purposes, set behind its firewalls and controlled by it (as distinct from open social media such as Facebook, Twitter and

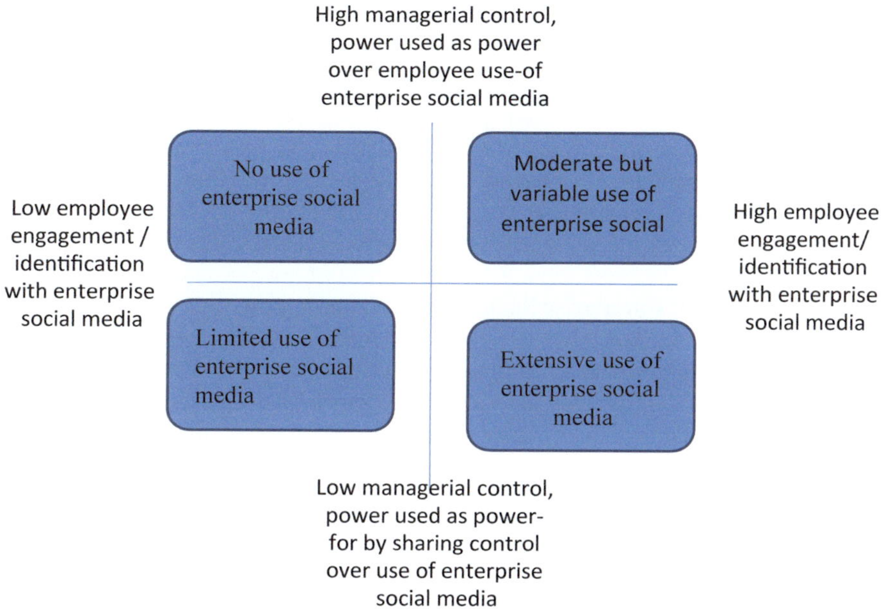

Fig. 11.1 Four scenarios of employees likely use of enterprise-based social media

other blogging sites). Both engagement and control can be expressed as two ends of intersecting continua. These categories of responses give rise to differences in employees' use of social media according to whether they see these media as (1) a means of improving two-way communications and information sharing, and/or (2) a means of improving decision-making.

These four archetypical scenarios give rise to different propositions regarding employees use of enterprise social media to improve communications and collaborative decision-making.

1. **Reject Enterprise Social Media**. In the top left-hand scenario, we propose that employees whose engagement and identification with particular forms of enterprise-based social media is low and who experience it as introduced and controlled by the organization in a power-over relationship are likely to make little or no use of these media to improve two-way communications or collaborative decision-making.
2. **Moderate but Variable Use of Enterprise Social Media**. In the top right-hand scenario, we propose that certain groups of employees, who engage and identify with certain types of enterprise social media and who see these media in a power-for relationship, are likely to make extensive use of these media to improve communications and decision-making. Other groups of employees in the organization, however, will either reject these media or use them in a calculative

manner or even asocial manner for two-way communications and collaborative decision-making.

3. **Limited Use of Enterprise Social Media**. In the bottom left-hand scenario, we propose that there will be limited/sporadic use of enterprise social media because they have low engagement/identification with the enterprise's social media, even although they perceive it as having been introduced for employees' benefit and with extensive consultation. These employees are likely to make minimal use of enterprise social media to improve communications and collaborative decision-making.
4. **Extensive Use of Enterprise Social Media**. In the bottom right-hand box, enterprise social media has been designed and introduced in a power-for manner (extensive consultation and input) by organizations to ensure that it allows them to express their identity, embodies the values they hold and gives them a sense of ownership and control over these media. Thus, we propose that employees will make extensive use of enterprise social media to improve communications and collaborative decision-making.

To provide a qualitative assessment of certain of these archetypes and to provide a partial test of the four propositions arising from them, we undertook research into six case studies of UK companies which had introduced enterprise social media. These are described and analyzed below.

11.3 Methods and Data Collection

Our short case summaries are based upon data from a project undertaken by the Involvement and Participation Association (IPA) on behalf of the Advisory, Conciliation and Arbitration Service (ACAS). The case studies are of six UK-based organizations in diverse sectors, including public, private and not-for-profit: Leeds Teaching Hospitals NHS Trust; Lloyds Register; London Borough of Lewisham; Nampak; Oxfam GB and Southeastern Trains. Data were collected using individual semi-structured interviews with senior managers and HR practitioners within the organizations and analyzed for key themes. A standard interview guide was developed for this purpose. In addition, relevant company information was analyzed and focus groups and interviews were run with employees.

11.4 Findings

Our cases point to enterprise social media being used to various degrees to promote employee voice as we proposed in our framework, namely: (1) as a means of improving two-way communications and information sharing, and (2) as a means of improving decision-making through enhanced collaboration between individuals and teams.

11.4.1 Social Media Used to Improve Two-Way Communications and Information Sharing

First, social media was used to encourage two-way communication and information sharing, particularly when the workforce was geographically dispersed or mobile. The cases of Nampak, Southeastern and Oxfam GB provide good examples of these uses of social media for employee voice.

11.5 Nampak

Nampak is a leading UK manufacturer of milk bottles, with 550 employees across nine sites. The company has a strong emphasis on employee engagement and employee voice and therefore saw it as important for employee communication tools to provide a voice for employees to share ideas and harness innovation. The organization had a number of existing voice initiatives including an annual conference and excellence awards evening, regular team briefings and an employee survey. The company also recognize a trade union at some of its sites. The company introduced online tool 'Yammer' as a tool that was readily available, engaging for employees, and easy to navigate and use. They encourage employees to submit ideas for process improvements and, if adopted, they receive 5% of the savings.

After 3 months take-up of Yammer was relatively slow, with only 145 employees signed up. Adoption by managers and office-based employees was relatively high but it was problematic to engage machine operatives on shift work, partly because these people do not have a Nampak email address and the process of registering a personal email address is somewhat drawn out. In addition, it was recognized that some employees were not familiar with social media and there was a lack of trust in the technology. Consequently, the company has undertaken marketing in order to increase adoption of Yammer, via their business conference, the company magazine and appointing 'champions' at each site. Nampak has also released some simple guidelines for using social media in order to reduce the chance of misuse.

The reactions of users to the tool has been generally positive with employees feeling valued and more up-to-date with company activities. Social media is seen by many employees and managers as a means for providing consistent messages and information across a geographically dispersed workforce and for bringing the sites closer together. It is also seen as increasing the visibility of senior leadership and breaking down barriers between senior leadership and employees. Yammer is also seen as important in facilitating innovation via an online innovation group where people are encouraged to put forward and discuss ideas. However, there was also a view expressed by some employees that the early use of the tool has been '*relatively corporate*', focusing on business issues only. To counter this perspective, senior management has been keen for employees to share more personal and informal posts to build '*a bit of community spirit and … a sense of belonging from being at Nampak*'.

11.6 Southeastern

Southeastern is a UK train operator which employs around 4,000 people. The company wanted to introduce social media to address a perceived deficiency in employee voice and to provide a mechanism to obtain employees' views on a range of issues from its highly dispersed workforce. Previously, the company used a staff survey and an intranet but management was unhappy with the effectiveness of these in promoting employee voice. Thus, they adopted 'WorkMate' (a version of 'Socialtext'), an enterprise social network in April 2012. WorkMate is similar to Facebook in that users have a personal profile and can look at activity streams, join groups and send private messages. The platform contained a news blog, the 'Worth a Look' section, for key issues and a library of key information and policies. The company made sure that WorkMate was integrated into other Voice channels, including promoting and reporting on a weekly phone-in with senior management and the staff survey. The trade unions also have their own pages on WorkMate. The company has developed a standard code of conduct for use of WorkMate but generally, have a self-regulating approach.

WorkMate has been relatively successful with 80% of employees registered and 2,200 visiting per month. However, the most common use was for passive access to information with only around 500 employees actively posting views and ideas on it per month. The company sees WorkMate as allowing them to communicate real-time information and to engage with a highly dispersed and mobile workforce, as well as to share expertise and information across the workforce. Employees can post questions or requests on WorkMate and receive responses from colleagues in other parts of the organization. In addition, WorkMate is used to obtain employee views and opinions on specific topics (e.g. a change in uniform policy). Southeastern encourage non-work discussions (around a third of topics are unrelated to work) in order to build a sense of community within the organization.

A significant challenge to using WorkMate has been senior management engagement with limited involvement of senior managers over the first few years. Interviewees saw this as the result of a '*what can it do for me?*' perception among senior managers. This calculative approach by senior managers to WorkMate is reflected by some middle managers, whose use follows a similar pattern.

11.7 Oxfam GB

Oxfam GB is one of 17 affiliate organizations that make up Oxfam, an international non-governmental organization working to reduce poverty and injustice across the world. Oxfam employs 5,000 employees worldwide. Oxfam has used Yammer for several years, alongside an intranet called 'Karl' which both provides information and allows employees to interact with each other and share information. Oxfam also uses a range of other online tools such as Skype, Webex, Blackboard and Collaborate. As Oxfam consists of a number of national 'silos' and joint working can be difficult, the use of social media is seen by employees as providing the opportunity to allow them to '*work across the organization much more*'.

A number of communities have been set up using Karl, for example, an IT group called 'Geek Speak' of around 120 employees across the world has been used to bring IT workers together. Social media generally is seen as being able to enable staff to share information, communicate and work together as well as to become less top-down and more inclusive. This is important given Oxfam's dispersed and diverse workforce. Social media is also seen as a vehicle for improving employee engagement.

Despite these positive views, social media have yet to have a significant impact on the organization. One explanation is that adoption might be restricted because Yammer was introduced informally with little central direction or support from HR or senior leaders or a communication strategy. Another, perhaps more important reason is the diversity of channels used within the organization. With affiliate organizations working relatively independently, they have been allowed to develop their own IT and internal communications systems organically using different platforms and networks. The use of a single global enterprise social network would allow them to improve internal communications. Because of these issues, Oxfam IT Directors have launched a 'Find, Connect, Collaborate, Consolidate' initiative in order to rationalize the approaches across the global organization so that the affiliates can be linked together more effectively.

11.8 Collaboration to Improve Decision-Making

Second, the case studies provided evidence of the use of social media to encourage collaboration between members of the workforce and the engagement of employees in organizational issues in order to improve decision-making. This use of social media can be illustrated through the case studies in Lloyds Register, London Borough of Lewisham and Leeds Teaching Hospitals NHS Trust.

11.9 Lloyds Register

Lloyds Register is a global engineering, technical and business services organization which employs over 9,000 people in 78 countries. In 2015, the energy team, including 2,500 employees globally, embarked on a business transformation programme to change from a regional matrix structure to a global service line structure. The company wanted to both make the change quickly and to involve employees in the new organization design so that it reflected local needs and fostered collaboration and employee engagement. Despite existing voice channels, they decided to adopt the social research tool 'Future of Work Lab' (FOWlab) in order to engage a large and geographically dispersed workforce in a focused discussion.

FOWlab allows large groups of employees to collaborate in developing business solutions to identified business issues, to have their say and shape the change process and to identify concerns, challenges and solutions. The tool is accessible online and users have named accounts because the company saw it as a means to ensure professional and constructive contributions. Lloyds Register posted a number of questions or provocations so that managers could frame the debate but also allowed employees to raise their own issues and questions. Each 'jam' was online for 72 h constantly in order to promote intensive involvement and discussion on a particular issue and to allow a narrow focus. The company undertook extensive marketing work via emails, messaging from senior management and line managers, and a video in order to facilitate take-up. The role of senior managers in both promoting the tool and in taking part themselves was seen as essential.

Out of 3,066 employees who were invited to take part, over 1,275 did so, posting 1,400 comments. Staff were seen to be co-creating ideas and projects together and as supporting innovation. The company also perceived an impact on employee engagement and perceptions of voice as employees felt '*genuinely consulted*' and that they had a greater buy-into decisions as '*when the solution comes out of the Jam, they're not surprised as that [the] solution they've identified*'. Interviewees in Lloyds Register emphasized the importance of acting on the information coming out of the Jam as '*if you're expecting people to give up their time, you need to do something with it*'.

11.10 London Borough of Lewisham

London Borough of Lewisham is a local authority based in South East London, delivering services to almost 300,000 people with 2,500 employees. The organization has undergone significant change due to cuts in Government funding and needed to review services in order to deliver further financial savings. Lewisham saw involving employees in the change process as essential to promoting understanding of the system and its benefits. In addition to existing voice mechanisms, such as regular team meetings, wider meetings led by the chief executive, formal consultations and a staff survey, the organization introduced the 'We.Create' social media tool in order to '*crowdsource ideas from staff*' on re-designing services and reducing costs while maintaining service quality and outcomes. Employees can suggest ideas, and vote and comment on other people's ideas so that suggestions are shaped collaboratively and managers can see which ideas resonate with employees. Employees who suggested ideas that were later taken up were invited to get involved in their delivery.

With the year up to July 2014, 533 staff members had used the system with over 100 ideas being suggested. As well as existing Voice channels, having a culture that '*encourages consultation and engagement*' was seen as important in this success. The ability of teams to work across services was seen as a driver of innovation, and the tool generally as promoting a sense of voice, involvement and employee engagement.

11.11 Leeds Teaching Hospitals NHS Trust

Leeds Teaching Hospitals NHS Trust is one of the largest NHS (National Health Service) Trusts in the UK, employing around 16,000 staff at seven different sites and treating approximately 1.5 m patients annually. Leeds' set up a crowdsourcing platform ('Wayfinder') as a means to create effective voice mechanisms to empower staff and allow them to collaborate and 'co-create'. Wayfinder allows people to anonymously share ideas and comments on ongoing organizational campaigns, as well as to read and rate other people's comments. For example, Wayfinder was used as a key channel to involve staff in a campaign to assess the organization's diversity and inclusion policies.

Interviewees at Leeds' emphasized the importance of the role of senior managers in promoting the social media tool and in 'becoming advocates' of the system. Interviewees felt that the clear support of senior managers meant that employees feel more comfortable using the technology. Also important was that Wayfinder is anonymized, allowing employees to speak freely and openly without fear of retribution. This is particularly important given historical concerns by employees of speaking up in the NHS. There were some concerns that this might lead to inappropriate usage such as excessive criticism or abuse, but this had not been the case at the time of the research.

Senior managers believed that Wayfinder had helped to develop networks and to deliver service improvements, e.g. Theatre Directors used the tool to examine different ideas to run their theatres more efficiently. In addition, interviewees believed that the initiative had been successful in both generating ideas and identifying concerns among the workforce.

11.12 Discussion

Our two questions were (1) why have organizations been less enthusiastic about using social media to help employees to collaborate, share their knowledge and give voice to their views about issues over which they are most concerned in their organizations? and (2) what options are best for organizations seeking to benefit from employee collaboration, knowledge sharing and voice? We drew on a range of literature on technological engagement and organizational control and power to answer these questions. Thus, we developed a framework of four scenarios of employees use of enterprise social media to express authentic voice, with four propositions concerning the use of enterprise social media to improve two-way communications and collaborative decision-making and data from six case studies to provide a test of the propositions.

The Problems of Organizational Control. Our literature review highlighted the importance of power and managers' need for control in most organizations. Organization and management are defined by the need for control, which is often based on the exercise by managers of power-over employees. The cases highlighted three findings relevant to the problems of control, the exercise of power-over and mistrust of managers by employees. Employee mistrust of technological innovation is quite widespread because such innovations are sometimes seen by employees as managers acting incompetently (without the necessary skills and ability), lacking benevolence (i.e. not seeking to do good for employees) or integrity (not adhering to principles that employees find acceptable), three important determinants of trustworthiness in organizations (Mayer et al. 1995). First, the introduction of Yammer in Oxfam was perceived to be restricted because of a lack of senior management competence in providing direction and communications support.

Second, a lack of perceived organizational benevolence was evident in the relatively slow adoption of Yammer into Nampak, which was attributed to a lack of employee trust in the technology because it was seen by some as a 'corporate tool' rather than seeking to benefit employees. This perception of social media as a corporate tool and the reluctance to see social media being introduced to do good for employees was also reflected in the relatively slow uptake of Workmate in Southeastern. Similarly, Lloyds Register's perceived needs to have its senior managers' 'frame the debate' by structuring the agenda for discussion falls into the category of lacking benevolence. This relates to the importance of employees' belief that their voice will be acted on (Burris et al. 2017) and supports our earlier work that emphasized the importance of personal control and perceived impact in the success of online voice tools (Martin et al. 2015). Some of the organizations in this study had attempted to address this need. For example, Lloyds Register allowed employees to suggest topics for discussion as well as to contribute to discussions on those topics suggested by senior management. London Borough of Lewisham encouraged those employees who had suggested the ideas that were taken up to become involved in their delivery and implementation.

Third, managers being viewed as lacking integrity was evidenced in perceptions of a lack of support from senior and middle managers in the case of Southeastern, some of whom were perceived by employees as viewing social media as a calculative method of enhancing their own power rather than introducing social media for the good of all. Arguably, Lloyds Register's requirement that employees who posted material on FOWlab record their names to ensure 'professional and constructive' contributions could be seen as a low trust initiative and violation of employees' preferences for anonymity. Interestingly, the opposite stance was taken in the case of Leeds NHS Trust by ensuring that employee posts on its crowdsourcing platform, Wayfinder, were anonymous. Arguably, this was an example of a high trust initiative met by a high trust response, since despite some early misgivings, there was little evidence of excessive criticism or abuse.

Technological Engagement. Our literature review suggested employees would use social media to the extent that it allowed them to express an identity, was consistent with their values and allowed them to express a degree of psychological ownership. Such a perspective is consistent with the notion of *power-to-do*, in which managers and employees can work together to create a positive-sum game where both parties benefit. Our cases provided a number of examples where power-to-do appeared to be the principle or aim underlying the introduction of social media. Thus, in cases where social media were perceived by employees and managers as facilitating two-way communication and information sharing, these seemed to characterized by positive outcomes and take-up. So, for example, Lloyds Register recorded more than 40% of its staff who were invited to take part in FOWlab did so actively by posting comments, with employees feeling 'genuinely consulted' and expressing greater buy-into decisions that came from the Jam in which they had participated (Burris et al. 2017). Similarly, the introduction of Wayfinder at Leeds NHS Trust as a means of ensuring collaboration and co-creation of ideas to benefit patient care appeared to have resulted in positive outcomes in generating ideas and raising workforce concerns. In this case, employees' engagement with social media seems to have benefitted from senior managers promotion and advocacy of the system, and high trust initiative in allowing for anonymity of responses.

Psychological ownership was also important in cases of successful implementation through the inclusion of non-work discussion to promote community and a sense that the media belonged to employees. A good example of organizational learning in this respect was the response by senior managers to the negative comments about the corporate feel of Yammer in Nampak, whereby they began to promote informal posting to generate 'community spirit'. Similarly, Southeastern's decision to provide a trade union page and allow self-regulation of posting appear to be underpinned by a desire to promote psychological ownership among employees.

11.13 Conclusions

Overall the case studies support the importance of organizational control and technological engagement in encouraging the use of social media as a means for promoting communication, collaboration and employee voice, and support our framework of four scenarios and associated propositions. This framework and the data from the cases provide important insights in relation to our two research questions. First, we can see that concerns related to organizational control and differing levels of technological engagement might provide an answer to our question of why some organizations have been less enthusiastic about using social media for collaboration, communication and employee voice. Promoting employee voice via social media technologies is not as simple as just introducing these tools and expecting employees to adopt them freely. Organizations might need to be prepared to relinquish a degree of control to their employees in order to encourage them to believe that engaging with the technology is worthwhile and will have a valued impact on the organization.

Second, we can provide some recommendations as to how organizations might best benefit from employee collaboration, knowledge sharing and voice. It is clear from both this study, our previous work (Martin et al. 2015) and the work of others on what employees seek to voice and why they do so (Burris et al. 2017) that the success of employee voice mechanisms, including those reliant on social media, is dependent on the willingness of senior management to value their input and engage in genuine dialogue with employees in an open and participative organizational culture. Without these prerequisites, employee voice mechanisms will not be successful regardless of how advanced they are technologically. The imposition of significant restrictions (outside of the 'light touch' guidelines used by our case study organizations) on the exercise of voice via enterprise social networks will result in employees perceiving a lack of both personal control and impact, which will in turn discourage them from engaging with social media. As suggested above, building such a culture requires senior management to share control and trust employees to exercise voice constructively. Such a culture may require, as Ricouer (1992) suggested, exercising '*power in common*', which suggests a system whereby managers and employees come together to articulate an organization's aims as being equally concerned with ethics and morality as economic outcomes, and with ensuring well-being at work for all.

References

Brown, A. D. (2015). Identities and identity work in organizations. *International Journal of Management Reviews, 17*(1), 20–40.

Budd, J. (2014). The future of employee voice. In A. Wilkinson, J. Donaghey, T. Dundond, & R. B. Freeman (Eds.), *The handbook of research on employee voice*. Cheltenham: Edward Elgar.

Burris, E., Rockman, K., & Kimmons, Y. S. (2017). The value of voice (to managers): Employee identification and the content of voice. *Academy of Management Journal*. https://doi.org/10.5465/amj2014.0320.

Dromey, J. (2016). Going digital? Harnessing social media for employee voice? Research paper, ACAS, 03/16.

Fox, A. (1974). *Man mismanagement* (2nd ed.). London: Business Books.

Hirschman, A. O. (1970). Exit, voice and loyalty: Responses to decline in firms, organizations and states. Harvard Business School Press, Cambridge, MA.

Lukes, S. (2005). Power: A radical view (2nd ed.). Palgrave Macmillan.

Martin, G., Parry, E., & Flowers, P. (2015). Do social media enhance constructive voice all of the time or just some of the time? *Human Resource Management Journal, 25*(4), 541–562.

Martin, G., Reddington, M., & Kneafsey, M. B. (2009). Web 2.0 and human resource management: Groundswell or hype? Chartered Institute of Personnel and Development, London.

Martin, G., & Siebert, S. (2016). *Managing people and organizations in changing contexts* (2nd ed.). Oxford: Routledge.

Mayer, R., Davis, J. H., & Schoorman, F. D. (1995). An integrative model of trust. *Academy of Management Journal, 20*(3), 709–734.

Parry, E., & Solidaro, A. (2013). Social media as a mechanism for engagement. In T. Bondarouk & M. R. Olivas-Lujan II (Eds.), *Social media in human resource management: Advanced series in management*. Emerald: Bingley.

Ricouer, P. (1992). *Oneself as another*. Chicago: University of Chicago Press.

Siebert, S., Martin, G., Bozic, B., & Docherty, I. (2015). Looking ‘beyond the factory gates’: Towards more pluralist and radical approaches to intraorganizational trust research. *Organization Studies, 36,* 1033–1062.

Wilkinson, A., & Fay, C. (2011). New times for employee voice? *Human Resource Management, 50*(1), 65–74.

Dr. Emma Parry is Professor of Human Resource Management and Head of the *Changing World of Work* Group at Cranfield School of Management, UK. Her research interests focus on the impact of the changing context on managing people, specifically the influence of national context, technological advancement and changing demographics on HRM. Emma has published widely in these areas including seven books and numerous articles in refereed journals. Emma is an Academic Fellow of the Chartered Institute of Personnel and Development (CIPD), an Honorary Fellow of the Institute for Employment Studies (IES) and a Visiting Fellow at Westminster Business School.

Dr. Graeme Martin is Chair of Management and Research Director of the University of Dundee School of Business in Scotland. He has published extensively in HRM, organizational studies and change management, including eight authored and edited books and numerous articles in refereed journal articles. He has held visiting appointments in Australia, the US, Italy and Sweden and works extensively with private and public sector organizations in a number of industries and countries. Currently he is working on projects in medical leadership and HRM in fast growth SMEs.

Joe Dromey is a Senior Research Fellow for the think tank IPPR. Prior to joining the IPPR, he worked as a political advisor. He has worked as head of policy and research for a charity focused on employee involvement, and as a senior policy officer at the London Borough of Newham. He has a first-class honours degree from the University of Warwick in history and politics, and a master's in history from UCL. He is a Councillor and Cabinet Member in the London Borough of Lewisham.

Chapter 12
The Politics of Voice: Voice and Volunteering in a Third Sector Organisation

Julian Teicher and Xiaoyan Liang

Abstract The study of voice has rarely examined a large part of the workforce and one of rising importance—Third Sector organisations which deliver important services on a not-for-profit basis. In this chapter, we commence an examination of voice among volunteers, particularly in the context of mixed employee and volunteer workforces. We establish that while there are differences between the two groups, there are a range of commonalities that suggest that having a voice is an important element of volunteering. Against this background, we examine a complex and long-running collective bargaining dispute in a rural fire service in Australia, that is staffed primarily by volunteers. In this case, a perceived lack of voice among volunteers underscored a legacy of poor management which also impeded the resolution of the dispute.

Keywords Volunteer voice · Employment relations · Third sector organisation

12.1 Introduction

While the literature on employee voice is burgeoning, the related area of voice among volunteers remains relatively unexplored in the wider management and employment relations literature. In an era of declining union density, employment relations scholars have expanded their field of inquiry to include issues pertaining to the multiple mechanisms for employee representation and influence at work. This expanded field often includes consideration of allied categories of workers such as dependent contractors (employees in most respects other than name) and the employees of labour hire organisations who are outsourced to third parties. Similarly, related disciplines like human resources management and organisational behaviour have concentrated on paid workers though unlike the employment relations discipline, their concerns are typically with the interests of management and the organisation.

J. Teicher (✉) · X. Liang
Central Queensland University, Melbourne, Australia
e-mail: j.teicher@cqu.edu.au

P. Holland et al. (eds.), *Employee Voice at Work*, Work, Organization, and Employment, https://doi.org/10.1007/978-981-13-2820-6_12

Historically, it was understandable that researchers concentrated on studying the employees and the employment relationship and the associated issues of control, power, rights and representation. The corollary neglect of volunteers may have originated in the very voluntariness of their labour because strictly they were not subject to management control. It may also have originated in the fact that most voluntary work occurred in the context of small-scale charitable endeavours largely separate from employees and in the non-traded goods and services sector. Over time, however, volunteering has become more prevalent in developed economies and is common in most age groups—particularly, among those who have retired from what is conventionally defined as the workforce employment. In many countries, volunteering is widespread and makes a large but usually unmeasured contribution to the national economy. For example, in 2017 volunteering was estimated to involve 31% of the Australian population, accounted for nearly 12.3 million $AUD 477.5 million (See volunteeringaustralia.org). In the US in 2013, 62.6 million are estimated to have contributed 7.7 billion hours of work which was worth $US 173 billion. And in the European Union 22% of the population volunteer each year (Alfes 2018).

At one end of the spectrum volunteers may be seen providing occasional labour on school and church cake stalls and at the other end of the spectrum volunteers workers are routinely deployed in large local, national and international organisations providing services including health care, environmental remediation, humanitarian assistance, distribution of food and clothing and providing tourist services. While volunteers may work alone, in Third Sector organisations, the workforce typically consists of employees and volunteers with the proportion and role of each group of workers varying widely. Moreover, the roles of volunteers and employees may be identical or overlapping and managerial and supervisory roles may be played by volunteers in such organisations. There are other similarities between the two groups of workers including the need for managerial functions such as recruitment, training, and occupational health and safety. In these circumstances, the dearth of research on volunteers is surprising and especially in relation to the issue of voice among volunteers. Also notable is that while Third Sector organisations have multiple stakeholders, by their nature these organisations are more transparent than private enterprises, especially if they receive government funding as is increasingly the case. Hence Brewster and Cerdin (2018, p. 7) comment that 'there is inevitably a degree of politics (and sometimes Politics) both internally and externally that can have a considerable impact on HRM in the organisation'.

For the present purpose, it is also important that there are some distinguishing features of volunteering. Volunteers are regarded as having a prosocial motivation in that they seek to benefit society or some part of society rather than having a pecuniary motivation. Consequently, their duties are not usually constrained by position descriptions and they are only loosely a part of the chain of command—though this is not the situation with the case study discussed below. But the motivation of volunteers does not by its nature preclude the need for voice—on the contrary, it may heighten it.

In this chapter, we consider first the nature and extent of the literature on volunteer workers and issues relating to voice among volunteer before turning to a case study which demonstrates the challenges of managing a mixed workforce. This discussion centres on a protracted dispute in an organisation that was historically a collection of locally based and separate rural fire brigades but has evolved into a Third Sector Organisation, the Country Fire Authority (CFA) in the state of Victoria in Australia. Over time a range of considerations have seen an increasing portion of the work undertaken by employees and in the context of bargaining for a new collective bargaining agreement for the career firefighters, the volunteers and their communities expressed concern and anger over their exclusion from decisions that bore directly on the organisation and management of the workforce and the conduct of CFA operations.

12.2 Management, Employment Relations and Voice in Third Sector Organisations

In view of the nature and significance of volunteering and the potential challenges of managing a workforce whether a volunteer only or more commonly a mixed workforce it could be expected that there would be a substantial academic literature. On the contrary, this literature is limited and mostly falls within the field of HRM as we outline below. The research themes of this literature highlight that voice has yet to be identified as particularly relevant to volunteers due to the prevalence of intrinsic motivation among volunteers.

There are undeniable differences between the management of volunteers and of employees, particularly as volunteers usually hold different job attitudes and motivations. Pearce (1983) indicated that social interaction and the opportunity to make positive social change are the motivators of volunteers. Accordingly, Third Sector organisations need to understand the importance of providing a 'rewarding experience of volunteering' to reinforce their level of motivation (Alfes et al. 2017). However, in practice, organisations employing volunteers do not usually have formal roles and processes in place that could achieve the organisation mission (Farmer and Fedor 1999). Consequently, volunteers exercise flexibility in interpreting and implementing their roles and this may not match the requirements of the job at hand (Alfes et al. 2017). This is compounded by the formal power structure, performance management and reward/punishment mechanism that would enable the organisations to shape volunteer behaviors (Alfes et al. 2017). The increasing trend of volunteering has engendered a need for a more professional and systematic approach to the management of volunteers.

In the literature on managing volunteers, the major topics covered are recruitment and selection (e.g. Bennett and Kottasz 2001), learning and development (e.g. Newton et al. 2014), motivation and reward (e.g. Phillips and Phillips 2011) or job design (e.g. Neufeind et al. 2013). A key theme of this literature is a consideration of the extent of the applicability of mainstream HRM practices to Third Sector organisations.

The process of attracting and recruiting suitable applicants is similar across both organisation types with the commonly used channels being social media outlets, advertisements, posters, and extending an invitation to friends and family (Broadbridge and Horne 1996; Randle and Dolnicar 2012; Whithear 1999). Selection processes differ in that in Third Sector selection of volunteers is usually based on suitability for the position with the element of competition for a job being absent (Wilson and Pimm 1996). Similarly, because rigorous selection may deter volunteers, selection processes are usually both less structured and stringent. Despite this application forms, background checks, and interviews are often used in recruitment (Lynch and Smith 2009). In some cases, the specificity of the job requirements entails the need to evaluate aptitude, skill and physical fitness.

Unsurprisingly, training and development is a core topic in volunteer management with a focus on the influence of training on job satisfaction, commitment and retention (e.g. Allen and Shaw 2009; Jamison 2003; Newton et al. 2014; Tang et al. 2009). In a study of hospital volunteers attitudes and satisfaction with the organisation's HRM practices Ferreira et al. (2012) found that training was the most highly rated HRM practice whereas reward and recognition, the lowest rated. Saksida et al. (2017) found that among volunteers role mastery, defined in terms of role clarity and self-efficacy could be enhanced by training and supportive work relationships with employees which in turn fosters organisational commitment among volunteers. Similarly, Cuskelly et al. (2006) study of the efficacy of volunteer management practices among Australian Rugby League clubs found that planning, training and support practices were predictive of volunteer retention.

A range of studies have considered the impact of intrinsic and extrinsic rewards on willingness to volunteer. Some studies found that extrinsic rewards (e.g. free medical services and meals, lump-sum payments and skills development) increased volunteering (e.g. Cnaan and Cascio 1998; Hunter and Ross 2013; Stirling et al. 2011) but others found a negative relationship between monetary incentive and volunteering (e.g. Anghelcev and Eighmey 2013; Tang et al. 2009). These seemingly contradictory results indicate the limitations of data collected at a point in time but also highlight that volunteers are not a homogenous group and they are likely to be motivated by different mixes of altruistic and self-serving motives (Phillips and Phillips 2011; Alfes et al. 2017).

Job design among volunteers has attracted limited research attention with most studies using the classic five 'core' job characteristics theory (Hackman and Oldham 1975). One approach is to explore the effect of a single job characteristic on volunteer's work-related outcomes; for example, autonomy has been found to positively influence volunteers' time commitment (e.g. Dailey 1986; Gagné 2003), satisfaction and retention (e.g. Güntert et al. 2015) and satisfaction and motivation (e.g. Allen and Shaw 2009; Oostlander et al. 2014). The other approach is to examine multiple job characteristics (e.g. Hidalgo and Moreno 2009; Millette and Gagné 2008; Nencini et al. 2016); however, these studies have not produced consistent findings. For example, Millette and Gagné (2008) found no relationship between job design and volunteers' turnover intentions while Alfes et al. 2015 and, Hidalgo and Moreno

2009 found a positive relationship between specific job characteristics and intention to remain.

Within mainstream organisations voice takes a variety of forms with informal individual voice being the most common form. By contrast, employee voice has attracted much attention across the HRM, employment relations and organisation behaviour literatures. For present purposes, it is relevant that the traditional focus of voice research was on unions and to a lesser extent other representative forms such as works councils. Contemporary research reveals a much more complex landscape of voice including the prevalence of direct or non-union employee voice and organisations with hybrid union and non-union voice (Wilkinson and Barry 2016).

Voice is arguably the least researched aspect of volunteering, yet it is potentially of great importance. Having a channel for volunteer voice could be beneficial to Third Sector organisations, particularly as these organisations are increasingly large and complex. While volunteers may have concerns that need consideration by management, these may go unnoticed given the typically relatively unstructured relationship between volunteers and the organisation. Further, as the literature considered above reveals, issues of motivation and management of volunteers are not uncomplicated. We were able to identify only one paper that directly addressed volunteer voice, Garner and Garner (2011). This paper applied Hirschmann's (1970) concept of exit-voice loyalty explaining that when volunteers are dissatisfied they have four options: they can exercise their dissatisfaction, exit the organisation, remain and 'silently live with the dissatisfaction, or to reduce the effort they put into their Duties'. Volunteer voice was categorised as 'constructive' or 'destructive' with an example of the former being to approach a supervisor with a solution to a problem while the latter 'would include venting to others, blaming, or making the problem seem worse than it really is.' (Garner and Garner 2011, p. 861). The authors found that volunteers' satisfaction made little difference to their voice behaviour but motivation to volunteer played an important role in voice choices. For example, volunteers who were motivated by the desire to gain increased understanding were likely to exhibit constructive voice in times of frustration. As with employees, it was found that volunteers' voice behaviour influenced turnover with constructive voice having a positive relationship with retention.

Indirectly the relevance of voice to Third Sector organisations is demonstrated by literature on organisational commitment and the psychological contract. Hence, Alfes (2018, p. 62) observes that although 'the psychological contract is often not explicitly written down, volunteers tend to have a very specific view of the mutual obligations that both parties are bound to'. Such contracts are more likely to be relational than transactional as the decision to volunteer is often based on altruistic motives. Bennett and Barkensjo (2005) found that volunteers' organisational commitment was positively influenced by the organisation's internal communication. Similarly, Presti (2013) reported that volunteers who were informed about their roles and the organisation exhibited a lower intention to leave and higher levels of satisfaction and commitment. Further, a study by Waters and Bortree (2012) highlighted the importance of organisational communication and inclusive behaviour in retaining both male and female volunteers. For females, social group inclusion and overall organisational events participation were positively related to intention to volunteer again. For males, being a part of the organisations decision-making process, information network, and events were strong predictors of their retention rates.

We conclude then that as with many HRM practices the concept of voice can be applied in Third Sector organisations in order to better understand this important sector of society. Accordingly, we now turn to an examination of an Australian firefighting organisation.

12.3 Voice and Politics in a Firefighting Organisation

12.3.1 Background

In the State of Victoria, fire services in the capital city, Melbourne, are delivered by the Metropolitan Fire Brigade (MFB), an organisation staffed entirely by employees. Outside the metropolitan area historically firefighting was conducted by separate volunteer fire brigades located across the state and which are closely linked to their local communities. Most of these firefighting stations operate under the management of the CFA which is a statutory body created under the *Country Fire Authority Act 1958*. The CFA is primarily funded by the Victorian government though individual brigades raise additional funding through donations. In 2016/17 total income was $AUD 590.5 million of which $AUD 4.5 million was donations (State of Victoria, Country Fire Authority 2017). Aside from those employed in management and support roles, the CFA firefighting workforce consists of 60,000 volunteers and 1200 employees.

In keeping with the size and complexity of the CFA and with its responsibilities for fire, emergency services and related matters, the organisation has a management and governance structure that is very similar to other corporations. However, the CFA is distinctive in being a government-owned and controlled entity, although its services are largely delivered by part-time volunteers primarily serving their local communities and who may be assigned to other fire and emergency events as required. This situation is complicated by the rapid population growth and increasing urbanisation surrounding Melbourne. Consequently, some former country towns on the fringes of suburbia are served by CFA units which are staffed by a mixed workforce of volunteers and career firefighters. These stations account for 32 of the 1,186 CFA controlled fire stations. In these locations both groups work alongside each other and in view of the hazardous nature of their duties, good working relationships are critical.

In the present case, our focus is a dispute over the re-negotiation of a collective agreement between the career firefighters represented by the United Firefighters Union and the CFA. However, as we will see below the matters in dispute impinged on the volunteer firefighters who are represented by the Volunteer Fire Brigades of Victoria (VFBV). The VFBV is a member organisation representing volunteer and which describes them as 'the unpaid professionals of our Emergency Services'. A Volunteer Charter with the CFA and the State government commits the latter parties to consultation with the elected representatives of the volunteer firefighters on all 'matters which might reasonably be expected to affect Volunteers' (CFAVolunteer-Charter_1.pdf). Interestingly, in view of the representative nature of the VFBV and its concern with a range of issues relating to fire and emergency services and the well-being of its members, its organisational and governance structure is remarkably like that of a trade union.

12.3.2 Poor Relationships and the Frontier of Control

Although the issue of volunteer voice was brought to the fore by an impasse in collective bargaining negotiations with the career firefighters, this was underscored by poor relations between the CFA management and the United Firefighters Union (UFU) and its members in a classic struggle over the 'frontier of control' (Goodrich 1920). This was brought to the fore in a February 2014 Federal Court decision (*United Firefighters Union of Australia ('UFU') V Country Fire Authority ('CFA')* FCA 2014) in a case brought by the UFU. In this case, the union sought orders that the CFA implement provisions of the 2010 collective agreement requiring it to: recruit an additional 341 career firefighters by 2016; employ a specified number of career firefighters on each shift; and use only career firefighters to perform certain work.

The Federal Court found this clause unconstitutional because it would unduly restrict the capacity of the State government to function, though its decision noted the CFA had given no cogent explanation of why it had agreed to the provisions in the 2010 agreement in the first place. In that case, the CFA had argued that the agreement had been reached under a different government and a different management, and that 'budgetary and demographic issues' had made the changes necessary. In effect, the CFA used the constitutional challenge to renege on an agreement, a move that dramatically increased tensions between the CFA and the UFU and its members but enabled management to portray itself as standing up for the interest of the organisation and the volunteer firefighters.

12.3.3 The Bargaining Dispute and Voice

Most important for the present purposes was the perceived dominance of union voice and the lack of volunteer voice. This situation was underpinned by the distinctive character of a contemporary Third Sector organisation, that is, the involvement of multiple stakeholders and high levels of transparency. The stakeholders, in this case, included the firefighters and the organisations representing them, rural communities, political parties and governments at state and national levels, courts and industrial and anti-discrimination tribunals.

Consequently, in 2016, a dispute that initially manifested as the breakdown of collective negotiations reached a flashpoint with the potential to undermine the effective delivery of fire services in Victoria. The parties had been unable to agree on all the terms of a new collective agreement to replace an agreement that had expired in September 2013. As events unfolded it became clear that there were deeper issues in contention including management failures, relations between volunteer and employee firefighters, gender equity and occupational health and safety.

Notably, pay was not one of the issues in dispute. Rather, the CFA management was concerned that the UFU's bargaining claims gave the career firefighters too much power to make decisions over volunteer firefighters and the equipment, processes and staffing of CFA stations. Superficially at least this was a plausible position as the Volunteer Charter gives the CFA the unusual responsibility to consider the interests of volunteer firefighters. The CFA had long been concerned with the marginalisation of the volunteers but also the cost to the CFA budget of increasing the numbers of career firefighters. During the 2014 state election, the Labor Party State government had promised to hire an additional 350 firefighters giving the CFA management concern that this would be at the expense of much-needed equipment and other priorities. The State government for its part was projected in the media as being close to the UFU and its leader and, as events unfolded, this enabled the union and the State government to be portrayed as having interests opposed to those of the volunteer firefighters.

With negotiations at an impasse, in November 2015 the union applied to the national employment relations tribunal, the Fair Work Commission, for assistance in the negotiation process. While the parties had progressively narrowed the areas of dispute the CFA opposed the issuing of final recommendations; however, in June, the Commission's decided this provided the 'best prospect for resolution of this long-running dispute' (Fair Work Commission 2016). Specifically, the recommendations were designed to: ensure the agreement would only apply to career firefighters and not impact on the role of volunteers; apply only to integrated volunteer and career firefighter stations; and maintain the discretion of incident controllers in managing resources in the interests of public safety. While these recommendations took account of the volunteers' interests and made concessions to management, the CFA persisted with its opposition to the making of final recommendations.

In view of the protracted nature of the dispute, on June 1 2016, the Fair Work Commission issued recommendations intended to resolve the dispute. It explicitly referred to the flashpoint issues of the 'relationship between paid and volunteer fire-fighters, and the … maintenance of the discretion of incident controllers in managing resources in the interests of public safety'. But, predictably, the CFA rejected the recommendations, arguing they did not meet their concerns about issues of discrimination, management's ability to deploy resources flexibly, management autonomy in decision-making, and the interests of volunteer firefighters.

Events escalated from this point. The Victorian government endorsed the draft agreement at least partly in an attempt to end the long-running dispute that could be used to embarrass its colleagues in the national Labor Party in the campaign leading to a federal election in July 2016. Showing unusual independence of the Victorian government the CFA management sought a Victorian Supreme Court injunction preventing the agreement being put to a ballot of career firefighters. In response, the Victorian government dismissed the board citing 'cultural and governance failures', its inability to resolve the dispute, concerns about occupational health and safety, and serious divisions between senior management and firefighters. (Victorian State Government 2016). This action was followed closely by the resignations of the Emergency Services Minister and the CFA chief executive officer which paved the way for the appointment of a new management team and board.

The new board consulted with the organisations representing both the volunteer and career firefighters leading to a further draft agreement. In its media statement the new board explained that it had 'consulted extensively with Volunteer Fire Brigades Victoria and the United Firefighters Union to ensure we fully understand their views' (CFA 2016) In addition the CFA and the UFU released a joint statement designed primarily to appease the concerns of the volunteers stating that: the agreement would only apply to the small number of integrated fire stations with paid and volunteer firefighters; does not require seven career firefighters on the ground before firefighting begins; and incident controllers maintain their authority in deploying resources. Each of these points was designed to address the concerns of the volunteer firefighters which were now being expressed not just through VFBV but increasingly in the mainstream media, on social media and through politicians.

At this point, VFBV endorsement of the agreement could have been expected but it again rejected the agreement and returned to the Supreme Court. There it secured an undertaking from the CFA that the agreement would not be put to a ballot of career firefighters until the Supreme Court had decided on the agreement's legality. As of late 2018, the agreement had not been put to a ballot and had been in part subsumed in a wider effort to reorganise the delivery of fire services in Victoria to create two separate firefighting organisations, one consisting of volunteer firefighters in rural areas and the other, of career firefighters in the rest of the State.

12.3.4 Voice, Volunteers and Politics

For reasons which remain unclear the State government's action in sacking the CFA board opened a new chapter in the efforts of the volunteers to exercise voice. Apart from the courts, there was increasing visibility of State and national politicians. Senior members of the State Opposition (Conservative) parties mounted a media campaign ostensibly in support of the (embattled) volunteers. Their interests were presented as being disregarded and the performance of rural firefighting services and the safety of communities as being jeopardised because of deals between the Labor Party Victorian government and a so-called 'rogue' union. At the national level, the Liberal (Conservative) prime minister who was facing an imminent election promised that if re-elected his government would legislate against this attack on the ethos of volunteering by the State Labor government. The proposed agreement was described as 'an assault not just on the safety of Victorians ... it is an assault on what is the very best in our Australian spirit.' (Herald Sun 2016).

Following the federal election the national government amended the Fair Work Act 2009 Section 195A to prevent the Fair Work Commission approving terms of an enterprise agreement (objectionable terms) relating to emergency services volunteers—if those terms restrict the emergency services organisation's ability to engage or deploy its volunteers, or provide them with support or equipment, or require the 'body to consult, or reach agreement with, any other person or body before taking any action' in relation to those matters. In an unprecedented move the amendments gave bodies representing volunteers right to make submissions to the Fair Work Commission in matters affecting the interests of volunteers, a provision in effect enabling volunteers to participate in future collective bargaining negotiations. Whether motivated by political opportunism or belief in the cause of the volunteer firefighters the media campaign waged by the volunteers and VFBV had succeeded in further entrenching the principal of volunteer voice at least in the Victorian CFA.

12.4 Conclusion

Whereas in the past, volunteering occurred largely in small charitable organisations, it is now also found in large and complex organisations such as hospitals and in firefighting. These Third Sector organisations usually have multiple stakeholders and they are more transparent than most other organisational forms, especially those which receive government funding. In the case of the CFA volunteers it was the multiple stakeholders and transparency which enabled the volunteers to prevent the CFA-UFU agreement being concluded and ultimately to gain an increased voice opportunity.

However, the literature on HRM in Third Sector organisations scarcely considers volunteer voice instead giving most attention to the applicability of mainstream HRM practices. For present purposes, however, it is important to note some distinctive features of volunteering, particularly that volunteers are considered to have a prosocial motivation; that is, they aim to benefit society or some part of society. But the motivation of volunteers does not by its nature preclude the need for voice—on the contrary, it may be heightened by the need to make volunteering a rewarding experience (Alfes et al. 2017). Allied with this training and development opportunities have been identified as a source of job satisfaction, commitment and retention (e.g. Newton et al. 2014).

Turning to the issue of voice, the HRM and employment relations literature presents a variegated picture of employee voice in contemporary organisations. At this point, in time little can be said about the nature and extent of voice in volunteering, but the notion of voice as either constructive or destructive (Garner and Garner 2011) is potentially useful. In the case of the volunteer firefighters in Victoria, at least publicly their voice was negative and conflictual. Also notable in this case was the mobilisation of support from politicians based on the opportunity to cast the vexed issue of operational staffing and management in terms of an attack on the Australian ethos of volunteering.

We observe also that in the CFA volunteer voice is legally enshrined in a Volunteer Charter and volunteers are represented by a union like organisation. During the period of the case study, the VFBV consistently campaigned to resist a perceived erosion of the position of volunteers in the CFA including the authority of volunteers to manage career professionals. When the CFA proved to be insufficient to achieve this end, the VFVB took their campaign into the public arena ultimately securing amendments to the Fair Work Act which effectively extend volunteer voice into a sphere that was hitherto confined to unions. In this, we see how in Third Sector and public organisations delivering key services, external stakeholders (audiences) may be mobilised to augment voice among volunteers.

References

Alfes, K. (2018). People management in volunteer organizations and charities. In C. Brewster & J. Cerdin (Eds.), *HRM in mission driven organizations* (pp. 47–78). Palgrave Macmillan.

Alfes, K., Antunes, B., & Shantz, A. D. (2017). The management of volunteers—what can human resources do? A review and research agenda. *The International Journal of Human Resource Management, 28*(1), 62–97.

Alfes, K., Shantz, A., & Saksida, T. (2015). Committed to Whom? Unraveling How Relational Job Design Influences Volunteers' Turnover Intentions and Time Spent Volunteering. *Official Journal of the International Society for Third-Sector Research, 26*(6), 2479–2499. https://doi.org/10.1007/s11266-014-9526-2.

Allen, J. B., & Shaw, S. (2009). Everyone rolls up their sleeves and mucks in: Exploring volunteers' motivation and experiences of the motivational climate of a sporting event. *Sport Management Review, 12*(2), 79–90.

Anghelcev, G., & Eighmey, J. (2013). The impact of extrinsic incentives on students' willingness to volunteer as peer mentors: Implications for advertising education. *Journal of Advertising Education, 17*(2), 5.

Bennett, R., & Barkensjo, A. (2005). Internal marketing, negative experiences, and volunteers' commitment to providing high-quality services in a UK helping and caring charitable organization. *Voluntas: International Journal of Voluntary and Nonprofit Organizations, 16*(3), 251–274.

Bennett, R., & Kottasz, R. (2001). Advertisement style and the recruitment of charity volunteers. *Journal of Nonprofit & Public Sector Marketing, 8*(2), 45–63.

Brewster, C., & Cerdin, J. (2018). The management of people in mission-driven organisations. In C. Breser & J. Cerdin (Eds.), *In HRM in mission driven organisations* (pp. 1 – 14). London: Palgrave Macmillan.

Broadbridge, A., & Horne, S. (1996). Volunteers in charity retailing: Recruitment and training. *Nonprofit Management and Leadership, 6*(3), 255–270.

Cnaan, R. A., & Cascio, T. A. (1998). Performance and commitment: Issues in management of volunteers in human service organizations. *Journal of Social Service Research, 24*(3–4), 1–37.

Cuskelly, G., Taylor, T., Hoye, R., & Darcy, S. (2006). Volunteer management practices and volunteer retention: A human resource management approach. *Sport Management Review (Sport Management Association of Australia & New Zealand), 9*(2), 141–163.

Country Fire Authority. (2016). Statement from the Chair, 16 August.

Dailey, R. C. (1986). Understanding organizational commitment for volunteers: Empirical and managerial implications. *Journal of Voluntary Action Research, 15*(1), 19–31.

Fair Work Commission. (2016). United Firefighters' Union of Australa v Country Fire Authority, Final Recommendations, PR51268.

Farmer, S. M., & Fedor, D. B. (1999). Volunteer participation and withdrawal. *Nonprofit Management and Leadership, 9*(4), 349–368.

Federal Court of Australia. (2014). United Firefighters Union of Australia ('UFU') V Country Fire Authority (CFA'). Fcaf1.

Ferreira, M. R., Proença, T., & Proença, J. F. (2012). Organisational influence on volunteer satisfaction and attitudes towards HRM practices: The case of hospital volunteers. *International Review on Public and Nonprofit Marketing, 9*(1), 27–42.

Gagné, M. (2003). The role of autonomy support and autonomy orientation in prosocial behavior engagement. *Motivation and Emotion, 27*(3), 199–223.

Garner, J. T., & Garner, L. T. (2011). Volunteering an opinion: Organizational voice and volunteer retention in nonprofit organizations. *Nonprofit and Voluntary Sector Quarterly, 40*(5), 813–828.

Goodrich, C. L. (1920). *The Frontier of Control A Study of British Workshop Politics*. Brace and How, London, London: Harcourt.

Güntert, S. T., Neufeind, M., & Wehner, T. (2015). Motives for event volunteering: Extending the functional approach. *Nonprofit and Voluntary Sector Quarterly, 44*(4), 686–707.

Hackman, J. R., & Oldham, G. R. (1975). Development of the job diagnostic survey. *Journal of Applied Psychology, 60*(2), 159.

Hirschman, A. O. (1970). *Exit, voice, and loyalty: Responses to decline in firms, organizations, and states*. Cambridge, MA: Harvard University Press.

Herald Sun. (2016). CFA dispute: Prime Minister promises to enshrine CFA volunteer rights in law if elected, https://www.heraldsun.com.au/news/victoria/cfa-dispute-prime-minister-promises-to-enshrine-cfa-volunteer-rights-in-law-if-elected/news-story/6125d6d8627a64a4808706496d6d2699.

Hidalgo, M. C., & Moreno, P. (2009). Organizational socialization of volunteers: The effect on their intention to remain. *Journal of Community Psychology, 37*(5), 594–601.

Hunter, K., & Ross, E. (2013). Stipend-paid volunteers in South Africa: A euphemism for low-paid work? *Development Southern Africa, 30*(6), 743–759.

Jamison, I. B. (2003). Turnover and retention among volunteers in human service agencies. *Review of Public Personnel Administration, 23*(2), 114–132.

Lynch, S., & Smith, K. (2009). The dilemma of judging unpaid workers. *Personnel Review, 39*(1), 80–95.

Millette, V., & Gagné, M. (2008). Designing volunteers' tasks to maximize motivation, satisfaction and performance: The impact of job characteristics on volunteer engagement. *Motivation and Emotion, 32*(1), 11–22.

Nencini, A., Romaioli, D., & Meneghini, A. M. (2016). Volunteer motivation and organizational climate: Factors that promote satisfaction and sustained volunteerism in NPOs. *Voluntas: International Journal of Voluntary and Nonprofit Organizations, 27*(2), 618–639.

Neufeind, M., Güntert, S. T., & Wehner, T. (2013). The impact of job design on event volunteers' future engagement: Insights from the European Football Championship 2008. *European Sport Management Quarterly, 13*(5), 537–556.

Newton, C., Becker, K., & Bell, S. (2014). Learning and development opportunities as a tool for the retention of volunteers: A motivational perspective. *Human Resource Management Journal, 24*(4), 514–530.

Oostlander, J., Güntert, S. T., & Wehner, T. (2014). Linking autonomy-supportive leadership to volunteer satisfaction: A self-determination theory perspective. *Voluntas: International Journal of Voluntary and Nonprofit Organizations, 25*(6), 1368–1387.

Pearce, J. L. (1983). Job attitude and motivation differences between volunteers and employees from comparable organizations. *Journal of Applied Psychology, 68*(4), 646.

Phillips, L., & Phillips, M. (2011). Altruism, egoism, or something else: Rewarding volunteers effectively and affordably. *Southern Business Review, 36*(1), 23.

Presti, A. L. (2013). The interactive effects of job resources and motivations to volunteer among a sample of Italian volunteers. *Voluntas: International Journal of Voluntary and Nonprofit Organizations, 24*(4), 969–985.

Randle, M., & Dolnicar, S. (2012). Attracting Volunteers in Highly Multicultural Societies: A Marketing Challenge. *Journal of Nonprofit & Public Sector Marketing, 24*(4), 351–369. https://doi.org/10.1080/10495142.2012.733668.

Saksida, T., Alfes, K., & Shantz, A. (2017). Volunteer role mastery and commitment: Can HRM make a difference? *The International Journal of Human Resource Management, 28*(14), 2062–2084.

State of Victoria, Country Fire Authority. (2017). *Annual Report 2016/17*. https://www.cfa.vic.gov.au/documents/20143/203205/CFA-Annual-Report-2017.pdf/92403a6f-9799-84cc-cc13-e76bbdac43ff.

Stirling, C., Kilpatrick, S., & Orpin, P. (2011). A psychological contract perspective to the link between non-profit organizations' management practices and volunteer sustainability. *Human Resource Development International, 14*(3), 321–336.

Tang, F., Morrow-Howell, N., & Hong, S. (2009). Institutional facilitation in sustained volunteering among older adult volunteers. *Social Work Research, 33*(3), 172–182.

Victoria State Government. (2016). Statement ofn the CFA Board, 10 June.

Waters, R. D., & Bortree, D. S. (2012). Improving volunteer retention efforts in public library systems: How communication and inclusion impact female and male volunteers differently. *International Journal of Nonprofit and Voluntary Sector Marketing, 17*(2), 92–107.

Wilkinson, A., & Barry, M. (2016). Voices from across the divide: An industrial relations perspective on employee voice. *German Journal of Human Resource Management, 30*(3–4), 338–344.

Whithear, R. (1999). Charity shop volunteers: A case for 'tender loving care'. *International Journal of Nonprofit and Voluntary Sector Marketing, 4*(2), 107–120.

Wilson, A., & Pimm, G. (1996). The tyranny of the volunteer: the care and feeding of voluntary workforces. *Management Decision, 34*(4), 24–40.

Julian Teicher is Professor in Human Resources and Employment and Deputy Dean (Research) in the School of Business and Law at Central Queensland University, Melbourne, Australia. In the early part of his career he worked as an industrial relations officer for two unions, one in the maritime and power industries and the other in nursing. His research is in two related fields: workplace (industrial) relations and public policy and management. He has published widely on a range of topics including: conflict management, employee participation, voice and industrial democracy, bargaining and dispute resolution, and training and skill formation.

Xiaoyan (Christiana) Liang is a lecturer in the School of Business and Law at Central Queensland University, Melbourne, Australia. Her research interests include business ethics, leadership, volunteer management and voice. She has experience working in the industry as a consultant in Shanghai before moving to Australia.

Conclusion—Or Some Thoughts on the Future of Work and Voice

As many of us know, when writing research papers, it is important to add a section on future issues to indicate the direction in which research in a particular field is likely to head or should head and what is worth considering. We attempt to take this approach in this final chapter. Rather than developing a summary of the book, we take the approach that we appear to be in the midst of a revolution rather than evolution in work and as such we look to some alternatives and how voice will play a part in these various scenarios. We hope this will help in the research considerations around the future of voice at work. We start first with a quote regarding the changing times we are living in:

> While the future is basically unknowable, one thing is certain. The world of work is not going to be disrupted, it is disrupted, with more disturbance to come (Ross et al. 2017).

The quote above highlights what we have attempted to show in this book that the broad and dynamic nature of communication patterns and practices that come under the umbrella of voice at work is evolving to meet these dynamic times. We hoped to illustrate the evolution of voice through examples like the case study on CarCo, where despite it staged closure, management introduced new voice practices. Through new communication channels such as social media (See Parry et al. and Holland et al.) that have emerged in the last 10 years, we have illustrated the impact these communication channels are already making. These changes are part of what is increasingly described as the fourth industrial revolution underpinned by (smart) technology, artificial intelligence (AI) and globalisation (Schwab 2016). Commentators such as Friedman (2016), described this revolution in work as potentially as radical as the first industrial revolution, in terms of changing when how and why we work. An emerging example of this change being the emergence of the 'gig' economy, whilst this sector is disrupting some of the most established industries in AMEs from taxi (see Uber) to hotels (see Airbnb), these changes are also having a profound effect on the employment relationship. As such what we have identified and explored in this book may be just the tip of the iceberg when it comes to the changing relationship between work and employment and by

P. Holland et al. (eds.), *Employee Voice at Work*, Work, Organization, and Employment, https://doi.org/10.1007/978-981-13-2820-6

inference the very nature of employee voice. A particular outcome of this change as the 'gig' economy highlights is the growing separation of work and employment in AMEs. So how will an increasingly fragmented workforce, with less employment regulation and following contemporary trends less organised labour support have a voice or we would argue, more specifically, what will voice look like?

The first scenario could be that voice will become less significant as employment (and the associated terms and conditions) and work become increasingly separated and individualised. As highlighted by the 'gig' economy, where individuals (labour) effectively bid against each other for work in this 'race to the bottom' scenario in terms of pay rates. However, we are already seeing forms of counter-action around these issues, whilst discussion about regulating these new employment relations like tradition employment have not gained much traction—with the exception of some high profile but sporadic victories to the worker. A combination of traditional labour institutions and the strategic use of social media appear to be emerging as the new voices in these markets, with increasing impact. For example, in the UK a new union has emerged out of the GMB and TWGU—know and the Independent Union of Great Britain (IUGB) to address the unique circumstances of the 'gig' worker, whilst only a new and relatively small union, successful campaigns with couriers, Uber drivers and cleaners, have seen the union attract new members including self-employed electricians to it ranks. What is notable about this new and agile union is their use of social media to generate publicity for their campaigns. This use of social media as well as being central to this new economy can also be a powerful tool if used strategically by the labour side of the equation.

An additional social media strategy at the individual level that is seen to provide a balance in the power of the 'gig' marketplace is the practice of naming and shaming of bad experience with certain clients. So what we may be seeing here is the emergence of electronic hybrid voice of institutional and social mechanisms, where the combination of these strategies enables the individual contractor and labour institutions (unions) to place some regulation into the market specifically through their voice.

A second scenario is that where workers are in stable employment, we could see little change in the current trend of hybrid voice with direct voice becoming increasingly the norm as technology enables individual to voice their issue on internal systems and algorithms identify and spot trend which the organisation can identify that are or could become issues for management if dealt within the traditional timeframe and processes. Where unions remain relatively strong in this hybrid model, their voice may remain central to the negotiating terms and condition of employment and grievance procedures—what might be termed the traditional role of trade unions. In addition, for employees, who believe they are being silenced or management is providing a deaf ear to their concerns, the new technology highlighted by social media, in this book such as Twitter, Facebook could provide a new voice in the context of individuals addressing workplace issues on open platforms or forum, providing a new technologically enabled countervailing influence on the employer. The power of these forums as noted in the case of HMV in this book is that the concerns are discussed in real time on these platforms and also provide a channel for whistle-blowing undertaken in real time, which creates an immediate and potentially global awareness of issue which generates pressure for management to act responsibly and respond accordingly.

A third scenario is that the further deregulation of the economy and employment sets in train a backlash and the push to legislate for more formal employment regulation and voice in this new and emerging economy in AMEs—see the comparison of the Anglo-American and European voice in this book, whilst, the most unlikely of the scenarios, what we have seen to date in the world economy and the changing nature of work less than 20 years into this century suggests that nothing should be ruled out. What is clear is that changes already moving through the employment relationship are having a profound effect but employee voice in one form or another is central to the functioning of the relationship and as a form of communication and countervailing power, and is likely to remain central to the work and employment relationship.

References

Friedman, T. L. (2016). *Thanks for being late: An optimist's guide to thriving in the age of accelerations*. New York: Allen Lane.

Ross, P., Ressia, S., & Sander, E. (2017). *Work in the 21st century: How do I log on?*. Bradford UK: Emerald Publishing.

Schwarb, K. (2016). *The fourth industrial revolution*. Switzerland: World Economic Forum.

MIX
Papier aus verantwortungsvollen Quellen
Paper from responsible sources
FSC® C105338

If you have any concerns about our products,
you can contact us on
ProductSafety@springernature.com

In case Publisher is established outside the EU,
the EU authorized representative is:
Springer Nature Customer Service Center GmbH
Europaplatz 3, 69115 Heidelberg, Germany

Printed by Libri Plureos GmbH
in Hamburg, Germany